D0857003

THE NIGHTINGHOULS OF PARIS

KRIÉGER
DE
PARIS

THE NIGHTINGHOULS OF PARIS

ROBERT McALMON

EDITED AND WITH AN
INTRODUCTION
BY SANFORD J. SMOLLER

UNIVERSITY OF ILLINOIS PRESS
Urbana and Chicago

Frontispiece: Graeme Taylor,
John Glassco, Robert McAlmon,
Nice, 1929. (John Glassco/Library and
Archives Canada/PA-188182)

Manufactured in the United States
of America
C 5 4 3 2 1

∞ This book is printed
on acid-free paper.

Library of Congress Cataloging-in-
Publication Data

McAlmon, Robert, 1896–1956.
The nightinghouls of Paris / Robert
McAlmon ; edited and with an
introduction by Sanford J. Smoller.
p. cm.
Includes bibliographical references and
index.
ISBN-13: 978-0-252-03135-9 (cloth : alk. paper)
ISBN-10: 0-252-03135-0 (cloth : alk. paper)
1. Paris (France)—Fiction.
I. Smoller, Sanford J. II. Title.
PS3525.A1143N54 2007
813'.52—dc22 2006022584

To the memory of
our daughter Deborah

CONTENTS

ACKNOWLEDGMENTS

My thanks first to Dr. Patricia C. Willis, the Elizabeth Wakeman Dwight Curator of the Beinecke Library Collection of American Literature at Yale University, and the excellent staff there. Without their archival care of Robert McAlmon's unpublished typescript "The Nightinghouls of Paris," this project would not have been possible. The Library and Archives of Canada provided the photograph of Graeme Taylor, John Glassco, and McAlmon at Nice in 1929. Special thanks to Brian Busby, John Glassco's biographer, whose diligent scholarship uncovered facts about McAlmon's life and associations that enabled me to correct a longstanding error and to identify some of the obscure characters who figure in *Nightinghouls* under fictitious names. I wish him all the best. Professor Robert E. Knoll, who pioneered McAlmon studies, and Professor Sandra Spanier, a leading modernist scholar and the general editor of Hemingway's complete letters, pointed out errors of fact and infelicities, and suggested improvements to my introduction and annotations. Rebecca Crist helped guide me through the rocks and shoals of electronic publishing. Angela Burton adroitly and graciously managed the editorial process. Julie Gay keenly spotted my gaffes and smoothed out my rough places. Those that remain, of course, are mine. Willis G. Regier was a staunch advocate of this work, and his attentiveness and wise counsel kept me on track from beginning to end. Thanks, Bill. Thanks, too, to my family and friends for their encouragement and support. In particular, Mike Burns, Peter Hargitai, Jack Pickering, Bob Saba, Don Shrager, and Shelby Stephenson answered the call. My wife, Merry Sue Smoller, bore the brunt of word processing and formatting my copy on the computer. An excerpt from *The Nightinghouls of Paris,* in slightly different form (entitled "A Night at Bricktop's"), appeared in *Dictionary of Literary Biography Yearbook: 2001.*

INTRODUCTION

Sanford J. Smoller

After living in Europe for almost twenty years, mainly in Paris with sojourns in London, Berlin, Nice, Majorca, and Barcelona, the American expatriate writer and publisher Robert McAlmon was repatriated from occupied France in the fall of 1940. He barely escaped internment, and with his health weakened by years of heavy drinking and the harsh German occupation, he probably would not have survived until France was liberated in 1944. His sisters and brothers prevailed upon their senators to look into his case, and after his brother Bert supplied the required five hundred dollars, McAlmon was permitted to go to Lisbon, where he took one of the last flights to the United States.

Among the first wave of Americans in Paris after World War I, he had arrived in the spring of 1921 with exuberance, a letter of introduction to James Joyce, and a bountiful allowance by virtue of his marriage of convenience to Annie Winifred Ellerman (who wrote under the name of Bryher), the daughter of Sir John Ellerman, one of England's wealthiest men. He returned at age forty-five, penurious and soon to enter a sanitarium for tuberculosis, with only the books and papers he had salvaged to show for all his years abroad. Once he was a prominent young American writer in Paris, whose fiction and poetry appeared in the avant-garde literary magazines of the time; throughout the 1920s his Contact Publishing Company was the foremost publisher of experimental expatriate writing. Now, in November 1940, going to work for his brothers George and Bert at their Southwestern Surgical Supply store in Phoenix, he was just Robert McAlmon, truss salesman. Reflecting on this reversal of fortune, Edward Dahlberg, who befriended McAlmon in the early 1950s, commented, "What an odd and bawdy occupation for a magnificent and lewd nature."[1]

Although McAlmon has been termed an expatriate by literary historians and biographers, he never considered himself an expatriate in the sense of one "who withdraws of his own free will" from his homeland.[2] Unlike Gertrude Stein, Ezra Pound, and T. S. Eliot of the older generation, and such Ivy League contemporaries as Malcolm Cowley and Archibald MacLeish, McAlmon was not enraptured by European culture generally and French literary and artistic achievements in particular. He might have agreed with the findings of Harold Stearns's symposium, *Civilization in the United States* (1922), which indicted all the institutions of American society for moral and spiritual corruption. Still, he had no illusions that people were any better in Montparnasse than in Madison, South Dakota, where he lived as a teenager. Circumstances of his marriage had taken him to Europe, not a willing rejection of his native country. Even after six years in Europe, very little of anything European had rubbed off on him. For, as he explained in his memoir *Being Geniuses Together* (1938) (hereinafter *Geniuses*), "I never felt myself an expatriate, or anything but an American, although not through excess of patriotism. My country is much too polyglot of race, type and varieties of faiths, political and otherwise, for me to discover exactly to which qualities one would remain loyal in being one hundred per cent American."[3]

However unromantic about Paris, McAlmon found the absence of cant about drinking and sex refreshing. The French knew that life was hard and that wine, beer, and spirits gave solace and pleasure. They understood, too, that men and women liked to have sex, and if they liked to have sex with the same sex, well, that was life. Musicians, artists, and especially poets were acknowledged as at least a little *fou*. There was a long tradition of wild and often violent poets dating to the troubadours and François Villon. In this live-and-let-live milieu, the hard-drinking, bisexual, sometimes pugnacious McAlmon felt right at home. In 1929, he responded to a questionnaire circulated among notable Montparnassians by *The Little Review:* "Like: some people and some things. Dislike: same answer. Like: music, mainly jazz, and dancing, mainly my own, and gregarious life and lots of it. Low, or high, but always salted with a little disreputability."[4] He had come a long way from temperate Clifton, Kansas, where he was born on March 9, 1895, the youngest of eight surviving children of the Reverend John Alexander McAlmon and his wife Bess Urquhart McAlmon.

An emigrant from Northern Ireland by way of Canada, the itinerant Presbyterian minister moved his large brood to South Dakota when Robert was a young boy. The experiences of his boyhood and teenage years provided McAlmon with the subjects of his short story collections, *A Hasty Bunch* (1921) and *A Companion Volume* (1922), as well as of the autobiographical novel *Village: As It Happened through a Fifteen-Year Period* (1924). In these works, his youthful characters struggle to free themselves from a provincial, repressive family and communal life in "a wild and dreary plains state" (McAlmon, *Geniuses*, 157).

Judging from his invariably autobiographical fiction, McAlmon's childhood was not a happy one. In a letter dated August 5, 1920, to William Carlos Williams, he listed his problems: "too precocious, too mature on realization for what I was in ability to create—too well read—too much family—too much poverty, and nasty experiences with life before I was eight years old."[5] Yet his sisters Victoria and Grace believed he exaggerated the severity of his childhood. In Victoria's remembrance, Robert was "loved and cherished," and their home life was relaxed and lively.[6] Nevertheless, whatever negative feelings McAlmon expressed about his childhood in his early writings, the further he got from it, the less onerous it seemed. Morley Callaghan recalled a night with the Joyces in which McAlmon evinced "rich pleasure" telling stories of his boyhood.[7]

To Gore Vidal, McAlmon's middle teen years in Madison were especially interesting because Vidal's father, Eugene "Gene" Vidal, was McAlmon's best chum. McAlmon renamed Gene Vidal "Gene Collins" in *Village*, and the opening scenes find Gene Collins and Peter Reynalds (McAlmon) in a deep and perplexing discussion of their first nocturnal emissions, followed by Peter's ruminating on his feelings for Gene: "He almost resented his affection for Gene; he wondered if he'd had liked him at all if many other boys his own age were about. . . . Gene had an attraction for him however that Lloyd never had. He wondered, was that simply now, and because both of them were adolescent? . . . He saw that Gene felt about him as he did about Gene; attracted, and antagonistic too. That was rivalry, and jealousy, because the two of them led their class easily."[8]

From these passages Vidal infers that McAlmon "had been romantically involved" with his (Vidal's) father, and that in the novel Peter "is in love with Gene."[9] In Peter and Gene, moreover, Vidal sees his own teenage infatuation with Jimmie Trimble, which is central to his novel about obsessive homoeroticism, *The City and the Pillar* (1948). Homoeroticism is certainly present in these scenes (which Vidal quotes in full in his 1995 memoir *Palimpsest*), but that is common among adolescent boys. Vidal asserts, however, that the boys expressed their affection physically, although his father never talked about McAlmon and, because Vidal did not read *Village* until 1990, he never asked Gene about him. McAlmon may have "loved" Gene Vidal, and vice versa, but it is extremely unlikely any "funny stuff" took place. The boys in *Village* look to girls, or their wet dreams, to relieve their sexual urges.

Conjecture about McAlmon's teenage sexuality aside, Vidal affirms that "he is plainly working from the facts in *Village*," for Vidal's aunt Margaret "testifies to the accuracy of his description of life in that box of a house where winters were arctic and summers hot . . ." (Vidal, 136). Here McAlmon would have been pleased, because his intent was to describe, in precise detail, what he himself had experienced and observed, without embellishment. This is one reason he resented Sinclair Lewis's caricatures, especially in *Babbitt*, of Midwestern people as "boobs." After all, his own family and friends gave the lie to Lewis. McAlmon's father was a graduate of Princeton Divinity School; his brother Will was a football star at the University of Minnesota and later coached his brother George at Grinnell College; his sister Victoria was an emancipated feminist, a founder of Minnesota's progressive Farmer–Labor Party, and a teacher at Los Angeles Community College; his brothers George and Bert were enterprising businessmen; and his sister Grace was a nurse. Gene Vidal, after excelling in sports at West Point (All-American quarterback), became an army aviator, taught aeronautics at the Academy, pioneered commercial aviation, and was appointed Director of Air Commerce by Franklin D. Roosevelt in 1933. Clearly, the Midwestern small town could produce people as bright, ambitious, and successful as people any place in the country.

When John Alexander McAlmon became ill, the family moved to Minneapolis, where McAlmon graduated from East High School in 1912. He entered the University of Minnesota but dropped out during his freshman year. Forced to make his own way, like his fictional counterpart Peter Reynalds, he worked for brief stints writing "sob stories" for a small newspaper, clerking in a lumberyard, and even harvesting wheat. McAlmon drifted back to Madison to pal around with his buddies, but he was bored and restless everywhere. After John Alexander died in 1915, McAlmon's family moved to Los Angeles. But still at loose ends and hankering for action, McAlmon crossed the border to Winnipeg, Canada, and on August 28, 1916, enlisted in the 190th Overseas Battalion of the Canadian Expeditionary Force and signed the oath to "be faithful and bear true Allegiance to His Majesty King George the Fifth." He gave his date of birth as March 9, 1895, and is described as five feet eight inches tall, with an expanded chest of thirty-seven inches, a fair complexion, blue eyes, and dark hair. He listed his religion as Presbyterian. Whether he actually reported for training is problematic, but there is no question that he deserted, for across the top of his enlistment papers is written "Deserter." Evidently having second thoughts about doing and dying for King George, or unable to take the discipline, he lit out for the States and joined his family in Los Angeles.[10]

He enrolled at the University of Southern California (USC), which had recently opened with a Methodist affiliation, but he was a desultory student. In March 1918, McAlmon enlisted in the Army, hoping to be posted to Europe, but he was assigned to the Army Air Corps's Rockwell Field in San Diego. He may have had pilot training, for he wrote poems on flying that were published in *Poetry* in March 1919. He edited and wrote for the camp newspaper, and back in Los Angeles after his discharge, he edited a short-lived magazine on flying called *The Ace*.

To please his mother, McAlmon re-enrolled at USC and joined a fraternity and the literary society. He chafed, however, at the hidebound professors and narrow-minded students. McAlmon later recalled reactions to a paper he read in class, wherein he noted "that of fifty great writers of the last half-century, all had been completely or partially agnostic. A girl left the classroom as I read; the professor was pale and wiped sweat from his brow; and a fraternity brother attempted to have me expelled as a heretic" (McAlmon, *Geniuses*, 225–26). Although he also had a solid job as a court reporter (accounting for his vaunted, rapid-fire typing), regular life was not for him. So quitting college and the job, and wanting to pay his respects to *Poetry* editor Harriet Monroe, he went to Chicago in early 1920. Among the Chicago bohemians was the doomed Italian poet Emanuel Carnevali, with whom McAlmon had corresponded. After Carnevali was stricken with encephalitis and confined to a sanitarium in Italy, McAlmon contributed to his expenses and later published Carnevali's febrile autobiographical writing titled *A Hurried Man* in 1925; McAlmon also wrote an unpublished novel about Carnevali, "Too Quick for Life."

By the spring of 1920, McAlmon was in Greenwich Village. His first job was posing nude for mixed art classes at Cooper Union. McAlmon was proud of his trim, well-formed body, which, to William Carlos Williams, "might have served for the original of Donatello's youthful Medici in armor."[11] According to Williams, McAlmon was introduced to his circle of friends—among them Lola Ridge, Alfred Kreymbourg, Marianne Moore, Djuna Barnes, Kenneth Burke, and Matthew Josephson—when the painter-poet Marsden Hartley, after "discovering" McAlmon at Cooper Union, brought him to a party at Ridge's. Poet and socialist, Ridge was the editorial force behind Harold Loeb's magazine *Broom.* To Ridge, McAlmon was "wild and daring and hard as nails," but for a poet he "drank too much."[12]

However, while this version makes a good story, the facts suggest that Hartley had prepared McAlmon's entrance into the Village scene. Townsend Ludington, in his biography of Hartley, reports that McAlmon attended poetry readings Hartley gave in Los Angeles in the spring of 1919. McAlmon introduced himself and they struck up a friendship. Liking McAlmon's intelligence and "radical . . . viewpoints about art,"[13] Hartley probably urged his young friend to go to the capital of bohemia and to look him up when he arrived. In this case, Hartley, plausibly, rather than chancing upon McAlmon at Cooper Union, got him the modeling job. McAlmon shared a room with the homosexual Hartley at his boardinghouse on West Fifteenth Street. And despite appearances, as McAlmon confided to Norman Holmes Pearson, "never in all the months did Marsden make a pass at me."[14] Much impressed by Hartley's talent and personality, McAlmon would model fictional artists on him in three stories and in his roman à clef of Green Village in 1920, *Post-Adolescence.*

In spite of differences in age, temperament, and personal history, McAlmon and Williams hit it off immediately and became the closest of friends for thirty years. In the late fall of 1920 they decided that the literary situation was ripe for a new magazine, which they called *Contact.* The first issue, a patchwork of mimeographed, cheap paper, appeared in December 1920. The editors' credo reflected their shared "conviction that art which attains is indigenous of experience and relations, and that the artist works to express perceptions rather than to attain standards of achievement. . . . For native work in verse, fiction, criticism or whatever is written we mean to maintain a place, insisting on that which we have not found insisted upon before, the essential contact between words and the locality that breeds them, in this case America" (1, 10). Here, then, is a prose formulation of Williams's famous dictum: "No ideas but in things." Thus the American writer must use the American language, whose words are rooted in the peculiar American experience.

In September 1920, two visitors from England would, for good or ill, turn McAlmon's life around. Williams's imagist poet-friend from Philadelphia, H. D., with her lover-companion Bryher, was stopping in New York on a transcontinental tour. Invited to tea by H. D., Williams brought McAlmon along to meet "the old gal." What happened when McAlmon set eyes on Bryher at the Hotel Brevoort—and the events leading to his consenting to her proposal of marriage in February 1921—has engendered conflicting accounts of intentions and motives not only from the principals but also from their friends and family. Did Bryher feel any affection for him? Did McAlmon feel anything for her besides respect for her intellect and a kindred disdain of convention? Friends of both differed on who exploited whom, if in fact there was manipulation. What role did H. D. play, if any, in arranging (as it turned out) strictly a marriage of convenience? Did the bisexual McAlmon discern that Bryher had no sexual interest in men? According to Bryher, she "put her problem [an overbearing father] before him and suggested that if we married my family would leave me alone."[15] Marriage would give her the freedom to travel respectably with H. D., and, in turn, she would share her 600-pounds-a-year (about $3,000 American) allowance with him. Except for occasional visits to her parents, they would lead separate lives. For whatever reason—recklessness, opportunism, compassion—by marrying Bryher, McAlmon was instantly transformed from a scuffling writer bound by economic necessity into the nominal husband of a wealthy wife, with no need to work at anything but writing and with the funds to come and go as he pleased. McAlmon wrote and said little about his marriage, but he maintained that he married Annie Winifred Ellerman under her writing name and had no inkling of her father's riches until he saw the family mansion in London.

Sir John Ellerman reserved the bridal suite (ironically) on the liner *Celtic*, which he owned, for the newlyweds, and they along with H. D. and her little daughter Perdita sailed to England at the end of February 1921. To Williams, his friend's going to Europe boded ill. As he wrote to Amy Lowell, "I wish I had the boy back with me and not lost there abroad, to no good purpose I feel sure. My God, have we not had enough Pounds and Eliots? *The Sacred Wood* is full of them and their air rifles. But perhaps

Bob will do better. He will do better on condition that he comes back to America soon."[16] But it would be five years before McAlmon returned to America, and by then his life's course was set.

Turned off by London's dinginess and stuffy upper-class society, McAlmon, true to form, ferreted out like-minded writers and artists. One was the iconoclastic Wyndham Lewis, who steered him through London's bohemia, giving him tips on whom to avoid. Lewis published two of McAlmon's poems in his magazine *The Tyro*, and McAlmon reciprocated by influencing his father-in-law to secure Lewis painting commissions. McAlmon also became acquainted with Harriet Weaver, feminist publisher and Joyce's main patron; Weaver's Egoist Press brought out McAlmon's first book, *Explorations* (1921), a collection of poems and prose meditations. Despite his low opinion of T. S. Eliot's "mouldy poetry," McAlmon telephoned him to arrange a meeting. During an afternoon drinking whisky with Eliot and the science journalist J. W. N. Sullivan, McAlmon was pleasantly surprised to find that Eliot the man was "very likeable indeed" (McAlmon, *Geniuses*, 8–10). A few months later McAlmon received a letter from Eliot advising him on how to deal with Paris: in essence, observe but do not partake of its lower pursuits, and emulate Joyce, who was "independent of outside stimulus."[17] That advice McAlmon, always a player and never just a spectator, rejected out of hand.

Arriving in Paris in the spring of 1921, after a short stay in Montmartre, McAlmon gravitated to the Left Bank, where most of his compatriots had dug in. With some exceptions, the Americans, McAlmon included, spoke French poorly and had little to do with the natives, other than *poules* and barmen, aside from spending their francs (at about the rate of 25 francs to the dollar throughout the 1920s) at the French cafes, bars, bistros, restaurants, and shops. That was quite all right with the proprietors, who were only interested in the francs anyway. Relations between the former allies were not always comradely in the cafes and bars. When the wine (and gin and Scotch and brandy) flowed too freely and tempers flared, each would insult the other's honor, and a brawl would often ensue. McAlmon both participated in and witnessed these donnybrooks, which frequently had to be quelled by the gendarmes. In 1923, for example, Malcolm Cowley was arrested for punching out the *patron* of the Rotonde, a mean and nasty type who jacked up his prices for the Americans. McAlmon joined Laurence Vail and others in testifying on Cowley's behalf, and the magistrate dismissed the charges.[18] To the French, the Americans seemed cavalier about France's suffering during the war. And though the United States did not enter the war until April 1917, some Americans acted as if America alone had defeated Germany. In fact, America's total battle deaths—53,402, according to the U.S. Department of Defense—were a drop in the blood bucket compared with French, British, German, and Russian losses (not to mention Italian and Austrian casualties). Indeed, it was not the American expatriates who were "the lost generation," but the young men of Europe who were killed or maimed physically and emotionally.

But McAlmon had not come to Paris to mourn. In short order he became Joyce's drinking buddy, sometime financier, typist, and hawker of subscriptions to *Ulysses.* Among the first young American writers to patronize Sylvia Beach's Shakespeare and Company bookstore, he would check in almost daily and used it as a mailing address. Beach regarded him with sisterly fondness and rued his dissipations. Djuna Barnes and others of the *Broom* crowd were in town, as were Wyndham Lewis and Ezra Pound. McAlmon's first meeting with Pound went poorly because Pound donned the mantle of the pedagogue, which McAlmon resented. They kept their distance for about a year, and then became respectful friends. No one championed McAlmon's writing more than Pound, in reviews and in exhorting editors to give McAlmon a hearing.

All was not *la vie bohème*, however. In about six weeks McAlmon wrote enough short stories based on his life in the Midwest, Los Angeles, and New York to compose a volume. For a title Joyce suggested *A Hasty Bunch*, referring to the "racy" language and, perhaps, the speedy production. After English printers refused to typeset such "obscenity," Joyce wondered if McAlmon would ask Beach to undertake the printing, or do it on his own. Why not on his own? So McAlmon paid Maurice Darantière, Joyce's printer in Lyon, to bring out *A Hasty Bunch*, which was ready by the end of 1921. Reviewing it in *The Dial*, Pound noted, "The stories show little skill, but they do show a very considerable determination to present, or at any rate a capacity for presenting, the American small town in hard and just light, no nonsense, no overworking, no overloading. . . . McAlmon has written in the American spoken language."[19] To Pound, McAlmon was a young writer with potential.

When the Parisian summer season ended, McAlmon returned briefly to London and then moved on to chaotic Berlin. Unemployment, rampant inflation, and war reparations were ravaging Germany. Predators of all nationalities swooped in to the exploit the desperate populace. The dollar was worth twenty times its value elsewhere, and in Berlin drugs and sex of one's choice could be bought for a relative pittance (a deck of cocaine, for example, cost the equivalent of a dime). Among the American enclave in Berlin were Barnes, photographer Berenice Abbot, sculptor Thelma Wood (lover of both Barnes and Abbott), and Hartley, flush from selling his paintings and enjoying the favors of Berlin's young men. Although McAlmon made the rounds of the Hotel Adlon and subterranean dance halls-cum-cocaine dives, he was depressed by the youths of both sexes selling their bodies to survive.

McAlmon recaptured his Berlin experience in what has been judged his most original and best work, *Distinguished Air (Grim Fairy Tales)* (1925). The book is composed of three thematically interlocked stories—"Distinguished Air," "Miss Knight," and "The Lodging House"—centering on physical, moral, and spiritual decay. A tour de force, "Miss Knight" exposes the misadventures of transvestite whore Charley Knight, whose confused sexual identity McAlmon renders by interchanging masculine and feminine pronouns. *Distinguished Air* had to circulate underground in English-speaking countries because it was considered obscene, and McAlmon was especially fearful of being prosecuted in England. How times change! In 1998, "Miss Knight" was accorded a high place in American writing about homosexuals in the early twentieth century when it was selected for *The Columbia Anthology of Gay Literature*. Editor Byrne R. S. Fone lauded McAlmon's treatment of type and his gay argot for being well ahead of their time.

From Berlin, with a stop in xenophobic Munich, McAlmon went to Italy, which he took "a hate on" when a couple of Mussolini's thugs accosted him and a friend for not showing the proper respect for the fascist anthem. He was repelled by Rome and the Roman men flaunting their virility. Capri, where he met Norman Douglas, gay author of *South Wind*, was better, and he lingered for six weeks before heading back to London and then to Paris. He wrapped a momentous first year abroad by helping Joyce celebrate the publication of *Ulysses* on February 2, 1922.

In early 1923, McAlmon received a gift of seventy thousand dollars from his generous father-in-law. (Whatever he thought about Bryher, he was a dutiful son-in-law and was well liked by her family.) He used much of the money to establish the Contact Publishing Company so that he could publish his friends' writings as well as his own. Before he folded the enterprise in 1929, McAlmon published advanced work by, among others, Hartley, Williams, Hemingway, H. D., Mina Loy, Stein, Barnes, and Robert M. Coates. Especially noteworthy in modern literary history are Williams's *Spring and All* (1923); Hemingway's *Three Stories and Ten Poems* (his first book, 1923); Stein's *The Making of Americans* (1925); and the *Contact Collection of Contemporary Writers* (1925).[20]

Throughout the 1920s, McAlmon's life in Paris followed a pattern. Living mainly in hotels, he would write and tend to his publishing business during the day. Then at sundown he would appear at the Dôme or Select for cocktails and begin to "do nightlife." After dining he would check out the cafes and dance halls, picking up and dropping companions along the way. He often made forays late at night across the river to Montmartre nightclubs such as Zelli's, the Grand Duc, and, later in the decade, Bricktop's.[21] A serious night out would end at dawn with onion soup and beer at Les Halles market. To Sylvia Beach, McAlmon's personality was galvanic. "He attracted people. . . . He was certainly the most popular member of 'the Crowd,' as he called it. Whatever café or bar McAlmon patronized at the moment was where you saw everybody."[22] His popularity was due not only to picking up bar tabs, but even more to his knowing where the action would be, causing it himself if need be. Whether it was his drunken wailing of his "Chinese opera," or his hoofing it at *bals musettes* (both straight and gay) or insulting blowhards and getting into fights, for which he was "disciplined" (thrown out) by the management, a night on the town with McAlmon was never dull.

Yet, when McAlmon wrote concertedly, he would be, in Sisley Huddleston's word, "invisible," largely because he would leave Paris for a rural retreat such as Rambouillet, dry out, and get down to work. When he really wanted to shape up, he would go to a Riviera village, such as Theoule, and swim and tan on the beach and live quietly. With time and money at his disposal, he would travel to wherever appealed to his restless nature at the moment: Scandinavia, Egypt, Spain, Ireland, Mexico. And it was on one such trip to Italy, in February 1923, when he visited Pound's home at Rapallo, that Robert McAlmon met Ernest Hemingway for the first time. Every Hemingway biographer has quoted McAlmon's first impressions of Hemingway, albeit written after their early friendship had descended to mutual enmity: "At times he was deliberately hard-boiled and case-hardened; again he appeared deliberately innocent, sentimental, the hurt, soft, but fairly sensitive boy trying to conceal hurt, wanting to be brave. . . . He approached a café with a small-boy, tough-guy swagger, and before strangers of whom he was doubtful a potential snarl of scorn played on his large-lipped, rather loose mouth" (McAlmon, *Geniuses*, 155). McAlmon also wondered why a grown man and father would shadowbox and shadow-bullfight on the streets of Paris. Still, they started off pretty well. Both were from the Midwest; both liked to drink; both enjoyed hearing and spreading "dirt" about people they knew. Commiserating with Hemingway over the loss of almost all his manuscripts, which were in a trunk stolen from Hadley Hemingway at a Paris train station, McAlmon offered to publish what remained: the stories "My Old Man" and "Up in Michigan," to which Hemingway added a new one, "Out of Season," and ten poems. Chiefly notable as Hemingway's first book, *Three Stories and Ten Poems* received a good review by Edmund Wilson, who marked Hemingway as an up-and-comer.

When McAlmon told Hemingway that he was going to Spain for the bullfights, Hemingway said he wished he could go too, but money was tight. McAlmon invited him to come along anyway, mostly at his expense. In *Being Geniuses Together*, McAlmon recounted Hemingway's studying maggots eating the carcass of a dead dog on a flatcar next to their train in Spain. This to McAlmon was a prime example of Hemingway's deliberate case-hardening. But to Hemingway biographer Michael Reynolds, because Hemingway was taking notes, he was actually "working at his craft."[23] Hemingway chided McAlmon for going "soft" when he went to the bar car for a brandy, but, as McAlmon recalled, Hemingway soon joined him. When they hooked up with Bill Bird in Spain, the atmosphere was already frosty. Bird, the peacemaker, put the onus for the "needling and baiting" on Hemingway.[24] Meyers, Lynn, and Reynolds speculate that McAlmon's approaches to good-looking young Spaniards riled his homophobic companion. But McAlmon was not a demonstrative homosexual, and he certainly would not have flirted with men in Hemingway's presence. As he wrote in a letter to Norman Holmes Pearson, he might not have been a "he-he" man, but he was not a "fairy."[25] Something sexual between them might have occurred one night when they had more than enough of Johnnie Walker: in 1929, McAlmon told Morley Callaghan (and others) that Hemingway had revealed his homoerotic nature on this trip. Perhaps McAlmon cooked up this story out of jealousy and vengefulness, as charged. And yet, thirty years after the fact, he would write to Pearson (sparing the details) about a "beauty of a dream scene in the room Hem and I had one night. But I was Vicky, the buxom, tough, and beautiful tart of the cabaret of the night before."[26] The truth, of course, lies in their graves.

Putting whatever happened in Spain behind them, McAlmon and Hemingway remained cordial through 1924. When Hemingway was short of cash, McAlmon lent him money, which was always repaid. That summer, McAlmon was among the group—the Hemingways, the Birds, John Dos Passos, Donald Ogden Stewart, and Chink Dorman-Smith—that attended the Pamplona festival. In stark contrast to the nastiness the following year, all had a fine time. In December, McAlmon asked Hemingway to contribute to an anthology of new American and British writing he was assembling. Hemingway submitted "Soldier's Home," which he appraised as "the best short story I ever wrote," and which was subsequently published in the *Contact Collection*.[27] Hemingway's letters to McAlmon at this time are breezy and gossipy, closing with regards from Hadley and "Always yours, Hem." In retrospect, "always" for Hemingway turned out to be about a year. By December 1925 he was calling McAlmon "a son of a bitch with a mind like an ingrowing toe nail."[28] From then on the dirt they spread was on each other.

Hemingway would probably have turned against McAlmon eventually, as he did with such early benefactors as Sherwood Anderson, Gertrude Stein, and Ford Madox Ford. But the rupture in their friendship was hastened by F. Scott Fitzgerald's arrival in Paris in the spring of 1925. Matthew J. Bruccoli and Scott Donaldson have devoted books to the Hemingway-Fitzgerald relationship, and other biographers of both writers have weighed in heavily on it as well. There is no need to dwell on it here, except to remark that Hemingway's admiration for Fitzgerald's talent and his liking for the man aside, he also had a practical reason for cultivating the friendship: Fitzgerald was promoting him to Maxwell Perkins, his editor at Scribner's.

A week after reviling McAlmon, Hemingway wrote to Fitzgerald about his effort to break his contract with Liveright and to publish *The Sun Also Rises* with Scribner's: "It's up to you how I proceed next. You can write Max telling him how Liveright turned it [*The Torrents of Spring*] down and why, and your opinion of it. . . . You . . . are an important cog in the show."[29] So where does McAlmon come in? Thinking that Hemingway would like the low-down on his new buddy, McAlmon told him that he had sized up Fitzgerald as a fairy. But this bit of dirt backfired, for Hemingway, as he informed Fitzgerald, "called him [McAlmon]" on it: "I told him he was a liar and a damn fool."[30] Surprised and miffed by this rebuke, according to Hemingway, "McAlmon went around for two nights talking on the subject of what a swine I was, how *he* had done everything for me, started me off etc."[31]

Although McAlmon was wrong about Fitzgerald's sexuality, Fitzgerald was cut to the quick, and the wound festered for years. Stung even more by Zelda's accusation that he and Hemingway had had a homosexual affair, in 1930 he would write to her, in sorrow and anger: "My instinct is to write a public letter to the *Paris Herald* to see if any human being except yourself and Robert McAlmon has ever thought I was a homosexual. The three weeks after the horror of Valmont when I could not lift my eyes to meet the eyes of other men after your stinking allegations and insinuations will not be repeated."[32] Yet Fitzgerald himself was not above joking about homosexuals and pegging men as fairies. "Norman Douglas is not here now and anyway I have the piles," he wrote to John Peale Bishop from Paris in 1925; of a mutual acquaintance he offered, "'Dodo' Benson is here. I think he is (or was) a fairy."[33] And after his friendship with Hemingway had unraveled, he took a swipe at his former idol's manhood in explaining that the "dying fall" ending of *Tender Is the Night* was designed to let the reader "come to bat for *me* rather than going out to shake his nerves, whoop him up, then leaving him rather in the condition of a frustrated woman in bed. (Did that ever happen to you in your days with Macallaghan or McKisco, Sweetie?)."[34] From this distance, these imputations and cracks about homosexuality seem frivolous. The consequences for McAlmon, however, were serious: a lost chance to publish with Scribner's and, reportedly, a punch in the mouth from Hemingway.

Leaving Paris for New York in the fall of 1929, McAlmon was armed with a draft of a long, autobiographical novel, "Family Panorama," which he hoped to place with an American publisher. Unbeknownst to McAlmon, Hemingway had written a letter of introduction to Perkins because, despite his animus, "I have tried to help materially everyone I know who is a writer whether a friend or an enemy."[35] At dinner with Perkins, however, McAlmon, ever impolitic, began to "say mean things about Ernest . . . both as a man and as a writer."[36] Taken aback by McAlmon's "malicious envy," Perkins wrote Fitzgerald in confidence about the incident. This gave Fitzgerald an opportunity to get in some licks of his own, replying to Perkins that "McAlmon is a bitter rat" who has "failed as a writer" and who "assured Ernest that I was a fairy" and "told Callaghan that Ernest was a fairy. He's a pretty good person to avoid."[37]

While dining with the Hemingways a few weeks later, Fitzgerald, his mouth loosened by drink, betrayed Perkins's confidence and blabbed about McAlmon's behavior, adding a "particularly filthy story" about Hemingway that he had heard from Callaghan who learned it first from McAlmon himself. On December 10, 1929, a seething Hemingway wrote Perkins a long, rancorous letter asking exactly what McAlmon had said about him. Were these "new stories"? Hemingway was aware of the current ones: that Pauline was a lesbian; that he himself was a homosexual; that he had beaten Hadley and caused Bumby to be born prematurely. (For the record, Pauline in later years had lesbian affairs, and Hemingway, who admittedly was quick to anger, verbally and physically abused his fourth wife Mary.)[38] Hemingway protested that this time McAlmon "has gone a little too far. There should be a limit what lies people are allowed to tell under jealousies." Therefore, even if there was no honor in beating up the overmatched McAlmon, "I will go through with it as I should have long ago because the only thing such people fear is physical correction—They have no moral feelings to hurt."[39] Apparently, Hemingway (a few years later) knocked McAlmon down and split his lip in front of Jimmie Charter's Falstaff bar. But he was wrong about McAlmon's fear of physical punishment, for according to Bill Bird, "Bob was quite cheerful about his wounded lip."[40] That was not the first time McAlmon had been slugged, and he could take shots as well as dish them out, both with his fists and his mouth.

After Hemingway asked Perkins not to "reproach Scott with breach of confidence" because "drunk he is no more responsible than an insane man,"[41] Perkins replied on December 26 and 27, 1929, to pacify Hemingway by revealing what McAlmon really said. McAlmon had not talked "the line you tell me about," but "actually . . . talked [t]he way the once brilliant newspaper reporter, no longer young, talks about one who has become a brilliant correspondent, implying that he is a darn sight the better of the two and that, in fact, the other one learned writing from him." To Perkins, who confessed to "lik[ing] the rascal," McAlmon's jealousy "was only too obvious." Perkins also thought that McAlmon had "something" as a writer in spite of being "terribly stubborn" and overvaluing his importance. As for telling Fitzgerald about McAlmon, he did so to show him what a good guy Hemingway had been "to play the friend to McAlmon." Because McAlmon's sour grapes "had no significance of any kind in reality," Perkins wished he had kept his own counsel. By his moral standard, McAlmon was certainly "not what you want a man to be, by a considerable sight, but everyone who knows him knows that, I suppose."[42]

Well, obviously not everyone: on learning that Perkins was still undecided about publishing McAlmon, Fitzgerald, either ignorantly or willfully, greatly depreciated McAlmon's literary contributions. After owning up to telling Hemingway "that McAlmon was at his own dirty work around New York," Fitzgerald claimed that besides publishing "Ernest's first book and some books of his own," his only other accomplishment was to "found some magazine but of no importance." Then he added that "if the ubiquitous and ruined McAlmon deserves a hearing then John Bishop [a friend from Princeton], a poet and man of really great talents and intelligence, does."[43] Whether or not Fitzgerald's railing against McAlmon influenced Perkins, McAlmon was nevertheless shut out of the house of Scribner. Perkins later informed Morley Callaghan, who liked McAlmon, as to why his friend had been rejected. "I don't care if you tell McAlmon. . . . I hope you do tell him," Perkins said.[44] Still, even if McAlmon had known beforehand the cost of his tongue wagging, because "he spoke his mind under all circumstances," he would not have retracted one word.[45]

In 1926, McAlmon took action to end his sham marriage to Bryher, and when the divorce became final in 1927, he received a hefty settlement from Sir John. Thereupon wags around the Quarter dubbed him "Robert McAlimony," which Sisley Huddleston, among others, thought "perfectly unfair."[46] After almost six years in Europe, McAlmon decided to renew ties to his native land. Taking the long voyage home, he sailed first to Los Angeles to visit with his family, surveyed the artist colonies in Taos and Santa Fe, and then reunited with Williams and other returnees in New York. As always, he partook strenuously of nightlife, quite content with the quality of the booze in the speakeasies. Yet, while New York had its pleasures, the fast pace discomforted him. So with the painter Marcel Duchamp for company, he returned to Paris in time to toast Charles Lindbergh's triumphal landing at Le Bourget Field on May 21, 1927. For some time McAlmon had been working on what he called a "transcontinental" novel; and in August 1927 the new magazine *transition*, though mostly devoted to surrealism, published an extract.

By 1927, the second wave of Americans had hit Paris, but McAlmon's old crowd had thinned out. Of them, only the artist and designer Hilaire Hiler, Bill Bird, and Djuna Barnes remained to provide companionship. Hiler was McAlmon's closest friend at the time, and over drinks they lamented the passing of the years and absent friends. "The good days of the Quarter were finished," McAlmon complained to Kay Boyle in 1928 (Boyle, *Geniuses*, 323). Answering *The Little Review*'s question—"Why do you go on living?"—he wrote: "Because living interests me, and I prefer something to nothing." This laconic endorsement of life is not that of a happy man. Forty years later, Boyle, in her autobiographical interchapters to her revised edition of *Being Geniuses Together* (1968), presented a highly romanticized version of herself and her relationship with McAlmon during this period. She portrays herself as a femme fatale, desperately seeking love after the death in October 1926 of Ernest Walsh, poet, coeditor of *This Quarter*, her lover, and the father of her daughter Sharon. She is determined to succeed as a writer despite all obstacles, but she keeps getting into jams with men and impetuously enters Raymond Duncan's cultish neo-Greek commune. Boyle is mesmerized by McAlmon's "icy blue" eyes and transported by his savage attacks against hypocrisy and pretension. But beneath his cold, bitter, cynical exterior lies a tender and generous heart. She is in love with him and is certain he feels the same about her. She depicts him as despondent, lonely, and aimless. During a party at Harry and Caresse Crosby's country house, Boyle and McAlmon go for a walk and she quotes lines from one of his 1923 poems. McAlmon explodes: "'For Christ's sake. Six years saying the same poem? . . . The God-damned, fucking quivering pieces of me! Good enough to be flushed like you know what down the drain! . . . I'm fed up with whatever it is I'm carrying around inside this skin, rattling around inside these bones! . . . For Christ's sake, don't care about me! Stop it, will you? Let the God-damned pieces fall apart!'" (Boyle, *Geniuses*, 368–69). Perhaps McAlmon did say something like that, but the placement of the obscenities and the histrionics suggest, if not invention, at least embellishment on Boyle's part.

Tellingly, no such encounter is in the original or in McAlmon's reconstruction of the years 1928 to 1931 in his thinly fictionalized unpublished memoir, "The Nightinghouls of Paris." In both works, McAlmon regards Boyle (Dale Burke in "Nightinghouls") fondly, helps her financially, and offers moral support, but nowhere does he indicate romantic feelings for her. In fact, he judges her a flighty, self-dramatizing, sentimental young woman with a penchant for trouble, especially from ill-chosen men. In believing McAlmon secretly loved her, Boyle denied his having sex with men. Indeed, in her edition of *Being Geniuses Together*, there is no hint of McAlmon's homosexuality. And yet Boyle had known of it at least since the summer of 1931. As she wrote her sister Joan on August 8 of that year, "all that filth about McAlmon . . . has so turned my stomach that I can't be civil to him. As far as being friendly with him ever again—that's finished!"[47]

Boyle's "ever again" lasted about as long as Hemingway's "always." In 1932 she selected the stories for *The Indefinite Huntress and Other Stories*, published by Caresse Crosby's Black Sun Press. Moreover, she leaped to McAlmon's defense after Waverley Root reviewed the book negatively in the *Paris Herald*. In a letter to Root that he printed in the paper, she stated, "Because I recognize in McAlmon the sound and almost heedless builder of a certain strong wind in American letters, I can see Hemingway as the gentleman who came in afterward and laid down the linoleum because it was so decorative and so easy to keep clean." To Root, however, who was repelled by McAlmon personally, the question was not who wrote first but who wrote best, and he believed Boyle was "disingenuous" because she herself chose the stories and was being "both partisan and judge."[48] In truth, McAlmon was not pleased with the selection and complained to her about it.

Whether Kay Boyle did McAlmon's reputation a service by revising and editing his memoir is debatable. More than half the book is devoted to her story, and in lopping off the years 1931–1934 she deprived readers of his insights into the social and political unrest in Germany and France during this period. In Munich in 1932 with Seldon Rodman, for example, McAlmon watched a Nazi parade led by Hitler and his Brown Shirts; and in Paris he witnessed riots, police aggression, and clashes between fascists and communists. "Potential war or revolution was in the air, and hate and distrust," he correctly predicted in 1934 (McAlmon, *Geniuses*, 372).

Boyle's posthumous pairing garnered raves for her parts and barbs for his. Malcolm Cowley, who disliked McAlmon as a man and as a writer (and vice versa), in the *New York Times Book Review*, praised both her editing and writing at McAlmon's expense: Her "chapters reveal by contrast . . . that McAlmon never mastered the craft of writing. . . . His story when set beside Kay Boyle's reminds one of Hogarth's twin fables of the idle and industrious apprentice." Yet Cowley conceded that the book was valuable because "it gives us an impression of depth and substantiality that have been lacking in other memoirs of Paris in the 1920's, and notably in McAlmon's original story."[49] Had Cowley known that Secker and Warburg, English publisher of the original, "cut much of it as too vulgar, dangerous, or American"?[50] Would he have changed his opinion if he had? Worse yet was Jean Stafford's hatchet job in the *New York Review of Books:* "One could, with little loss, expurgate McAlmon altogether, for his postures are offensive, his literary dicta dictatorial, he is acidulous and patronizing and his writing is repetitious and boring."[51] Ironically, Stafford is right for the wrong reason: Boyle would have shown more respect for McAlmon's talent, in which she fervently believed, by influencing a publisher to bring out the uncut version (presuming it existed) or to reprint the complete 1938 edition. If no trade publisher would undertake it, she would have almost certainly placed it with an academic press. After all, the University of Nebraska Press published a generous selection of McAlmon's prose, including excerpts from *Being Geniuses Together*, in 1962, which she reviewed. She then could have written a foreword attesting to McAlmon's importance in literary history and recounting her relationship with him. In this way her name would have still been linked with his for posterity.[52]

Besides deleting and emending, Boyle performed some creative editing by inserting a passage involving John Glassco and his boon companion Graeme Taylor that is not in the original. She had been corresponding with Glassco and knew that he was writing a memoir of his Paris days. Conceivably, she wrote him in as a friendly gesture.[53] They had been lovers briefly in 1928, when the eighteen-year-old Glassco, having dropped out of McGill University in Montreal, with his older friend Taylor, came to Paris to pursue a literary career. Glassco's well-to-do, albeit censorious, father agreed to provide him with a hundred-dollars-a-month allowance.

With their subsistence assured, Glassco and Taylor, bored by Montreal's provinciality, sailed off to realize their writing ambitions "in the city of Baudelaire, Utrillo, and Apollinaire."[54]

Settling into a cheap hotel on the Rue du Montparnasse, they gradually worked their way into Quarter life. Giving up poetry, Glassco began writing his autobiography, while Taylor embarked on a novel. One night at the Dôme they were introduced by Diana Tree, as Glassco calls Kay Boyle in *Memoirs of Montparnasse*, to "a small, handsome, carelessly dressed man" who regarded them with "humorous contempt" and offered them a drink. After learning they were Canadian, Robert McAlmon told them, "I was in the Canadian army during the war but I deserted."[55] Cottoning to the boys, McAlmon led them on a tour of Paris nightspots. In a gay dance club on a "mysterious, sinister street," an American Negro gave Glassco and Taylor "genuine Cuban cigarillos," which turned out to be laced with hashish, nauseating Glassco. After Glassco sobered up, McAlmon herded them to Bricktop's by way of the notorious Place Pigalle, whose name prompted an obscene song by McAlmon. At Bricktop's, McAlmon proceeded to get drunk, insult the clients, screech his "Chinese opera," pass out when slipped a mickey, wake up crying at the Coupole, and finally to be carried, asleep, to Glassco's bed at dawn. While bunking with Taylor, Glassco was awakened by McAlmon's body between them, and he "began to wonder if [McAlmon] had been quite as helpless as he appeared to be in the Coupole bar."[56] That was certainly a memorable night. Did it happen the way Glassco reported it in *Memoirs?* Not likely.

In a prefatory note to *Memoirs*, Glassco explains its composition. The first three chapters, he says, were written in 1928; the rest during the winter of 1932–33, based on notes "taken on the spot" while he was awaiting surgery for advanced tuberculosis. He set the manuscript aside for thirty-five years, dusted it off, revised some phrases and supplied, in certain cases, fictitious names for living people, then sent it to be published. He changed nothing from the original, he avers, however unbecoming, because he is now "less like someone I have been than a character in a novel I have read."[57] To astute readers the last sentence gives the show away. *Memoirs* is more fiction than fact and is therefore untrustworthy as a reliable account of the people and events Glassco purportedly recorded.

As scholars of modern Canadian literature have disclosed, Glassco perpetrated a deception about when and how the book was written. Except for the first chapter, which was published in *This Quarter* in 1928, as Thomas E. Tausky reveals in a comparative analysis of the notebooks, manuscript, and published text, Glassco wrote the entire book between 1963 and 1964.[58] After his agent returned the manuscript as unpublishable, Glassco was seized by self-doubt and guilt. He confesses to himself in his journal "that one-quarter of this book was lies."[59] "People and things" did not appear "altogether as they did: I have *rearranged* many events, telescoped still more, & invented much of the dialogue—but the facts are all true, & and the tenor of the life in those days, and the behaviour of everybody, faithfully reproduced."[60] Glassco's confusion about facts and fictions is evident: a fact is true by definition.

Having abandoned the project for three years, Glassco was spurred to renew it after his contact with Boyle, whose chapters in *Being Geniuses Together* he was helping by sending her photographs and his renderings of McAlmon's speech. On September 9, 1968, he wrote her that the revision was finished: "It has the form of fiction . . . and is more a montage of those days than literal truth."[61] Of Glassco's portrayal of McAlmon, Tausky observes that it "remains one of the memorable features of the book. . . . McAlmon is the only individualized voice Glassco created. In a manuscript passage deleted from the final text, Glassco says of McAlmon: 'His was the most genuine personality I have ever known.'"[62] Why, one wonders, would Glassco excise such an encomium for a dead friend?

What Glassco also deleted—doubtless for protective reasons—was that after Taylor returned to Canada, Glassco was McAlmon's kept boy. Supported by McAlmon and because of his real affection for him, Glassco "was only too happy to lend myself to whatever fictive [sexual] role he wanted to cast me in."[63] Similarly, in the book Glassco obscures his homosexual relations with Taylor, who, according to Glassco, was the one with homoerotic desires. As with McAlmon, Glassco tolerated sex with Taylor out of friendship, and though he "simulate[d] reciprocity, such practices were alien to his essential heterosexual nature."[64]

With his obscenities, sarcasm, and hectoring, McAlmon does command *Memoirs*, but how close to the real man is Glassco's depiction? Here Philip Kokotailo notes the disparity between the manuscript and the book. In the manuscript, McAlmon has sympathy for others, especially fellow writers, and is not simply a "bitter and cynical exile." Glassco treats McAlmon's feelings of being a "lonely outcast" with compassion, and McAlmon, rather than being constantly drunk, is "fully sober." In his revision, however, Glassco "eliminated virtually all expositions of the private, inner man, leaving only the public persona." To Kokotailo, then, "the manuscript, especially with its candour about McAlmon's sexuality, private thoughts, and personal feelings, resonates with honesty. The book, with what it leaves unsaid, its subtlety, and its suggestiveness, resonates with artifice."[65] In Glassco's conception, as he wrote to Boyle, "the real value of 'memoirs' [was] not so much a record of 'what happened' as a re-creation of the spirit of a period of time." And for him the way to recapture this spirit was through "artifice," "subterfuge," and "invention."[66] While these techniques are used by fiction writers and so-called literary journalists (who have at times blurred the lines between reportage and fiction by concocting dialogue, for example), one who purports to be a memoirist has the moral obligation, both to his own time and to the future, to be as factual as possible, and not to distort for artistic purposes. Verisimilitude is the stuff of realistic fiction, but history, the genre to which memoirs and autobiographies belong, demands verity. The Robert McAlmon in *Memoirs of Montparnasse* is thus a caricature, not a rounded portrait of the person he was.

In a March 10, 1969, letter to William Toye, Glassco's editor at Oxford University Press Canada, Glassco disparaged *Being Geniuses Together* as "mostly name-dropping" and "faded literary gossip."[67] Yet, in letters to McAlmon in December 1941 and March 1942, he complimented both the title and the book for "sum[ming] up a certain life pretty well." (A mark of Glassco's shoddiness as regards McAlmon's writing is that, in *Memoirs*, he said he first read *Being Geniuses Together* in 1928 and found it to be like all of McAlmon's books.) Tastes change, of course, especially if one is making a case for one's own parallel book by putting down the competition. But perhaps Glassco had disliked it from the first and was merely being nice to an old friend.

On June 16, 1947, Glassco wrote to McAlmon that he was looking forward to reading the draft of "The Nightinghouls of Paris" that McAlmon had recently sent him. Regarding *Being Geniuses Together* as "most disingenuous, 'genteel,' and lacking in frankness," as Glassco remarked to Toye in 1969, was he more receptive to "Nightinghouls," which candidly recounts his and Taylor's frolics and foibles in Paris and Nice from 1928 to 1931? For McAlmon is perfectly direct about sexual couplings and uncouplings not only of Glassco and Taylor but also of fellow expatriates Kay Boyle, Djuna Barnes and Thelma Wood, Gwen Le Gallienne and Yvette Ledoux, Hilaire Hiler, Laurence Vail and Peggy Guggenheim Vail, Louise Bryant and William Bullitt, and Duff Twysden. The only person McAlmon is reticent about is himself. During this time his persona, Kit O'Malley, though tempted by a buxom adventuress in Nice and a slattern whom Glassco and Taylor pick up, is sexually abstemious. This was, of course, not the case. The evidence suggests that Glassco was not at all pleased by McAlmon's candor.

In a December 2, 1964, letter to a book dealer, Glassco asks if Northwestern University Library "has the manuscript of McAlmon's last novel *The Susceptible Boy*. He sent me a copy here in Foster [Canada] in 1946 or 1947, which I returned without comment: it ended our friendship. These old things seem mistaken and rather saddening now. But the existence of this book still troubles me." With his poor memory of McAlmon's titles, Glassco is here confusing McAlmon's 1929 short unpublished novel "The Susceptible Boy" (and such variant titles as "The Promiscuous Boy") with "Nightinghouls," which, as noted above, he read in 1947. According to Glassco biographer Brian Busby, Glassco's distaste for "Nightinghouls" explains "the abrupt ending to their correspondence."[68]

Although many of the same figures appear in Boyle's, Glassco's, and McAlmon's renditions, their characterization and speech are so unlike as to be about different people. In Boyle's, for example, McAlmon is a desperate man, with inexpressible longings not even alcohol and love can assuage. In Glassco's, he is a bitter, hopeless, manic boozer, a slipshod writer who never reads anything and yet knows everything. In "Nightinghouls," however, Kit O'Malley is a perceptive observer, a judicious advisor, fond of his drink but in control, at home with people of all stations, races, and nationalities, a classy dancer, scornful of pretense, an attentive reader of the great nineteenth-century Russian novelists, a connoisseur of painting. Though he uses expletives for emphasis, he speaks rationally in sentences and paragraphs. He is admittedly at times moody, irascible, and restive, but he is unquestionably an able man.

What of the Glassco and Taylor characters, whom McAlmon calls Sudge Galbraith and Ross Campion, in "Nightinghouls"? Except for incessant snickering at their elders, they are almost unrecognizable compared to Glassco's published text. Whereas McAlmon describes Glassco as "wistful," "boyish," "reticent," and deferential, Glassco casts himself as brash, sophisticated, and adept with women. Just as Glassco transfigured McAlmon in his revision, so he made himself a hard-boiled, experienced guy. But the Glassco in the manuscript is much like Sudge in "Nightinghouls"—"a shy and polite youngster," deferring to older writers such as Djuna Barnes (Willa Torrence in *Memoirs*). In his love affair with Diana Tree (Kay Boyle), he is not a confident, practiced ladies' man but an "impressionable and romantic" youth. With Stanley Dahl (Sanka in "Nightinghouls"), he is hesitant and callow, not an accomplished lover. In fact, in the manuscript, Stanley tells him: "I thought you were a fairy."[69] Nor does Ross resemble Taylor in *Memoirs*. In "Nightinghouls," he is fearful, neurasthenic, wimpy, moony, and ineffectual with women. In *Memoirs*, however, he has sex with the demimondaine Caridad and whores and is a two-fisted drinker who supplements Sudge's allowance by boldly hustling poker dice at bars. What Glassco omitted altogether from *Memoirs*, though planning to use it, was the fight he had with Taylor over the girl, with Taylor crying after Glassco strikes him, and Glassco apologetically consoling. McAlmon describes the fracas in full, and it formed the basis of Morley Callaghan's story "Now That April's Here" in *This Quarter* in 1929. Indeed, to the experienced women in "Nightinghouls," Sudge and Ross, far from young rakewells, are "babies," nice to play with but not to be taken seriously.

While garbling the titles and contents of McAlmon's books, Glassco makes a telling point about his method. McAlmon's stories, he discerns, "were obviously literal transcriptions of things set down simply because they had happened and were vividly recollected. There was neither *invention* nor *subterfuge*; when the recollection stopped so did the story."[70] From an artistic standpoint, the lack of imagination may be a liability; but in the context of social and cultural history, literal transcription is a virtue. Whatever its stylistic and organizational shortcomings, "Nightinghouls" accurately records expatriate life in Paris and on the Riviera at the end of the 1920s. While it may not always delight, it nevertheless instructs.

Perhaps in his fictionalizing, Glassco did "recapture the *spirit* of those days," but this spirit was only that felt by a young man. The spirit was entirely different for the old hands, whose own effervescent youth had flattened out by years of dissipation, failed marriages and love affairs, poverty, and rejection of their work. By 1929, for example, Hemingway, while attaining literary success, had suffered a wrenching divorce and a not altogether happy remarriage. Djuna Barnes and Thelma Wood had broken up, as had Janet Flanner and Solita Solongo, Laurence and Peggy Vail, and Louise Bryant and William Bullitt. Zelda Fitzgerald had begun her dementia, with attendant woes for her husband and daughter. And McAlmon himself, because "what Paris once offered she no longer gave," went back to the States en route to Mexico City (McAlmon, *Geniuses*, 304–5). As Sisley Huddleston recalled, one Montparnasse denizen said plaintively, in 1930 or 1931, "One never sees the old figures nowadays. . . . The Quarter without Ernest Hemingway has lost something. . . . And one does not see Ford Madox Ford any more. Bob McAlmon has gone."[71] Thus for McAlmon and his contemporaries the late 1920s was somber, and a dark tone pervades "Nightinghouls," as it does Fitzgerald's "Babylon Revisited" (1931) and *Tender Is the Night* (1934), both set in the same period and both concerned with American expatriates in France.

Although almost all of the now-celebrated American expatriate writers, with their prominent British counterparts, appear in speaking roles or by reference, the historical importance of "Nightinghouls" lies not only in McAlmon's anecdotes (sometimes snide) about them, but also in his representing their daily lives and those of the people they interacted with. Here are barmen like Gaston and Jimmie Charters; *patrons* of Riviera *pensions* like Poggi; fishermen and "old soaks" who get mellow on wine and "croak" ditties in a rope and wine shop in Nice; a commercial artist from Chicago with his wife and teenage daughter on a cultural sabbatical; a *patronne* of a bistro who recites Laforgue; a Russian "countess" and her young Chilean lover whom she discards for not being "brutal" enough; the brazen, flaming-haired Caridad (Hilaria) who lusts after beautiful male bodies, insults bragging Sinclair Lewis, and yet mothers young Jacques dying of tuberculosis. Then there are the deracinated pensioners at Poggi's: a retired British major and his wife; an eccentric South African matron and her offbeat daughter; the obese Cockney woman who stinks up the communal toilet; a fussy, carping Indian woman whom Sudge and Ross gleefully lock in the bathroom. Here too are the dogs—Woo-Woo, Clan, Dockie, Sultan, and Sadie—as fully realized (and in some cases more so) as the people. And finally there are the *poules* in Paris and Nice, whom McAlmon respects as honest professionals and with whom he enjoys talking and dancing. Though unsaid, perhaps he used their services as well, for, unlike the "amateur" Sanka, he knows that they have regular checkups for disease. (When Kit first meets Sudge and Ross, Sudge is in the throes of gonorrhea he contracted from a girl they picked up. Kit sends Sudge to a "reputable doctor" and warns him that the disease is not to be trifled with.) "The Nightinghouls of Paris," then, in contrast to memoirs focusing solely on expatriate writers and the literary life of the 1920s, embraces a cross section of common Left Bank and Riviera types, of many nationalities and social levels, and in so doing gives them a presence and a voice that redeems them from oblivion.

Throughout the Thirties, McAlmon, restless and adrift, traveled incessantly. With his friends scattered, Paris no longer appealed to him. So he bounced around two continents, crisscrossing America twice, with sojourns in Mexico, and roaming Europe from France to the Balkans, with extended stays in Majorca and Barcelona. He began writing *Being Geniuses Together* in Barcelona in 1933. Finishing it in the spring of 1934, he read the manuscript to Joyce, who was displeased by McAlmon's treating him less as a great writer than as, in Richard Ellman's words, "a member of the heavy-drinking bohemian set." When Joyce remarked that it should be called "*Advocatus Diaboli*" (Devil's Advocate), McAlmon replied, "What in hell you think the title means, that I take genius without salt." But to the offended Joyce the book was merely "the office boy's revenge," and it caused a rift in their friendship.[72] McAlmon took the manuscript to London and obtained an agent; Katherine Anne Porter, who admired the tone, style, and veracity, tried to place it with her publisher, Harcourt Brace. But with the world in turmoil, there was no market for a chronicle of Jazz Age high jinks. And when Secker and Warburg published its bowdlerized edition in 1938, all hell was about to break loose in Europe. Reportedly, most of the unsold copies were destroyed during the Blitz by a bomb on the warehouse storing them. McAlmon continued to write and publish stories, extracts from novels, and poetry in literary magazines in America and England. In 1937, James Laughlin brought out *Not Alone Lost,* collected poems, one of the earliest New Directions books, to mixed reviews. When the Germans invaded France in 1940, McAlmon was living in Dampierre, a small town about 75 miles southeast of Paris. He went to Paris to retrieve stored books and papers, but because the buses and the Métro were not operating, he had no means of transporting them. Even worse, back in Dampierre he was consternated to discover almost everything had been stolen. Though some material later turned up, which he managed to bring home, much of what he had written, published, and collected for twenty years became a casualty of war.

Was "Nightinghouls" among the survivors? The provenance is difficult to establish with certainty. Letters by and to McAlmon in the Beinecke Rare Book and Manuscript Library at Yale University might pinpoint when he wrote it. It is clear, however, from his sending a typescript to Glassco in June 1947 and from the address on the title page—the Southwestern Surgical Supply Co., Phoenix, where he worked from 1941 to 1947—that he had completed a draft by mid-1947. (In a letter dated February 3, 1953, to Pearson, he mentions "Nightinghouls" in reference to Glassco.) Possibly he started writing it in Europe and then worked on it during the war years in Phoenix, where he lived in a hotel and frequented bars packed with servicemen. If he had completed it before 1947, he would have no doubt sent it to Glassco earlier, since they had resumed corresponding in 1941. In all likelihood, writing to Glassco, Hartley, Hiler, and other old friends stirred McAlmon's memory and energized him to relive in words what, in retrospect, had been their last good years. He might also have used parts of *Being Geniuses Together* excised from the original. Moreover, in his letters McAlmon refers to a sequel he is planning to write, and perhaps "Nightinghouls" is that book. However circumstantial, the evidence suggests that McAlmon wrote "Nightinghouls" between 1945 and 1947.

What is rather odd, considering McAlmon's devotion to the American vernacular, is that he uses British orthography in "Nightinghouls," for example, "colour," "towards," "grey," and so forth. That might lead one to speculate that he had written it in Europe. More probable is that he assimilated British spelling during his years abroad. Evidence for this is in a February 12, 1953, letter to Pearson expressing his desire to go again to Europe on a ship "from San Francisco, San Diego, Los Angeles Harbour, or wherever—towards London, Antwerp, Rotterdam, doesn't matter a damn." By his own admission McAlmon was insouciant about spelling and grammar, ironically noting that he never could proofread and that, typing, "my fingers go everywhere."[73] A quirk, McAlmon's British spelling has no bearing on when he composed his recollections of his and his friends' pell-mell days. A writer from experience, at age fifty-two and isolated in the Valley of the Sun, McAlmon had only old stories to tell.

Handwritten on the title page is the date 1929. McAlmon may have wanted to add it to the title to signify the time of the major events. He provides no dates in the text, though he alludes to the stock market crash in October of that year. The chronology can best be determined by letters (his and others'), memoirs and autobiographies, and biographies of his contemporaries. Glassco and Taylor arrived in Paris in the spring of 1928. McAlmon is not altogether clear about when they first met, but it was probably in late 1928 or early 1929. In Boyle's edition of *Being Geniuses Together*, McAlmon remarks, apropos their time in Nice in February or early March 1929, that he "had known them in Paris when they spent a year in the Quarter" (Boyle, *Geniuses*, 307). But he does not say specifically when they met. Boyle assigns the Nice episodes to 1928, the year she dates a photograph of Glassco, Taylor, and McAlmon. But she erred: the same photograph in *Memoirs* is dated 1929, and Leon Edel, who knew "Buffy" Glassco in Montreal, states in his introduction to the first edition of *Memoirs* that, in 1929, he moved into the room McAlmon had vacated on leaving Nice. McAlmon spent the spring, summer, and much of the fall of 1928 in Le Canadel, a village near Villefrance. He went often to the Vails' nearby villa for parties and took trips in Vail's Hispano-Suiza to St. Tropez and Nice "for an occasional bust." At Le Canadel he met Edwin M. Lanham, who married Kay Boyle's sister, Joan, in 1929, and whose autobiographical novel, *Sailors Don't Care*, one of the last Contact Editions, McAlmon published in the spring of that year.[74] The domestic clashes between the Vails (Felix and Sally Lutyens), some instigated by Vail's sister Clotilde (Consuela), McAlmon recounts in "Nightinghouls." Glassco describes a night out with McAlmon and the Vails in which Laurence drives them to meet Frank Harris and, afterward, McAlmon falls asleep during a pornographic movie they go to see. None of this is in "Nightinghouls," and in any case the incident had to occur in 1929 when McAlmon and the boys were in Nice.

In the spring of 1929, McAlmon shared his studio apartment with Glassco and Taylor, and down the hall lived Gwen Le Gallienne and Yvette Ledoux (Laura Bradley and Colette Godescard). The scenes with Hemingway (Forest Pemberton) and Duff Twysden (Lady Mart) happened in 1929, when Hemingway, Pauline, and her sister Jinny spent the spring in Paris, as had those with the Callaghans (Flannagans), who had come to Paris in April 1929. The notorious sparring match between

Callaghan and Hemingway, which Flannagan puzzles over to Kit and the boys, took place in June.

McAlmon went alone to the Riviera seaside village of Theoule in the summer of 1929. There he befriended the Meyer (Groper) family and played the big brother to seventeen-year-old Felicia (Freddie). The Lanhams (Hal and Kate Meng) were also part of his social circle. In "Nightinghouls," Ross makes a brief appearance, but sullen and out of his element, he hurries back to Paris and Sudge. When Hilaire Hiler (Gaylord Showman) joins the group, everyone is invigorated by his floridity and bonhomie.

By the late summer, however, tourists had overrun Theoule, so McAlmon retreated to Paris, and then headed for New York and his fateful dinner with Perkins. He spent most of the next eighteen months in Alamos, a small Mexican town in Sonora.[75] But Paris beckoned again, and he returned in early 1931. In "Nightinghouls," Kit runs into Sudge on the Rue de Vaugirard and finds him much subdued. At that moment Sudge is preparing to go to Spain with Katherine Montoon, his older mistress. Sudge wants to buy Kit a farewell drink, but Katherine, who has him in tow, rushes him away. Before a parting handshake, Kit asks Sudge what he did with his memoirs. "Tore them up. They were disgustingly idiotic," Sudge replies. And yet, in another neat bit of subterfuge in *Memoirs*, Glassco maintains that he guarded his "pile of scribblers" (that is, his memoirs) by his bedside in the American hospital at Neuilly. All the rest of his juvenilia, however, is destroyed by his mistress, Mrs. Quayle (probably a composite of Margaret Whitney and Marguerite "Peggy" Lippe-Rosskam, McAlmon's Katherine Montoon).[76] Glassco claims that she burned his plays, poems, and stories because, she tells him, "'They were quite unworthy of you, my lovely child.'"[77]

In the end, Mrs. Quayle breaks Glassco's heart by jilting him in Majorca for a married Englishman. In despair, he begins to cough blood and has to have thoracoplastic surgery to save his life. In contrast, "Nightinghouls" closes quietly and sardonically. Awakening a drunken English novelist who had latched onto him during the voyage back to France, Kit says, "'Let's go on to the Quarter. There's an Irishman, several Russians, and a Pole there, all of whom delight in talking religion, mathematics, higher thought, and the power of evil. I'll locate one of them for you surely, and then I must be on my way, doing the rounds.'"

In the nine years remaining to McAlmon after he left Phoenix in 1947, none of his plans—to reprint early work, to publish any of twenty manuscripts, to revisit Europe—came to fruition. He worked in his brothers' El Paso store until 1951, when with help from his family he bought a duplex in Desert Hot Springs, California. In the late 1940s, to augment his salary he began selling books, letters, and memorabilia to Norman Holmes Pearson and Donald C. Gallup, professors at Yale. He also started a regular correspondence with Pearson in which he reminisced about the 1920s and tried to set the record straight. He was struck a body blow by Williams's *Autobiography* (1951), which he deemed filled with errors, distortions, and misquotations. He especially resented being portrayed as emasculated by H. D. and Bryher. Hurt to the core, he would inveigh against his dearest friend for thirty years to Pearson as well as to mutual friends. From time to time he would be uplifted by letters from Kay Boyle, Djuna Barnes, Josephine Herbst, Bill Bird, and a few other surviving friends. His family would visit from Los Angeles, and, during 1953, Edward Dahlberg, sympathizing with McAlmon's loneliness, would come from Santa Monica to keep him company. Kenneth Rexroth was another writer who came to see him. By 1955, his health failing, even writing letters was arduous. On February 2, 1956, he succumbed to pneumonia, a little more than a month shy of his sixty-first birthday. In 1961, Dahlberg eulogized McAlmon: Despite the "great faults" in McAlmon's writing, he said, "you will not look in vain for that rare ore in human character, honesty, which is lacking in the volumes prattled about in the public whorehouse directory of literature, American newspaper book columns."[78]

What of McAlmon's reputation fifty years after his death? In biographies of Hemingway, McAlmon starts out being a good guy for taking Hemingway to Spain and publishing his first book, then becomes a bad guy for gossiping maliciously about him. Usually, as in Kenneth S. Lynn's estimate, he is considered a writer who never "fulfilled" his "early promise" but is credited for his publishing.[79] Michael Reynolds, though calling him a "gossip virtuoso" and a "bitchy man," agrees with Hemingway's initial positive opinion of McAlmon's talent. After quoting McAlmon's description of Hemingway on first meeting, he observes, "Just how well McAlmon wrote can be judged by the way he caught Hemingway's physical presence with the short, deft, envious strokes of a caricaturist."[80] Reynolds follows the standard line on McAlmon and Hemingway: "[W]hen he and Ernest were both promising young men, it was an even bet as to which writer would make it big. By 1934, the question was decided, and Robert McAlmon must have wondered how his balloon lost its air."[81] Commercial success, of course, does not always equate with talent. And it is arguable that Hemingway fell short of his promise, too. For after *A Farewell to Arms* (1929), which was published when Hemingway was only thirty, he never wrote as well again except for a handful of stories and passages in *For Whom the Bell Tolls* (1940).

At least Lynn, and to a greater extent Reynolds, regard McAlmon as a serious writer. On the other hand, Jeffrey Meyers, in his slapdash, flippant biography of Hemingway, styles him as a "minor *littérateur*" homosexual with whom Hemingway became friends "not on mutual respect, but on McAlmon's money and his willingness to help Hemingway."[82] Where Meyers got this notion is a mystery. After reading McAlmon's stories in Rapallo, Hemingway praised them to Pound on March 10, 1923: "If I was in the tipster business I would whisper into the shell like ear of a friend, 'go and make a small bet on McAlmon while you can still get a good long price.'"[83] And in a letter to Edward J. O'Brien, dated September 12, 1924, Hemingway commented: "McAlmon is writing better all the time. He has written a really fine long poem [probably "The Revolving Mirror" published in *Portrait of a Generation* (1926)] and some really promising prose in a thing called Village."[84] Apparently, Meyers was less interested in quoting from Hemingway's published letters than in paraphrasing the unpublished ones, which he was not permitted to quote. Here is how he paraphrases an unpublished 1926 letter to Pound: "Hemingway threatened to beat that thin, disappointed, half-assed, fairy ass-licking, fake husband, literary type." It is hard to believe that Hemingway wrote anything like that—to Pound, especially—but if he did, his scurrility exceeded even McAlmon's. But perhaps Meyers is simply displaying his mastery of invective. Before dismissing a writer as "minor" (whatever that means), one should at the very least read his or her writing, which Meyers, other than the parts about Hemingway in Boyle's edition of *Being Geniuses Together*, gives no sign of having done with McAlmon. Thus, in these biographies of Hemingway, McAlmon is presented in three different, mostly uncomplimentary ways, and of them only Reynolds shows some respect for his writing and treats him with a measure of human understanding.

Humphrey Carpenter accords him his due, if not altogether as a writer, as the hub of expatriate social life in Montparnasse in *Geniuses Together: American Writers in Paris in the 1920s*. Besides alluding to McAlmon's title in his own, Carpenter quotes extensively from his memoir as well as from his narrative of Bastille Day 1923, "Truer Than Most Accounts," that Pound published in *The Exile* 2 (1927). In the main, Carpenter is less concerned with the writers as artists than he is with their nightlife, and in this respect McAlmon had no peer. While Carpenter is faithful to his sources, he takes Glassco's memoir at face value, and cites Glassco's invented dialogue and opinion of McAlmon's writing without qualification. Still, unlike Hemingway's biographers, he is nonjudgmental about McAlmon's character.

Listing McAlmon as the arch "slanderer" of Hemingway and Fitzgerald, Scott Donaldson, in *Hemingway vs. Fitzgerald* (1999), which rehashes Matthew J. Bruccoli's *Fitzgerald and Hemingway: A Dangerous Friendship* (1994), labels him a "writer-dilettante" and reprises his gabbing to Perkins, and Hemingway's and Fitzgerald's anger. Of Fitzgerald's lament that the "fairies . . . spoiled" his real affection for Hemingway, Donaldson comments, "Among the fairies whose malicious talk 'spoiled' things was, surely, Robert McAlmon."[85] To Donaldson, McAlmon was an epicene dabbler in literature whose only importance was breaking the "manly bond" between a latter-day Damon and Pythias. In McAlmon's favor, however, is that he did not assume Fitzgerald and Hemingway "were lovers," as Zelda charged.[86] In any event, what did McAlmon's sexuality have to do with his accusations? If he had been totally heterosexual, would the accusations have been more valid or any less hurtful? Would he have then not been a "spoiler"? Truth and falsehood have no logical connection to a speaker's sexuality. Here Donaldson seems, at least implicitly, to stereotype homosexuals and bisexuals as intrinsically deceitful.

While McAlmon is grist for Donaldson's mill, Anton Gill, in *Art Lover: A Biography of Peggy Guggenheim* (2002), takes the cake for fatuity, writing: "While his wife traveled, McAlmon stayed in Paris, drinking too much and indulging in some minor writing and a memoir, later revived by his friend Kay Boyle, of his life and the artistic life of the time."[87] It was McAlmon, of course, who traveled while Bryher, other than occasional trips, was ensconced in Switzerland with H. D. In Gill's confection, McAlmon would awaken from a debauch in Paris and ask himself, "Am I in shape to indulge in minor writing today?" Just so: a minor writer does minor writing. But, to be fair, Gill does acknowledge McAlmon's publishing contributions.

So at the start of the twenty-first century what is the critical line on Robert McAlmon? An unfulfilled, querulous, envious, malicious, slandering, deviant, tippling dilettante. He must certainly be the most vilified unread writer in modern American literature. Secondhand criticism of his fiction prior to 1990 might be pardoned because until then, except for *McAlmon and the Lost Generation: A Self Portrait* (1962), edited by Robert E. Knoll, and *A Hasty Bunch* (1977), edited by Harry T. Moore and Matthew J. Bruccoli, his books were available only from rare-book dealers (at great cost) or from a few major research libraries. But critics after that have no excuse for ignorance. For between 1990 and 1992 the University of New Mexico Press reissued *Village* (1990), *Post-Adolescence: A Selection of Short Fiction* (1991), and *Miss Knight and Others* [*Distinguished Air* plus "The Highly Prized Pajamas"], with a foreword by Gore Vidal (1992), each edited and with an introduction by Edward S. N. Lorusso. Critics who judge a writer's work without reading it subvert the scholarly principle of fair assessment. But perhaps McAlmon is destined to be a literary pariah, both as a man and as a writer, whose unsavory reputation, despite countervailing evidence, is engraved in stone. Will the publication of *The Nightinghouls of Paris* cast him in a better light and perhaps lead readers to his fiction so that they can judge for themselves? Hope springs eternal.

The story of how "Nightinghouls" surfaced is one of literary executorship, archival care, technology, and coincidence. During four days in December 1973, I sat long hours in the Beinecke Library at Yale feverishly taking notes, with pencil on yellow tablets, from letters by and to McAlmon from Williams, Boyle, Glassco, Hartley, Herbst, and others, generously put at my disposal by Norman Holmes Pearson, McAlmon's literary executor. Courtly and gracious, Pearson even gave me McAlmon's letters to him, which were invaluable in accounting for McAlmon's thoughts and feelings in his later years. None of the material had been catalogued; instead, it reposed in manila folders in shopping bags. Besides helping me with McAlmon's papers, Pearson corrected my misconceptions and flat-out errors, and he steered me to his dear friend Norman Macleod, who had known McAlmon. (Afterward, I corresponded with the two Normans until their regrettable deaths, untimely in Pearson's case.) Nevertheless, Pearson withheld McAlmon's unpublished manuscripts because he believed that they might injure the feelings and harm the reputations of then-living people. I knew from references in McAlmon's letters that some of the works dealt with homosexual themes and situations. Anyway, I had no real need for them since I had enough about sex (straight and gay) for my literary biography of him: *Adrift Among Geniuses: Robert McAlmon, Writer and Publisher of the Twenties* (Pennsylvania State University Press, 1975). Over the years I thought occasionally about McAlmon's archive, but I had no desire to inquire into its status. I figured that I had had my say on McAlmon. The reviews were mostly good, and I was pleased that some scholars of the period had found my book useful.

In 2000, I decided that the time had come to secure Macleod's and Pearson's letters to me. So I called Patricia C. Willis, curator of the American Collection at the Beinecke, to ask if the library would like to have them, stipulating that photocopies be returned to me. Very much so, she said. When I asked about Macleod's file, she said I could peruse it on the Beinecke's website. And when I did, lo, there listed was voluminous correspondence spanning almost fifty years of his life as poet, novelist, and editor of literary magazines. His letters to me would be alongside those to Eugene O'Neill, Allen Tate, Lincoln Kirstein, Babette Deutsch, James Dickey, Harriet Monroe, McAlmon himself, and many other notables whose lives intersected his. Just out of curiosity, I asked my wife, my Internet operator, to punch in McAlmon, and among the august correspondents were Barnes, Beach, Boyle, Hilda Doolittle (H. D.), Hemingway, Joyce, Wyndham Lewis, Macleod, Marianne Moore, K. A. Porter, Stein, and Williams—a biographer's treasure trove. And even more of a delight was to see under "Manuscripts" such titles as "Hangovers of the Gay Nineties," "One More to Set Her Up," "Roman à Clef," "School for Unrest," "Too Quick for Life," and "The Nightinghouls of Paris." In addition were typescripts of published work: "The Lodging House," "Miss Knight," and *Village*. Eldorado! It was there for the taking, for, as Ms. Willis informed me, the restrictions had been lifted and, provided copyright law was adhered to, anything could be published.

Not having the funds for a stay in New Haven to comb the file, I chose the most intriguing title and asked Ms. Willis if she would scan its length and subject. Gladly complying, she told me over the telephone that the typescript of "The Nightinghouls of Paris" was 268 pages, and then read me the first paragraph:

> It was a clear afternoon such as puts a wander-bird at loose ends, but I meant to have it alleviate my social appetites and sense of problems. Coming the night before from months in a quiet Spanish town I quickly realized anew that Paris was really another city of hometown souls perplexed by village woes. At the New York bar Tony Crane informed me that his wife was unwell, and they both worried about finding a suitable school for their twelve-year-old daughter. Tony also mourned the lack of news to make up a weekly letter for his syndicate. He hoped I might give him news but had no such luck. We drank.

Tony Crane? Wait a minute. A crane is a bird. McAlmon, sly dog, Tony Crane is really Bill Bird. "The Nightinghouls of Paris" was just what I hoped it would be: a book-length account of expatriate Paris in the 1920s. I had to have it.

Well, the Internet took me to "Nightinghouls," and the flo-copy duplicating process prepared it for me. Because the sheets were too fragile to photocopy directly, a microfilm copy had to be made first and then the hard copy was reproduced from the microfilm. After sending a check in advance to cover the processing cost, in due course I received a bound sheaf of words exactly how McAlmon typed them more than fifty years before.

As I read along and began identifying the characters—Bird, Barnes, Wood, Boyle, Glassco and Taylor, Hemingway, Twysden, and so forth—I realized that while McAlmon, in assigning fictitious names and re-creating dialogue, may have conceived of the work as a novel, it was actually a memoir of his experiences in the late 1920s and early 1930s. As such, it was very likely the last, unpublished, firsthand exposition of American expatriate life in France. On that score alone, I believed, it deserved publication. When I informed Matthew J. Bruccoli of it and sent him an edited sample, he concurred and published an extract, entitled "A Night at Bricktop's," in *Dictionary of Literary Biography Yearbook: 2001*. With McAlmon's file now open, other nuggets in his wordhoard surely await the enterprising literary digger.

The typescript of "Nightinghouls" is obviously a first draft, as evidenced by typographical, spelling, syntactical, and mechanical errors. There are also cross-outs, inserts, and inconsistencies. As an example of the last, Sudge's and Ross's native city is first identified as Toronto, but this is crossed out and Quebec written in above. A few pages later Toronto is crossed out again and Montreal written in. Then in chapter seventeen Sudge tells Kit that his father wants him to return to "Toronto," which recurs thereafter. Did McAlmon forget that Glassco and Taylor came from Montreal? Or did he change the city to disguise their identity?[88] McAlmon's energy appears to have flagged in writing the last third of the book, because uncorrected errors of every type abound.

One presumes that if McAlmon had written a second draft, he would have corrected typographical errors and inconsistencies. But whether he would have caught spelling, punctuation, and mechanical mistakes, cut out redundancies, used synonyms for overworked words, and straightened out tangled syntax is questionable. Though Carpenter exaggerates by saying that "McAlmon put down the first thing that came into his head and never revised,"[89] he is close to the mark in one respect: McAlmon, like Jack Kerouac, another keyboard wordslinger averse to rewriting and revising, operated on the principle of first thought, best thought. While it leaves him open to the charge of sloppiness, McAlmon's writing (again like Kerouac's) has the virtue of spontaneity and authenticity. To Sisley Huddleston, McAlmon's writing, though "rather formless," nevertheless "was strong because it was natural."[90] Indeed, rewriting and revising have been overrated by academic literary critics and instructors of writing workshops. One can "cut" and "polish," in Carpenter's words, a zircon ad infinitum, but it will never be a diamond. Talent, not speed of composition, determines quality in art. And for a writer, talent has perhaps as much to do with perception as it has with verbal skill. Hugh Kenner recalled a conversation with Ezra Pound in St. Elizabeth's Hospital in Washington, D.C., when Pound compared Hemingway and McAlmon: "'Hem always believed you should get yours *in*side the system.' . . . Ezra's mind was on Bob McAlmon, who was never inside the system. . . . 'And whereas Hem would polish . . . and polish . . . McAlmon would rip the sketch off and start a new one. Because McAlmon was curious about human variants. Whereas Hem . . . never knew one human being from another . . . and never much cared.'"[91]

There is a difference in kind between an author polishing a rewritten draft and an editor confronting a rough draft, by a dead writer, filled with compositional errors. Correcting typos, spelling, and mechanics is routine, but what about errors in punctuation, grammar, and syntax? Does the regularizing of punctuation—such as inserting commas after long prepositional phrases and subordinate clauses—corrupt the author's text? Similarly, does moving misplaced modifiers nearer their objects constitute tampering with an author's style? What of deleting redundancies and replacing, for variety, an overused word with a synonym? In short, the line between preparing intelligible, coherent, grammatical, nonfiction copy for publication and taking liberties with, or skewing the meaning of, a writer's original expression is very fine.

Now, I have chosen to make such copyediting corrections in McAlmon's narration and description, but not dialogue, solely for the sake of clarity and proper grammar. I have tried in every instance to be faithful to his tone and meaning. I have written nothing into his draft to "improve" it, nor have I imposed my "style" on it. This is in no sense a collaboration: *The Nightinghouls of Paris*, with all its strengths and weaknesses as literary art, belongs to Robert McAlmon alone.

NOTES

1. Edward Dahlberg, *Alms for Oblivion* (Minneapolis: University of Minnesota Press, 1964), 7.

2. Frederick J. Hoffman, *The Twenties: American Writing in the Postwar Decade* (New York: The Free Press, 1966), 55.

3. Robert McAlmon, *Being Geniuses Together* (London: Secker and Warburg, 1938), 224. Hereinafter cited as McAlmon, *Geniuses*.

4. *Little Review* 12 (May 1929): 52–53.

5. Unpublished letter, McAlmon Archive, Beinecke Rare Book and Manuscript Library, Yale University, New Haven, Conn. Hereinafter cited as McAlmon Archive.

6. Victoria McAlmon to Norman Holmes Pearson, May 6, 1965, Norman Holmes Pearson Archive, Beinecke Rare Book and Manuscript Library, Yale University, New Haven, Conn.

7. Morley Callaghan, *That Summer in Paris* (New York: Coward-McCann, 1963), 143.

8. Robert McAlmon, *Village: As It Happened through a Fifteen-Year Period*,

ed. Edward N. S. Lorusso (Albuquerque: University of New Mexico Press, 1990), 9.

9. Gore Vidal, *Palimpsest: A Memoir* (New York: Penguin, 1996), 135.

10. Robert McAlmon's enlistment papers, National Archives of Canada. McAlmon told W. C. Williams and, later in Paris, the Canadians John Glassco and Graeme Taylor that he had joined the Canadian Army and then deserted. Robert E. Knoll, who wrote a monograph on McAlmon and edited an anthology of his prose (see notes 40 and 45, below) found "no evidence of this." Assuming Knoll was correct, I also discounted McAlmon's story as a fiction to make himself appear dashing and mysterious. Knoll and I were both wrong. Brian Busby, Glassco's biographer and himself a Canadian, wondering if what McAlmon told Glassco was true, searched the National Archives on the Internet, discovered McAlmon's enlistment papers, and mailed me a copy. I am grateful for his scholarly diligence in setting the record straight.

11. William Carlos Williams, *The Autobiography of William Carlos Williams* (New York: Random House, 1951), 176.

12. Robert McAlmon, *Being Geniuses Together 1920–1930*, revised and with supplementary chapters by Kay Boyle (Garden City: Doubleday, 1968), 24. Hereinafter cited as Boyle, *Geniuses*.

13. Townsend Ludington, *Marsden Hartley: The Biography of an American Artist* (Boston: Little, Brown, 1992), 147.

14. McAlmon to Norman Holmes Pearson, July 15, 1953, McAlmon Archive.

15. Bryher, *The Heart to Artemis: A Writer's Memoirs* (New York: Harcourt, Brace and World, 1962), 201.

16. Williams to Amy Lowell, March 6, 1921, *The Selected Letters of William Carlos Williams*, ed. John C. Thirlwall (New York: McDowell, Obolensky, 1957), 51.

17. T. S. Eliot to Robert McAlmon, May 2, 1921. In addition to being in *The Letters of T. S. Eliot*, vol. 1, ed. Valerie Eliot (San Diego, Calif.: Jovanovich, 1988), this letter is quoted in full in Boyle, *Geniuses*, 8–9.

18. Malcolm Cowley, *Exile's Return* (New York: Viking, 1965), 164–67; McAlmon, *Geniuses*, 114.

19. Ezra Pound, "Paris Letter," *The Dial* (February 1922): 192.

20. For a full discussion of McAlmon's publishing activities, see Hugh Ford, *Published in Paris: American and British Writers, Printers, Publishers in Paris 1920–1939*, with a foreword by Janet Flanner (New York: Macmillan, 1975).

21. Bricktop (born Ada Louise Smith) credits McAlmon and F. Scott Fitzgerald for their early patronage and for steering wealthy clients to her establishments, in *Bricktop*, with James Haskins (New York: Atheneum, 1983), 95, 126. In Fitzgerald's "Babylon Revisited" (1931), Charley Wales rues his costly sprees

at Bricktop's. McAlmon and Fitzgerald apparently first met at a party in London, where Fitzgerald reportedly "saved McAlmon from a beating he probably deserved" (Fitzgerald to Hemingway, November 30, 1925, *The Letters of F. Scott Fitzgerald* [hereinafter *Letters*], ed. Andrew Turnbull [New York: Charles Scribner's Sons, 1963], 295). Because McAlmon and Fitzgerald belonged to different social sets, they crossed paths only occasionally in Paris and on the Riviera (McAlmon to Pearson, June 11, 1953, McAlmon Archive).

22. Sylvia Beach, *Shakespeare and Company* (New York: Harcourt Brace, 1959), 25.

23. Michael Reynolds, *Hemingway: The Paris Years* (Oxford: Basil Blackwell, 1989), 131.

24. Reynolds, *Hemingway*, 128.

25. McAlmon to Pearson, January 4, 1954 [1955?], McAlmon Archive.

26. McAlmon to Pearson, February 28, 1952, McAlmon Archive.

27. Hemingway to McAlmon, December 10, 1924, *Ernest Hemingway: Selected Letters 1917–1961*, ed. Carlos Baker (New York: Charles Scribner's Sons, 1981), 139.

28. Hemingway to Fitzgerald, December 24, 1925, *Hemingway: Selected Letters*, 181.

29. Hemingway to Fitzgerald, December 31, 1925–January 1, 1926, *Hemingway: Selected Letters*, 184.

30. Hemingway to Maxwell Perkins, December 10, 1929, *The Only Thing That Counts: The Ernest Hemingway/Maxwell Perkins Correspondence 1925–1947*, ed. Matthew J. Bruccoli, with the assistance of Robert W. Trogdon (New York: Scribner, 1996), 133.

31. Hemingway to F. Scott Fitzgerald, ca. December 24, 1925, *Hemingway: Selected Letters*, 181.

32. Fitzgerald to Zelda Fitzgerald, Summer[?] 1930, *F. Scott Fitzgerald: A Life in Letters*, ed. Matthew J. Bruccoli, with the assistance of Judith S. Baughman (London: Penguin, 1998), 198.

33. Bruccoli, ed., *Life in Letters*, 98–99.

34. Bruccoli, ed., *Life in Letters*, 264 (June 1, 1934). By yoking McAlmon's and Callaghan's names, Fitzgerald's pun was certainly calculated to rekindle Hemingway's ire. McKisco (perhaps modeled in part on McAlmon) is a smarmy writer in *Tender Is the Night*.

35. Hemingway, *Only Thing*, 132.

36. Perkins to F. Scott Fitzgerald, October 30, 1929, *Dear Scott/Dear Max: The Fitzgerald-Perkins Correspondence*, ed. John Kuehl and Jackson Bryer (New York: Charles Scribner's Sons, 1971), 157–58.

37. Fitzgerald to Maxwell Perkins, November 15, 1929, Fitzgerald, *Letters*, 216.

38. Hemingway biographers Jeffrey Meyers and Kenneth S. Lynn both state that Pauline had lesbian affairs after divorcing Hemingway. According to Meyers, the poet Elizabeth Bishop was one of her lovers (*Hemingway: A Biography* [New York: Harper & Row, 1985], 346). Lynn conjectures that she may have had lesbian encounters before meeting Hemingway (*Hemingway* [New York: Simon and Schuster, 1987], 301).

39. Hemingway, *Only Thing*, 133.

40. William Bird, quoted in Robert E. Knoll, ed., *McAlmon and the Lost Generation: A Self Portrait* (Lincoln: University of Nebraska Press, 1962), 234.

41. Hemingway, *Only Thing*, 132–33.

42. Hemingway, *Only Thing*, 137.

43. Fitzgerald, *Letters*, 217–19.

44. Callaghan, *That Summer*, 85.

45. William Carlos Williams, foreword to *Robert McAlmon: Expatriate Publisher and Writer*, by Robert E. Knoll (Lincoln: University of Nebraska Press, 1959), vii.

46. Sisley Huddleston, *Paris Salons, Cafés, Studios* (Philadelphia: Lippincott, 1928), 89.

47. Joan Mellen, *Kay Boyle: Author of Herself* (New York: Farrar, Straus, and Giroux, 1994), 148.

48. Waverley Root, *The Paris Edition 1927–1934*, ed. Samuel Abt (San Francisco: North Point Press, 1989), 184–85.

49. Malcolm Cowley, "Those Paris Years," *New York Times Book Review*, June 9, 1968, pp. 34–35.

50. McAlmon to William Carlos Williams, April 17, 1939, McAlmon Archive.

51. Jean Stafford, review of *Being Geniuses Together 1920–1930*, by Robert McAlmon and Kay Boyle, *New York Review of Books* (April 24, 1969): 28.

52. In a May 1968 review in *Library Journal*, Glenn O. Carey argued along the same lines: "Miss Boyle, it seems, has enough material here about the 1920's for a separate book of her own, and McAlmon is much too fast company for most authors to keep up with inside the same jacket covers, whether it be a Hemingway or a Boyle."

53. Michael Gnarowski observes that Glassco welcomed Boyle's revision because "he hoped that he and Graeme would have a place in it, since McAlmon had excluded them" from the original memoir. He cites a March 1942 letter from Glassco to McAlmon expressing disappointment at being left out. "'I do wish you had found space for Graeme and me in the book, now! It would have helped along my individual legend in Can. Lit'" (introduction to *Memoirs of Montparnasse*, by John Glassco, 2nd ed. [Toronto: Oxford University Press, 1995], xviii, xxv).

Gnarowski conjectures that McAlmon omitted them "because of the homosexual overtones of the friendship between McAlmon and Glassco," and goes on to say that "McAlmon . . . never admitted his homosexuality publicly" (228). Yet in *That Summer in Paris*, Morley Callaghan reported a scene with drunken McAlmon, who, after defending creative homosexuals such as Plato and Michelangelo, shouted, "I'm bisexual myself, like Michelangelo, and I don't give a damn who knows it" (134–35). More likely, McAlmon overlooked Glassco and Taylor because they were personal friends and had no literary significance at the time.

54. John Glassco, *Memoirs of Montparnasse* (Toronto: Oxford University Press, 1970), 13.

55. Glassco, *Memoirs of Montparnasse*, 50–51.

56. Glassco, *Memoirs of Montparnasse*, 50–62.

57. Glassco, *Memoirs of Montparnasse*, xiii.

58. Thomas E. Tausky, "*Memoirs of Montparnasse:* A Reflection of Myself," *Canadian Poetry: Studies/Documents/ Reviews* 13 (Fall/Winter 1983): 59–84. March 19, 2002, http:/ /www.arts.uwo.ca/can poetry/cpjrn/vol13/tausky.htm 1–40. See also in this issue Stephen Scobie, "The Mirror on the Brothel Wall: John Glassco *Memoirs of Montparnasse*": 43–58. My thanks to Tausky, Scobie, and Philip Kokotailo for acknowledging that, in 1975, I noted that *Memoirs* is "fictionalized history."

59. Tausky, "Reflection of Myself," 4.

60. Tausky, "Reflection of Myself," 3.

61. Tausky, "Reflection of Myself," 6.

62. Tausky, "Reflection of Myself," 11.

63. Philip Kokotailo, *John Glassco's Richer World: "Memoirs of Montparnasse"* (Toronto: ECW Press, 1988), 98.

64. Kokotailo, *Richer World*, 100.

65. Kokotailo, *Richer World*, 46–47.

66. Kokotailo, *Richer World*, 117.

67. Kokotailo, *Richer World*, 91.

68. My thanks to Brian Busby for sharing this letter.

69. Kokotailo, *Richer World*, 52–53.

70. Glassco, *Memoirs of Montparnasse*, 79 (emphasis added).

71. Sisley Huddleston, *Back to Montparnasse: Glimpses of Broadway in Bohemia* (Philadelphia: Lippincott, 1931), 278.

72. Richard Ellmann, *James Joyce* (New York: Oxford University Press, 1959), 684.

73. McAlmon to Pearson, 4 January 1954 [1955?], McAlmon Archive.

74. In 1937, Lanham published a novel, *Banner at Daybreak* (New York: Longman's Green, 1937) in which McAlmon appears as a character composed

of himself, Hilaire Hiler, Glassco, and Hart Crane, according to a December 12, 1943, letter Glassco wrote to McAlmon. Lanham's partly autobiographical novel, set in the early 1930s, centers on Clayton Hall, a young Texan who goes to Paris to paint and live freely. A close friend is the American expatriate poet Guy Hart. Lanham borrowed and contracted the name from Guy Urquhart, McAlmon's mother's maiden name, under which Kay Boyle submitted some poems by McAlmon to Eugene Jolas, editor of *transition*, to test his integrity, which McAlmon doubted. (Jolas published McAlmon's "The Silver Bull" with that pseudonym in the summer 1928 issue devoted to American writers.) Like McAlmon, Hart is a heavy drinker, argumentative, cynical, violent when drunk, lonely, restless, and "somewhat homosexual." Clayton Hall says of him, "Guy's life had always been one of quick departures, of sudden flights to new places, of constant search for new faces, feeling the need to complement himself, to complete the agonizing void in his own personality" (131). Together at a hotel in southern France, Hart gets drunk, dances grotesquely, wails his "Chinese opera," smashes a glass of rum on a table, and goes to bed sobbing. Curiously, Lanham seems to have grafted Hiler's thick, ungainly body, the opposite of McAlmon's slim, supple one, onto all the negative aspects of McAlmon's personality.

In 1934, Hall and his wife, Hilda, run into Hart in a Greenwich Village restaurant, and Hilda notices his "softer" features, arched eyebrows, and "mannerisms more definite" (279). Implicit is that Hart has become more effeminate. Almost always drunk now and abusive, Hart gets arrested for soliciting a boy in a public toilet, but he is not charged when the boy does not sign a complaint. However, he is humiliated by the cops who pretend to "camp." "God damn America," Hart rages to Hall, and wants to return to France, where he can live "like a human being," away from "primitive, brutish" America (304).

After Hall tells him he is going back to Texas, Hart, desolated, implores him to stay. When Hall leaves, Hart is stricken by "self-revulsion," belts down whiskey, and summons comforting memories of Berlin and southern France in the 1920s. As he goes for more ice, he turns on the gas jets of the stove, not intending suicide but as a "morbid counter to his unhappiness." Nodding off with the jets on, he awakens thinking of a young pianist in Paris who tried suicide by gas, is revived, but remains comatose. (According to Lanham's entry in the *Dictionary of Literary Biography*, he knew a young artist who committed suicide, perhaps in this way, in Paris in 1927.) But just as Hart lurches to the stove to shut the jets, the apartment explodes and he is physically as well as morally and emotionally disintegrated (303–6). Regarding this gothic ending, Glassco remarked wryly to McAlmon: "Anyone who was that kind of composite would have to blow himself up anyway: a case of spontaneous combustion" (December 12, 1943).

Thanks to Brian Busby for sharing this letter and for identifying Lanham's book, which, to my surprise, I checked out of the Miami–Dade County Public Library.

75. On May 28, 1930, McAlmon wrote to Glassco from his hotel in Alamos. First noting how cheaply one could live in Mexico, he asked him "to say hello to Louise Bryant, Gwen, Yvette, Caridad, Draquy, etc. if you see them, and tell them to write to me if they will." He also mentioned that Lanham placed *Sailors Don't Care* with Cape and Smith publishers through his agent. Thanks to Brian Busby for sharing this letter.

76. Brian Busby, *Character Parts: Who's Really Who in CanLit*, with a foreword by Bill Richardson (Toronto: Knopf Canada, 2003), 210.

77. Glassco, *Memoirs of Montparnasse*, 240.

78. Dahlberg, *Alms for Oblivion*, 47.

79. Lynn, *Hemingway*, 195.

80. Reynolds, *Hemingway*, 107.

81. Reynolds, *Hemingway*, 130.

82. Meyers, *Hemingway: A Biography*, 88–89.

83. *Hemingway: Selected Letters*, 80.

84. *Hemingway: Selected Letters*, 124.

85. Scott Donaldson, *Hemingway vs. Fitzgerald: The Rise and Fall of a Literary Friendship* (Woodstock, N.Y.: Overlook Press, 1999), 154–56.

86. Donaldson, *Hemingway vs. Fitzgerald*, 156.

87. Anton Gill, *Art Lover: A Biography of Peggy Guggenheim* (New York: HarperCollins, 2002), 95.

88. Gnarowski thinks Glassco used fictitious names for most of his characters perhaps "because he was afraid of being sued or that others still alive could" dispute "his 'facts'" (Glassco, *Memoirs of Montparnasse*, xvi). The same reasons might be applied to McAlmon's use of fictitious names, especially the former.

89. Humphrey Carpenter, *Geniuses Together: American Writers in Paris in the 1920s* (Boston: Houghton Mifflin, 1988), 82.

90. Huddleston, *Paris Salons*, 89.

91. Hugh Kenner, *The Pound Era* (Berkeley: University of California Press, 1971), 527–28.

ROSTER OF MAJOR CHARACTERS

The following roster of major characters is alphabetized by first names. Literary and historical figures and minor characters mentioned in passing are annotated, beginning on page 185.

CHLOE ANDREWS. Djuna Barnes (1892–1982), journalist and novelist who became friends with McAlmon in 1920 in New York; they remained so for life. Her novel *Nightwood* (1936) is set in the same period as *Nightinghouls*, which also records Barnes's breakup with her lover Thelma Wood, caused by Wood's promiscuity. Barnes's part satire and part defense of lesbianism, the roman à clef *Ladies Almanack* (1928), was published by McAlmon. John Glassco calls her Willa Torrence in *Memoirs of Montparnasse* (1970).

COLETTE GODESCARD. Yvette Ledoux, Canadian nurse who stayed in Paris after World War I. Living with her lover Gwen Le Gallienne in the same building as McAlmon, they would sometimes prepare meals for him as well as being good companions. She is called Angela Martin in *Memoirs.*

DALE BURKE. Kay Boyle (1902–92), novelist and short story writer who chronicles her relationship with McAlmon in her chapters of her 1968 edition of *Being Geniuses Together.* She was a loyal friend of McAlmon's and zealously guarded his reputation after his death. She is called Diana Tree in *Memoirs.*

ELLERY SANDERSON. Sisley Huddleston (1883–1952), Paris correspondent of the *London Times* and later editorial correspondent of the *Christian Science Monitor.* He was a prolific writer on French social, political, and cultural life. McAlmon figures in his studies of bohemian Paris: *Paris Salons, Cafés, Studios* (1928) and *Back to Montparnasse: Glimpses of Broad-*

way in Bohemia (1932). He became a naturalized French citizen under the Vichy government, dividing his time between Switzerland and France after World War II.

FELIX LUTYENS. Laurence Vail (1891–1968), American writer and painter who was married to Peggy Guggenheim at the time of *Nightinghouls*. After she divorced him, Vail married Kay Boyle. This marriage also dissolved. Vail was noted for his quick temper and aggressive behavior. Consuela Lutyens in *Nightinghouls* is his sister Clotilde. He and Peggy Vail are called Terence and Sally Marr in *Memoirs*.

FOREST PEMBERTON. Ernest Hemingway (1899–1961), who arrived in Paris in December 1921 with his first wife Hadley Richardson Hemingway (1891–1978) determined to be a fiction writer. After meeting McAlmon in Rapallo, Italy, in 1923, the two young writers from the Middle West became friends. They went to their first bullfights together in Spain in 1923, and McAlmon helped start Hemingway's career by publishing his *Three Stories and Ten Poems* (1923). But their relationship turned ugly in 1925, with mutual enmity thereafter. Olive in *Nightinghouls* is Hadley.

FRANK PENRYN. William C. Bullitt (1891–1967), American diplomat and writer. His interest in psychology led him to collaborate with Sigmund Freud on a psychoanalytical study of Woodrow Wilson. He was a close associate of Franklin D. Roosevelt's during the Second World War.

GAYLORD SHOWMAN. Hilaire Hiler [Hiler Harzberg] (1896–1966), American musician, designer, and painter. Hiler was respected not only as a painter but also as an imaginative designer. He decorated the Jockey Club, the Jungle, and the College Inn, popular nightspots for Americans in Paris in the 1920s. He also wrote a history of costumes. Hiler and McAlmon corresponded regularly after they returned from Europe and tried to help each other financially. He is called Sidney Schooner in *Memoirs*.

HAL AND KATE MENG. Edwin M. Lanham (1904–79) and his wife Joan Boyle Lanham, who were married in 1929 and divorced in 1936. Born in Texas, Lanham attended private schools in Maryland and New York and then Williams College in Massachusetts. With aspiration to paint, he also took art classes in New York. In 1923, he shipped out on a freighter to cruise the world, and his experiences formed the subject of his first novel, *Sailors Don't Care*, which McAlmon urged him to write and published in 1929, after they became friends on the Riviera the previous year. At the time, Joan Lanham (Kay Boyle's sister) was fashion designer for *Vogue*'s London edition. Lanham would cast McAlmon as Guy Hart, American expatriate homosexual poet, in *Banner at Daybreak* (1937). Lanham wrote populist novels during the 1930s, then turned to writing murder mysteries that were serialized in magazines and later published as books. He was also a friend of John Glassco's.

HILARIA. Caridad, a demimondaine in Montparnasse during this period. She appears to have been a flamboyant and ubiquitous presence. Glassco calls her Caridad de Plumas (feathers in Spanish) in *Memoirs*. Michael Gnarowski suggests that she may have been Caridad de Laberdesque, a dancer and mistress of, among others, painter Georges Malkine. In *Being Geniuses Together*, McAlmon, without naming her, describes Caridad as "a Cuban girl with ashen skin and bright mahogany hair" who "loved the vaudeville." Sisley Huddleston recalled seeing McAlmon drinking with her—"a red-haired beauty whose father had been in the diplomatic service"—at the Parnasse bar.

JAMES FERNLEY JOHN. Ford Madox Ford (1873–1939), poet, editor, memoirist, and novelist whose maternal grandfather was the pre-Raphaelite painter Ford Madox Brown. A friend of Joseph Conrad's, Ford collaborated with him on two novels. He was the first editor of the *English Review*, which published work of Lawrence, Pound, Hardy, Wells, James, Bennett, and Galsworthy, among others. Ford founded the *Transatlantic Review* in Paris in 1924 and thereby gave a hearing to such young America expatriate writers as Hemingway, McAlmon, and Nathan Asch. He was treated shabbily by the Americans in spite of his efforts on their behalf. Hemingway's portrait of him in *A Moveable Feast* (1963) is particularly cruel. Ford's ironic novel *The Good Soldier* (1915) is a modern classic, and his *Parade's End* tetralogy (1924–28) is a major fictional account of English life immediately before, during, and after World War I.

KIT O'MALLEY. Robert McAlmon (1895–1956). McAlmon evidently chose to stress the Irish side of his Scots-Irish heritage in selecting a name for his persona.

LADY MART. Duff Twysden (1893–1938), who acquired her title through marriage to her second husband in 1917, lived from hand-to-mouth in Paris. Infatuated by her looks and insouciance, Hemingway immortalized her as Brett Ashley in *The Sun Also Rises* (1926). McAlmon, who had known Twysden for a number of years, took a dim view of her, writing in *Being Geniuses Together* that she was "the most imitated, the least witty or amusing of the various 'ladies' on the loose in Paris." And commenting on the models for Hemingway's characters, Huddleston observes (in *Paris Salons*), "I saw one of them later—a dismal bedraggled figure, sunk to still lower depths of degradation, and I was saddened." Since Huddleston's description closely matches McAlmon's depiction of Twysden in *Nightinghouls* as ruined and lost, it is likely that he was referring to her.

LAURA BRADLEY. Gwen Le Gallienne, painter and sculptor. She was the stepdaughter of the fin de siècle poet and novelist Richard Le Gallienne and the half-sister of the famous actress Eva Le Gallienne. She is called Daphne Berners in *Memoirs*

REYNER. Edward Titus (1870–1952), bookdealer, publisher, editor. Titus was married to the cosmetics queen Helena Rubenstein. He owned the Black Manikin bookstore in Montparnasse and edited *This Quarter*, which he bought from Ethel Moorhead after Ernest Walsh died in 1926. He published the risqué *Memoirs of Kiki* with an introduction by Ernest Hemingway.

ROSE MORGAN. Louise Bryant (1885–1936), journalist and great beauty much in demand, with whom McAlmon socialized in the late 1920s and early 1930s. Her first husband was the radical John Reed, and at the time of *Nightinghouls* her marriage to William C. Bullitt was strained. A romantic figure, she has been the subject of three biographies, the latest in 1999 by Mary Dearborn, *Queen of Bohemia: The Life of Louise Bryant.*

ROSS CAMPION. Graeme Taylor (1905–57). John Glassco's lifelong friend and companion whom Michael Gnarowski calls "unrealized and obscure." Brian Busby has pieced together an account of his life from Glassco's unpublished "Intimate Journal" and conversations with William Toye, Glassco's editor at Oxford University Press Canada. Taylor's father was, like McAlmon's, a Presbyterian minister. He and Glassco met at McGill University, Montreal, and both dropped out to go to Paris in 1928. After returning to Canada alone, Taylor reunited with Glassco in 1932, and from 1935 they lived together until Taylor's death. In the late 1930s they supported themselves on a small farm Glassco bought southeast of Montreal. Glassco and Taylor then formed a ménage à trois with Mary Elizabeth Wilson, whom Taylor married in 1941. Taylor enlisted in the Canadian Army in 1941; after being discharged a year later, he returned to his wife and Glassco. But after a good deal of unpleasantness, Mary Elizabeth divorced him in 1950. In 1956, Elma Koolmar moved in with Taylor and Glassco and would later become Glassco's first wife. Afflicted with Buerger's disease in 1956, Taylor died in February 1957. Although Taylor published a few pieces in *transition* and *This Quarter*, he gave up writing to devote himself to Glassco, providing emotional and moral support and helping to edit his writing.

SALLY LUTYENS. Peggy Guggenheim Vail (1898–1979), niece of immensely wealthy art collector Solomon Guggenheim. After divorcing Laurence Vail, she went on to become a notable patron (and lover) of modern artists and a collector and dealer of modern art, especially the surrealists and abstract expressionists. Her own collection is housed in Venice, Italy. She recounts her life and times up to 1946 in *Out of This Century*.

SHAWIN FLANNAGAN. Morley Callaghan (1903–90), Canadian short story writer and novelist. Callaghan graduated from Toronto University intending to be a lawyer. Though he was called to the bar in 1928, by then he had decided to be a writer. For a short time he and Hemingway were reporter colleagues on the *Toronto Daily Star*, and Hemingway encouraged him to write fiction, as did McAlmon, with whom Callaghan corresponded before coming to Paris in 1929. His first novel, *Strange Fugitive* (1928), in a hard-boiled style, centering on a bootlegger, was published by Scribner's—Hemingway's, Fitzgerald's, and Thomas Wolfe's publisher. He recaptured his experiences among the expatriates in 1929 in *That Summer in Paris* (1963). After returning to Toronto, during the 1930s he established his reputation as a fiction writer by publishing five novels and two collections of stories. Maggie Flannagan is his wife Loretto.

STEVE RATH. Thelma Wood (1901–70), silverpoint artist and Djuna Barnes's lover-companion during the mid- and late 1920s. She was notable for her stature (nearly six feet tall and muscular) and sex appeal to both men and women, with whom she slept indiscriminately. Wood began as a sculptor but followed Barnes's advice and turned to silverpoint. She is the model for Robin Vote in *Nightwood* and is called Emily Pine in *Memoirs.*

SUDGE GALBRAITH. John Glassco (1909–81), Canadian poet, editor, translator, and erotic novelist who tells his life story, with some license, up to 1932 in *Memoirs of Montparnasse.* In his youth he was called "Buffy" by his friends. His father was bursar of McGill University, and his mother was from a very wealthy family. His literary production and reputation increased as he aged, and at his death he was acknowledged as one of Canada's most accomplished lyric poets. He and McAlmon wrote to each other during the Second World War, recalling friends and events from their time together in France. But disappointed and displeased by a draft of "The Nightinghouls of Paris" McAlmon sent him in 1947, Glassco broke off the correspondence and ended the friendship. Glassco published three books of poetry: *The Deficit Made Flesh* (1958), *A Point of Sky* (1964), and *Selected Poems* (1971). He also wrote erotic novellas under pseudonyms and edited *The Poetry of French Canada in Translation* (1971). Brian Busby, a Montreal native, is preparing a biography of John Glassco for Knopf Canada.

TONY CRANE. William "Bill" Bird (1889–1963), American journalist and printer in Paris. One of the "good guys" among the expatriates, Bird was born in Buffalo and educated at Trinity College in Hartford. In 1920, he was European manager of the Consolidated Press in Paris. He accompanied Hemingway and McAlmon, keeping the peace when they squabbled, on their first trip to Spain in 1923; he and his wife Sally were in the group that attended the Pamplona festival in 1924. Acquiring an old hand-letter printing press, he established Three Mountains Press (named for the three hills around Paris) to bring out fine, limited editions of advanced American and British writing as recommended by Ezra Pound. In addition to Hemingway's *in our time* (1924), Bird printed William Carlos Williams's *The Great American Novel* (1923) and Pound's *Indiscretions; or Une Revue de deux Mondes* (1923). Bird shared for a time his office and secretary with McAlmon's Contact Publishing Company. He remained a fond friend of McAlmon's and spoke well of him to scholars and biographers after McAlmon's death.

THE NIGHTINGHOULS OF PARIS

CHAPTER ONE

IT WAS A CLEAR AFTERNOON SUCH AS PUTS A WANDER-bird at loose ends, but I meant to have it alleviate my social appetites and sense of problems. Coming the night before from months in a quiet Spanish town, I quickly realized anew that Paris was really another city of hometown souls perplexed by village woes. At the New York bar Tony Crane informed me that his wife was unwell, and they both worried over finding a suitable school for their twelve-year-old daughter. Tony also mourned the lack of news to make up a weekly letter for his syndicate. He hoped I might give him news but had no such luck. We drank.

I sauntered with an eye alert to detect somebody to chat and drink with on a terrace cafe: a *poule*, barroom hound, artist, worker, passable-looking girl, or even an intellectual since Paris always allows one to escape when the mood demands. With a just-having-arrived emotion I liked the light on city buildings, the dazzle of traffic, and the flicker of passing ankles beneath light-colored dresses.

It was right that Hilaria should appear, radiating a let's-go quality. "Allo Kit, my darleeng friend," she greeted me, running a pale hand through her flaming hair to make me aware that it shone, newly shampooed. That alone proved her in one of her queen-of-all moods, and she felt literary too, for beneath her arm she carried three books. Of Cuban blood and Paris birth, Hilaria knew herself to be a great woman, and was sure that the world would soon know so. It was a problem to her whether to look more like Duse or Bernhardt, and a Greek boy once complicated her life further by saying that, should she desire, Argentina had no chance of retaining her laurels as pre-eminent Spanish dancer. For this Hilaria had permitted the boy to love her, but only for one night, *mon dieu.* He was beautiful, but that is not all in a man, and he had no money, and his attention wandered. Surely with a touch of Negro blood, Hilaria had ashen skin, and rimmed her eyelids with green or purple maquillage, and her lips with cerise or plum color, according to her moods. Her face she left pale. The legends that Hilaria would create about herself varied, but I guessed that she was the daughter of a former Cuban diplomat who had been quite a lover in his day, for Hilaria constantly remembered that this or that famous woman of the '90s had been one of his women, and any girl with red hair who had style, Hilaria suspected of being one of her half-sisters. Her father's wife, a woman of position, evidently did somewhat look after Hilaria's economic security, and bothered little about Hilaria's will to emulate her father's career as a person with a lively love life.

We kissed with fond meticulousness, not to besmear me or disarrange her makeup. She sighed upon accepting my invitation to drink, and sighed again lusciously to express her appreciation of the literary beauties of Comte de Lautréamont's style. Soon she was elaborately casual when informing me that Blaise Cendrars had given her one of his books with a dedication. I understood that, while a pleasure for her, it was exacting to have so many great friends as a girl of her caliber came to know. Some of them had been or might be her lovers, but today she was ready to relax with her rounder friend, Kit.

The chairs on the various terraces were empty now, but soon the jam of French bourgeois and moiling Quarterites would permit little peace should we sit outside. "Let's sit at the bar," I suggested. "I've been leading a steady life for so long that abandon is a necessity to bring me back to balance."

"*Mais oui*, Kit," Hilaria said, tenderly coquettish. It pleased me that Hilaria was free. She might readily have been living with a lover, and she fitted magnificently into the routine of each present lover's conventions.

"For you I weel get drunk this night," she said, "but I have not been drinking. It sometimes ruin my complexion, and that is not good. It does not do in the life to lose the beauty, but then, a woman with the character has not need for the beauty. For me, if I were a man, I should have the pretty woman once, and feenish. Ha, ha, ha, that is not for me. Once I try a man and if I no like, goodbye. If I think I like, I try five nights, and wait. If I remember, I live with him till I see a new man with the beauty. Today I see every man beautiful. It is spring and I am hot in the legs."

Hilaria was proudly conscious of her lithe body and put added wiggle into her hip movements. We did not get to La Coupole before she stopped to speak to men of various nationalities, impressing on spectators that she, queen of the Quarter, had come out for the afternoon, gracious, and all the world knew her with adoration if she bothered to let it.

Good barmen are a species dear to me. Regarding humanity in many phases they become understanding. Gaston, of La Coupole, was such a man, and we were numbered among his pet clients. He greeted me with courteous professional joy, and offered drinks to honor my return. Seated at the end of the bar was a lone blondined *poule*, who was, Hilaria said, in love with Gaston. "Such a trouble he has with silly women, because he is a barman and also a beautiful man. The bums in the Quarter have no money but the barmen have plenty." She puckered her lips, looked in the mirror, brushed back her hair, and allowed herself a moment of tenderness to assure me of her loyal regard. That over, she sighed with satisfaction. "Aren't I beautiful? *Mais oui.* If I were a man, I would be crazy about a girl like me. I am no beautiful," she said gravely, "but I have more, the character. What we drink? Tonight I feel for being crazee, with you, Kit."

"The heat bores you, doesn't it, Gaston?" I asked.

"*Mais oui,* Monsieur Kit." Gaston smiled, sweetly resigned. "I take no vacation for two years, and can't go now. The other boys do well, but they cannot handle the clients." Gaston had a prima-donna barman's fear of having some under-barman gain the affection of clients should he be gone from his bar long. It was his career, and seaside vacations made him restless, however overworked his nerves might be.

"Now Gaston, I have many ideas. We do raise hell in your bar, particularly at this season. You keep an eye on me tonight. I'm cutting loose."

"But surely," Gaston assured me. "But you have the heart, and much goodwill."

"Toward most, that's me—a man of heart and impulse. But give me a whiskey soda. I won't be in bed this night, not even with you, Hilaria."

Hilaria laughed, mildly taunting. "Last year I love you, but now . . . *mais oui*, I love you. You are crazee fool but beautiful man."

"You feel that way toward us all today."

"I am happy tonight," Hilaria chortled. "We will talk the ideas. I study acting now. It is not good, the life I have been living. Such boring people for a woman of character. Why should I waste me with people who no have the intellect?"

Betty and Arlette, two *poules*, came into the bar. Betty's face was swollen and her eye black from her having fallen down a flight of stairs when drunk a few nights before. Hilaria became reflective."Terrible," she said austerely. "Once Arlette had the beauty; now she is a cow. It is no good that these girls do not use the mind. They do not read; they do not think. One year, or two, then they are feenish, thinking to hold men with bodies. Ha, ha, ha," she laughed gaily. "But me, I do not think that to sleep with people is enough. For to be a great *poule*, a woman must have character. I read, I dance, I sing. Kit, I have wrote a book of poems, I have one on you, with your *corps comme* . . ."

"Hey Hilaria, don't get too descriptive about me in print. I won't be able to live up to your poetic flights."

"Yes, I am feenish with the Surrealists. I write my memoirs, till now, and for twenty-two they are not bad. I will have more books to write. I shall live the great life, not caring for the people alone. I don't dance the Spanish dance anymore. It is banal."

"The world needs great souls, Hilaria."

"Hi-lo, my friends say to me, you waste yourself. But I don't mind being poor. Someday I won't be. I was not always so, but to be is nothing. Now I work. Hi-lo, people ask, what are you doing? I don't tell all. At the theater they say I am great actress. I should waste myself alone with song and dance. I do all things. I am great woman. Someday the world knows it."

The bar began to fill with people of the summer variety. Two collegiates drank aperitifs, not knowing the effect of the amerpicons they gulped. One of them lifted his glass to Hilaria and shouted, "Hey Redhead, dance for us."

"Tamn fool," Hilaria muttered. "Last night I let him buy me drinks. He is fresh guy." She narrowed her eyes to slits and tilted her head back upon a slender, elegant neck. Slowly for dramatic effect, she got up from her stool and walked toward the boy, swaggering haughtily. "Sonofabeetch," she hissed. He did not fall back. "I should dance for you! When I dance it is for my pleasure, not for leetla boys who have grown quicker than they can handle." As her remark brought laughter from others in the bar she came back triumphantly. "Aren't I marvelous? Today so I feel and so I am. I tell you about the poem to you, with your body slim like a girl's and firm like an athlete's, and the caress which has tenderness sympathetic."

"You got going strong, didn't you? But hell, with the summer supply of virgins and frustrated old ladies arriving, no man can afford to have his abilities exploited."

Hilaria was thinking of her beauty again until suddenly she exclaimed, "Oh, the leetla boys. They touch me in the heart. Come, have a drink with me, leetla boys, so wistful."

I saw the boys for the first time. They would touch Hilaria's gallivanting heart which had a tincture of the maternal within it. Reticently they approached, shyboyishly eager. Hilaria took Ross's hand to shake and her strong grip threw him off balance. She laughed with tender delight. "Drink with Hilaria. I am the education for all leetla boys who wander lonely in Montparnasse, if they are of beauty. Last night I would speak to you, but sorry, I drink and forget. Now you know Hilaria, and Kit O'Malley, the crazee Irish, but he is good sport."

The boys seated themselves beside us. They were perfect visual examples of Etonesque schoolboys, with gray trousers, pink and white reticence, and grave, palpitating courtesy. Sudge looked fifteen but claimed to be eighteen, and Ross was twenty-two. With bashful curiosity they admitted not knowing how to get acquainted with people in the Quarter. I felt aged and dissipated, sure that Hilaria and I would horrify their ideas of correctness. Hilaria, of quick wit and reflexes, was too natural to be vulgar, but she used whatever words came to her, for laughter.

At the invitation to drink Ross looked at Sudge. Sudge looked at Ross and said, courteously questioning, "Whiskey?"

"Sound," Ross agreed, his bright face beaming as it broke into an inclusive smile about his granite-hued eyes. His skin was of the freckled blond variety that will not tan or merely flush. Instead, it grows lobster red under the sun or emotion. He was a delicate and wistful boy. I noticed that Sudge did not touch his whiskey, which Ross finally took. It struck me that Sudge did not drink, so that Ross, being kind, drank it so as not to refuse Hilaria's invitation. Sudge, seeing that I had noticed, said, "I'm not drinking. I'm sick."

"You do drink then?" I asked.

"Oh yes," he said with confiding directness. "It's rotten luck, just as Ross and I are beginning to know Paris. I don't know how long it will last. The doctor says he can cure me in a few days."

"You mean you have a social disease?"

"Yes."

"I'll give you the name of a reputable doctor. Don't fool with that sickness. Many a man has been cured in a few days, every time but the first time. The aftermath can be rotten."

"Sound," Sudge said with polite relief. I knew then I had somewhat adopted the boys. "I've heard about you," Sudge said. "Somebody pointed you out as you passed the Dôme and said you knew everybody. That's why we came down here. Ross and I have festered all spring trying to know Paris."

Sudge spoke with appealing earnestness, and I judged that both he and Ross were on their heels to explore. "Sure, stick with me," I told him. "I'll be barging about town for a time without purpose. There's no need not knowing whoever you wish in Paris at this season."

Ross beamed his bright smile in a way to make us old friends at once. "Sound," he said. "Stout," Sudge added. I wanted to chuckle as I observed Sudge looking at me with a sparrow-curious glance. He hadn't much chin, and his mouth was babyish, so that he looked bravely on the world with mystification. I thought he was pained with anxiety about his illness, but his brown eyes glinted and he snorted at some crack of Hilaria's. It was that snort and the simultaneous gruff titter of Ross which gave me a flash of knowing that between themselves the boys had much amusement at the expense of the world. We had dinner and the boys proved they knew how to live cheaply in Paris, for as regards hotels and reasonable eating places, there was nothing Hilaria or I could tell them.

They were from Montreal, and full of disdain for family and college life. They were mainly one. Whatever one said the other seconded with a devoted look of agreement and a "sound" or "stout." No two people could be more in accord or considerate of each other than these boys. They both had literary aspirations, although Sudge gave Ross the laurels and looked upon himself as a barrier between Ross and circumstances that interfered with his art's development. Ross was so quiveringly considerate, with such a wistful appeal, that he was the more likeable, immediately. His smile was disarming, and his delicate frame with his wistfulness made one gentle toward him, as did his air of intense interest in whatever one said. Sudge soon revealed an ironic tongue, and he brooded, but his sickness undoubtedly exasperated him. Soon after dinner we went back to La Coupole, where Sudge drank more colored water and looked unhappy.

Hilaria felt more the great woman than ever and sounded off all over the bar, as though appointed to entertain guests with her temperament and wit.

A flushed young Frenchman with a shock of blond hair came into the place, and at once began to flirt with Hilaria. She was tolerant until he tried to fondle her. "You should love me? Ha, ha, ha, what do I care? I don't like men who are too much men to think every woman loves them," she taunted.

"You are marvelous. I adore you," the French boy teased, catching her arm to kiss her.

"Careful," she warned. "Sonofabeetch, I am not for handling unless I wish it."

The boy was mockingly insistent, and kissed her bitingly, wanting her to play her role. She did.

"Bah!" She pushed him away, rubbing her mouth with a sour grimace. When he tried to catch her again, she jumped from her stool, broke a glass against the bar, and threatened to cut his face with its jagged edges. But she dropped the glass and struck his face with the back of her hand. "*Cochon, ordure, putain,*" she triumphed. "Don't play the fool with me."

The boy desisted, knowing that she would stop play-acting and become really angry. She liked to make vaudeville of life, as did he, but would not play the second role. "Him I put in a taxi one night and give him money when he was drunk and had none. He would sleep with *une grue.* I save him, telling him she is *sale.* He is nice boy, but I don't like he should kiss me that way. Sonofabeetch, I scare him. Ha, ha, ha." Hilaria rocked on her stool, delighted at having made a scene.

Sudge snorted and said, "Sound"; Ross tittered in baritone and added, "Stout." Hilaria was encouraged. She rocked her slender body and dismounted from the stool to writhe across the floor in a dance. "I feel gay," she sang. "I think I go across and tell Madame Select what I think of her. She is a pig, stupid woman. She always say, 'Don't do this. Don't do that,' to her clients. A beetch woman, but she would like the love with some of the pretty boys who drink in her place. Does she think she tell me how to behave?"

Things subsided and Sudge looked babyishly worried and tired. "You'd better go home, don't you think?" I advised. "You'll get well quicker if you're quiet."

"Yes, but Ross."

"Must he suffer confinement because you're sick? Maybe he wants a night out."

Sudge went. Soon Steve Rath appeared, and later went away with Hilaria clucking confidences. I guessed that Chloe Andrews, who was given to suffering without cause, now could suffer because Steve elected to adore Hilaria. Steve was a handsome boy-girl, with a boy's predatory curiosity, sentimental and unaware of conscience. That Chloe worried about her weak heart meant little to Steve, who found it trying to cope with Chloe's starved-mother idealizings. Under a hard-boiled mask Chloe so idealized whomever she loved that others than the susceptible Steve believed her incapable of wanting the "truth" she spoke of, however it was presented. It was natural that Steve and Hilaria should like being together, for both girls liked a roustabout life. Chloe had become painfully domestic and worried about Steve's heart now that they lived together, but this did not rob Steve of her desire for adventure.

Sudge left. Ross had another drink and told me about Sudge and himself. They had both worked in a lumber office in Montreal; they hated the grind as both had been brought up in families used to wealth. When Sudge's father allowed him a hundred dollars a month, Sudge was sure that he and Ross could live on that in Paris, so they shipped on a freighter. They discovered Paris haunts together, and as they had in Montreal resorted to a variety of tricks to have more spending money. It was from a girl they had picked up at La Noctambule, to share together, that Sudge contracted his disease. Only luck spared Ross. As Ross talked he revealed that life in Montreal had not left them without worldly awareness. He was also amused by Hilaria and other Quarter characters they had observed through dreary winter months while sitting at tables in the Dôme. Already their "stouts" and "sounds," and their snorts and snickers, began to echo in my mind.

I got beautifully lit that night and went to Zelli's, and from there to other places in Montmartre. Ross was along, quietly ready to smile his bright, crinkly smile about his granite-clear eyes that, I was later to learn from Sudge, had a mesmerizing effect on women. Sudge, loyally supporting and protecting Ross, found much satisfaction in assuring people that Ross was a genius.

I don't know how I got home, because when I left the jazz gaiety of a

Negro cabaret I forgot to remember. When I lifted my head from the pillow in the morning, I saw Ross sleeping in rosy peace beside me. He woke up as I wondered what we had done the night before. He sat up and smiled winningly. "Sound night we had?" he questioned with staunch cheer.

"Stout," I answered. "Let's get up and go to the Dôme for coffee."

"Sound," Ross seconded.

CHAPTER TWO

IT WAS PAST NOON WHEN WE GOT TO THE DÔME, AND the day was too clear for anything so common as sense. I let coffee go and started drinking beer, sure that this was to be another day of Montparnasse circus. Hilaria drifted by and greeted us, but swung down the street to see an artist: "a great man," who might give her a drawing because she had posed for him. "Ten thousand francs it will sell for someday when I need the money. And I have never sleep with him. He gives me it for my beauty," she said gaily.

Beer is soothing and Ross was a calm companion, but more scornful of most writers than the usual college literary youth. With his wistful-boy air of rosy sweetness, he dismissed D. H. Lawrence for neurotic prophetic idiocies, psychoanalytic blah, and other-than-whichness of magnetic attraction between electric-kneed males. Virginia Woolf he found derivative, pretentious, country-English, and impressed, really, by society and Bloomsbury preciousness. He didn't read Dorothy Richardson to discover what she finally made Miriam think through a novel, while washing the dentist's instruments. Aldous Huxley he brushed aside as lacking a sense of life or of character: a mere encyclopedia of anemic and undigested erudition. He drily searched for mere information, in boredom, so hadn't even a fanatical scholarliness.

"Do you care for Rimbaud?" I asked defensively.

"Sound enough," Ross said. "Hysterical though."

"He left a frenzy of beauty in his wake, and stopped young enough for adolescence to excuse the hysteria. Any such intellectual passion is neurasthenic, but we're all cases for the psychologic laboratory," I fenced, feeling caught and made to be precious. "He didn't sputter."

The silence suggested a scoff from Ross. I tried him on Laforgue. He indicated interest, and I had a bright moment of knowing he could be detected at not knowing the works of many writers. Later I couldn't disagree when he found the febrile way the consumptive Laforgue caressed wan moons precocious. Ross did not intend to be *fin de siècle,* and it was just as well that he found no glamour in the cry that intellect will not let passion realize itself. No more did he respond to the bravery of hard-boiled realism which, in American writing now, conceals mawkish softness beneath the frozen gelatine of staccato phrases, with maimed caution before delicacy or tenderness. Ross had me stalled. I had misgivings about my lost generation, which is thwartedly illusioned and in revolt to such an extent as to be incapable of detachment. Our lostness consists in our knowing ourselves lost while viewing older or younger lost generations and types as unaware of their lostness and mediocrity. Were the boys of the new generation free of the sentimental complexities that once bothered us? With youth still in me I didn't want to feel a grandfather while readjustment and flexibility were possible.

Lucienne, a Spanish girl, who some years before had been known as the queen of the Quarter, came along to save me. Remembering how she had once come in autos, regally, to the Quarter, and knowing she was my age, I was bothered by her broken-tormented quality now. Things were not breaking well for her, neither financially nor in her love affairs, and worse, she felt her beauty and vitality departing. She clutched my hand as she kissed me, and said, "Kit, my old friend, you are adorable. I need to hear you be droll." My heart sank. I switched quickly from beer to pernod, which would give the uplifting effect that might make me, if not droll, at least lively. Still, her presence was comforting. Her smoky hair was a fine veil about her smoldering darkness. She was beautiful enough, but she no longer gloried in her ability to conquer, which made her depressing, and I had praised her to Ross. As I watched, his gaze met mine. He smiled and muttered, "Sound." Lucienne was not another one he found "hardly important."

After a drink she left, seeing the bulky sculptor she lived with. He was trying to break from her, but she wanted marriage at last. Hilaria came back, less gay than before because the painter had not been in to give her a drawing. Also she had seen Lucienne, and these girls, ostensibly friends, regarded each other's *réclame* jealously. "Lucienne is going off in looks and doesn't dress as well as she did," I observed, to comfort Hilaria after she had ordered a vermouth.

"*Oui,*" Hilaria said curtly. "I like Lucienne. She is beautiful but not happy, and beauty is not all in the life. She has no education, and has let herself get old. Now she will not find a rich lover, and why should a man marry her when he does not have to? She has lived with Benoit for five years. He is bored. What has she to occupy herself, or to interest him?"

Hilaria was off again, analyzing and philosophizing, but she felt better when Ross assured her that Lucienne wasn't as vital as she was. "Lucienne, *ma belle*," she called in dulcet tones, "come and sit with us."

"I bore myself," Lucienne said as she sat down, a fretful look on her face. She wasn't managing Benoit and it disturbed her. "But Kit is droll. I adore him. One night he reads the hands of people when he was drinking, and I laugh for the way he makes them afraid of what he says. He told one he was not intelligent; another he said was a fabric clerk; a third he told not to try to be an artist. It was *formidable.* Always he was right. How I did laugh."

Lucienne made animated conversation, unready to have Hilaria appear livelier. I was sheepish because of my foolish trick, when I have been drinking, of pretending to read hands. It always amazes me how naively they believe and worry.

"Kit is crazee, like you and me," Hilaria chortled, leaning back to watch a passing man. "Ah, there is a beautiful man. I will have to take me the spring tonic."

"I am angry. I shall not wait," Lucienne stated. "Never will I wait half an hour for a man. Domingo said he would be here at five and it is half past. I will go on. If he comes, say I am downstairs."

"Poor Lucienne," Hilaria said with satisfaction. "She plays silly. She is in love with Domingo, the barman, and Benoit begins to understand. He doesn't care. Domingo is nice, for an animal one likes to pet. He is beautiful to sleep with once, and goodbye. He is amiable, but it is for him to laugh that Lucienne loves him. His passion is to shake the cocktail. He no cares too much what little girl's tra-la-la he shakes. Ha, ha, ha, like me. Prod once, and goodbye. There is a world of some very beautiful people, and I don't care."

Domingo loitered up. We knew Lucienne would be back. It was easy to see why Domingo infatuated Lucienne. He had the quality of a faun, the alertness, beauty, drollery, and wandering curiosity of whimsy which could not center itself long. His black eyes were deep with animal light. His silken black hair over a low brow was that of a nice animal. Seating himself, he smiled to show his white teeth in droll good nature as he looked around, comically alert. "*Alors*, Monsieur Kit," he said, quaintly bronchial-voiced, "you no come drink with me anymore."

"I've been in Spain, and looked up the places in Barcelona you spoke of."

"You come tonight for the cocktail with me, with Mademoiselle Hilaria. We play dice."

"And I'll read your hand."

"No, no." Domingo hid his hand shyly. "You don't tell me the good fortune. You say I have more heart than mind and that is not good in the bar business." Evidently the simple Domingo believed my bluff at palm-reading, and his peasant superstitions were aroused. But Domingo was a debonair and forgetting boy. He got up and went with Lucienne when she came back. She didn't scold him. Instead, she looked happy and relieved, and he was nonchalant with a swagger, as ready to have a rendezvous with Lucienne as with any passable girl.

"A beautiful man," Hilaria said, squirming, finding him desirable only since Lucienne had found him so. "Cute! He has the nice smile. Sweet! But for Lucienne I would have him once, but she would hear. She has not the mind like me, to take the man once and be done. There are always the beautiful men, and for me who feels strong character like a man, I let them do the suffering. It is nothing in the life to make grand things out of love."

"Hell, Hilaria, you're slated to be a fat married woman before long," I teased.

"*Merde*, what you say? Fat, never shall I be fat," Hilaria scolded. "But you say the fool things to tease me. I will tell you something funny just the same. The other night the leetla Danfield girl followed me like a puppy dog. She is a sorry leetla rabbit. She gets on my nerves, but that night I felt me wild. 'Come on, Mae,' I said, 'we take a taxi to the Bois.' We went, and there two men tried to talk to us. One man tried to force me to kiss him. Tamn fool. He was not bad looking. Had he sense I would have maybe gone with him, but they no can act rough with me. 'Look out, I shoot quick,' I warned him, and I had only my cigarette case in my hand. But he was frightened. I laughed like hell when we got a taxi, and Mae knew I was wonderful, with guts. Hilaria can act the apache when she likes. But Kit, I am through with women. It is men I like. The girls talk too many histories. That is not intelligent, for me, I am curious. I am not a woman for the limitations. To Steve I say it is Chloe who loves her, and Chloe is beautiful but stupid with Steve. I give Steve to her. I no can bother for the love with her when she has no money and I have none also."

I asked Ross where Sudge was. "Oh, he's probably writing his memoirs which he began last week."

"Having read Moore's *Confessions of a Young Man?*" I guessed.

Ross chuckled. "They're sound. He probably hasn't known where to find us."

"You're a hell of a friend. Why don't you go get him. He's probably despondent over his sickness."

Ross didn't go, however. He beamed his smile and regarded Hilaria and other types about. Conversation wasn't his long suit, but I knew that when he and Sudge got together, they would have a grand session of snickering and chattering about me, Hilaria, Lucienne, and others. Hilaria informed me that already Sudge was excited by my *degage* air and my profile, which made him think that I resembled his favorite actor. Inclined to like me as he was, he nevertheless wondered: Apart from my amiability and easy way of offering people drinks, was I to be taken seriously?

At last Sudge appeared on the scene, walking absent-mindedly with a tiptoeish gesture of secretiveness. He was all schoolboy, nonchalant, but neatly groomed. He didn't see us until Ross hailed him. The joy in Ross's voice made me glance quickly at him. At once he became animated, and when Sudge sat down, the two told each other every detail of what had happened since Sudge had gone home last night. Hilaria and I said out loud that they twittered like love birds They did not hear us, so engrossed in snickers, snorts, and detailed revelations. Never in years of knowing the Quarter had I seen so fine an example of schoolboy love and accord. It brought back memories of similar friendships of my own when I was between fourteen and eighteen, but never had my intentness on the details of the other's life been so complete as theirs.

A pathetic incident occurred on the terrace which made us change our rendezvous. Seated at a table nearby was a group, one of whom was a successful American novelist of mediocre realism. Hilaria knew him but didn't like his looks. I knew him, but seeing that he was drunk, and knowing him insistent upon taking off boob types when in that condition, didn't speak. I regretted it later. He was proclaiming himself a great artist. A companion suggested that he created character well, but had not the style of Flaubert. The novelist insisted that he was a better stylist as well as a better psychologist than Flaubert.

Sudge wasn't a bold child, but he muttered, "Oh, tell him to keep quiet. He's only a best-seller."

Hilaria had paid little attention, but hearing Sudge's remark, she suddenly came to life. "Who is it you are better than?" she called out. "What you think? You look like a withered carrot and you write books only for the stupid people. Why for you come to France and act a tamn fool?"

The man turned to look at Hilaria. He grew white, wounded to the quick at her slur on his appearance. "Are you a woman of importance?" he asked. I gasped and started to put out my hand to quiet Hilaria, knowing that he would have little chance in a wordy combat with her. She didn't care what she said, was female, quick to react, and as ready to be rude as she was quick.

"Important?" she taunted. "What is important that you should know it?"

"Do you know that I am a person of international reputation?" he responded.

The situation was cruel. Hilaria was primitive and used to combat and exaggerated insults. "Ha, ha, ha." She leaned back, rocking in her chair tauntingly insolent. "You are a famous joke. The dried vegetable with a rusty top who makes the great literature. Come, funny man, I will buy you a drink. Never since the Fratellinis have I seen a clown funnier with the pathos."

The man was so struck in his vanity that sweat stood on his forehead. His hand shook and he could not lift the glass to his mouth.

"Hilaria, for Christ's sake," I said, "clamp down. The poor fish wouldn't be sounding off if he wasn't trying to bolster himself up. Let's get away from here."

"Oh, I have hurt him really," Hilaria said naively, becoming tender as quickly as she had become rude. "I will go and tell him I am sorry." She went to his table.

"Go away, you Cuban half-breed bitch," another man at the table said as she started to apologize. Quickly the table was overturned. Hilaria hit the speaker in the face with her fist. "Come out on the sidewalk and I will break your face, *putain*," she swore. "For why that I a Cuban half-breed bitch did you cry in your beer for me to love you the other night? I spit on you."

The man did not go to the walk, realizing that already a mob of Frenchmen was ready to make a big scene which might have a nationality element. The French would defend their Flaubert whether they knew his books or not. They would resent Hilaria's being called a half-breed bitch, and they already resented the Americans' attitude that they owned the Quarter. Hilaria came away, raging but triumphant.

"Poor fellow, she shouldn't have done that," Sudge said gloomily, overcome by the awfulness of existence.

"Yes, but she was right to soak the other fellow," Ross for once disagreed. Sudge didn't respond with his usual "stout" or "sound." Instead he asked about Hilaria.

"She's all right," I answered. "She would do anything she could for someone she likes. Such scenes break out often in the Quarter. That idiot shouldn't shout about his talent because nobody is less important than a writer whose books one doesn't like. Hilaria is too Parisian not to get a French mob on her side. I think she's the illegitimate child of somebody who once had position. She's batted about the town for years, managing not to be merely a *poule*. She'll be a bum all her life, but racially and from experience she can think ten times while that poor cuss can think once. It doesn't go, calling girls who are on the borderline bitches and half-breeds, especially when the man doing it gets as lousy drunk as the man she punched. With so many writers about, that novelist erred in revealing his megalomaniac need to bolster up his failing self-belief. Someone is always sure to get caustic."

Sudge went mournfully to his hotel, but Ross stayed. I didn't feel good, sensing there would be antagonism in the atmosphere this night. It seemed that Ross would be delighted to join Sudge at the hotel to chatter further over events during their hours apart, but such was not the case. I didn't leave the Quarter either, for an architect friend of mine from Chicago had a wealthy client and his wife in tow. They wanted to be shown around. Later at dinner I tried to be racy without shocking Mrs. Barton. She was a matron, worried in her complacency because in Paris her delicate health and children didn't suffice as conversation, and nobody knew much of her bridge game. She indicated that she read the latest books, without shock, but even these Paris people didn't discuss. Her last resort was to look modern and smart as couturières advised. Mr. Barton, an engineer, knew much he wouldn't reveal before his wife, who was not a woman for intellectual companionship. He was kindly, robust, with a keen humor that surely would have revealed itself away from her. I liked him, thinking how healthy and keen the sensibilities of a good commercial-executive person can be. He lacks the limited art-is-all attitude of specialists in any of the mediums, and arrives at intelligent conclusions regarding psychology, social states, and literature without precious theorizing. Several times he spotted the false note in novels we mentioned that were satires of their authors' limitations more than satires of society.

Evidently I looked hungover, for Mrs. Barton insisted that I must visit them at their "little home" outside Chicago. There she would see that I was given proper food. The idea wasn't unpleasant. "Our home is not pretentious, but we keep the grounds in order. There are twenty-five rolling acres, all of which are mowed daily except for the flower beds and hedges. It costs us six hundred dollars a month merely to keep those acres mowed. You could be free, and quite tranquil. We wouldn't interfere with your work." Naturally I pictured myself in the center of those twenty-five acres of manicured lawn, coiffeured hedges, and clipped flower gardens. I need no further quest for Elysium, but, crassly human, I parried acceptance of her invitation. Doubtless, the wail of my architect friend, to which I had listened before the lady arrived, wrongly influenced me. But if I were to believe him, the normal, sane, and settled friends we had in common spoke with pathetic envy of my freedom. Yet, if they knew that the only freedom I have is to visualize few human situations to envy, they might be more free themselves.

The party left me by ten o'clock, and as I always do at whatever hour of the night when I have no dinner appointments in Paris, I went back to the Quarter for that last drink, which multiplies and keeps one up till early morning. Striving to summon what small strength of character I have, I concluded that I felt empty and not self-sufficient and was unready to sleep then. Cities have that effect on me. As do many, I wanted companionship, and heady with wine I endeavored to find almost anybody agreeable. It was thus with relief that I encountered Ross, who had at last decided to join Sudge, but now he joined me.

As we walked toward La Coupole Ross was silent, until he finally said, reticently, "I hope you like Sudge and take him around with you. He needs to have you like him. He wants that."

"Yes, I do like him," I said, wondering at the way these boys so sweetly wanted to share everything. "Won't he be lonely now?"

"Poor little Sudge." Ross's voice was flooded with tenderness. He felt so tenderly toward Sudge without it occurring to him to stay with his ill friend when Sudge took a deep, bird-twittering joy in having him present. "He's having a dementia, though, and I can't bring him out it. We don't interfere with each other's pastimes."

There was much I had to learn about the boys' dementias, phobias, and manias. Sudge, given to melancholia which once would have been dubbed merely adolescence, glibly analyzed all their moods in the manner of the generation brought up on psychoanalysis. Ross had a most sympathetic appreciation of his own "dementia praecox" moments. The Campion family had all been victims of that disease which often, in Ross's case, struck me as simple Irish temper. The Galbraith family, Ross assured me, were middle-class dumbheads, and only because of him had Sudge come through to this present state of illumined understanding.

La Coupole was crowded. Tonight the gathering was more than usually mixed. Three Japs sat at a corner table; several Egyptians were at the bar; some Scandinavians were growling against Americans who acted as cocky as the Scandinavians themselves. Later a group of Frenchmen drifted in, and at once one began to damn Americans in a loud voice. It appeared that he had come to the Quarter to indulge his antagonism against Americans.

It is hard to draw the line where intoxication begins. I know that many acquaintances came into the bar and that we drank gaily. Two girls talked gleefully of various barroom fights they had seen. I began to feel that a real barroom scrap is one of life's fine spectacles: comparable to the dance, the theater, the opera, a boxing match, or a bullfight, and with the added charm of hot reality.

Some American slapped me on the back, and I hate that. It calls up a sense of collegiate swaggering and hard-boiled artifice. He called me a "swell guy," and I hate that, with no responding feeling that he was "regular." He might let whoever could find out that I was "swell," which one decidedly is not when irritable. Unfortunately I didn't voice my protest. I simply felt cranky.

Drinking with Felix Lutyens I was sitting upon but half my barstool when I felt myself displaced. Turning, I saw that the Frenchman who had been talking against Americans had rudely taken my seat. When I told him it was my place, he remarked, "You Americans are without civilization."

Now that is no remark to make to a man who actually is uncivilized, and my reflexes told me to take advantage of my barbaric state. My foot got entangled with one leg of the stool, and I pulled. The Frenchman landed neatly on his behind upon the floor. People in the bar roared with laughter and he arose raging. I didn't like his face and assured him that he was no honor to France, had not been elected by the French people to speak for them, and that his civilization was that of a dog which eats out of gutters.

May providence bless such French as have irony, love fights, and won't stand injustice. Within a minute the bar was in an uproar. The Frenchman was loudly declaring himself a soldier who had been wounded in the war while America was not doing her duty.

A *poule* interrupted him violently, telling him how little of a hero he had been, and what she knew about his mode of living. One man with him wanted to beat me up, but two of his companions sided with me, and one whispered that Jean had an evil disposition, that I was not to think that all Frenchmen regarded politeness as little as he did. Nevertheless, the fight raged, with about equal numbers in the bar defending each of our causes. Outside the door the gendarmes released me, as Gaston had indicated that I was a good boy, and these gendarmes were doing their best to avoid arresting me. I realized, however, that a Polish painter whose work I thought lousy had slapped my face and commented that I was insolent. For years he and I had looked at each other with antagonism. I hurtled back into the bar and sloughed the Pole. It was all very uncivilized, but it was a hot spring evening, and things can be trying. The battle was on again. Plump Madame Coupole, in a black evening dress with a pearl necklace dangling over her ample bosom, fussed about tearfully. Gaston tried to pacify ten people at once, since the girls who liked to see a fight were in the battle, verbally at least. Dale Burke said later that she had slammed the Frenchman in the ribs and called him a pig. Again we were ejected but, having slugged my man, I felt triumphant. It wasn't until we arrived at the College Inn that I noticed Sudge's presence. He snickered ashamedly. It seems that he had lifted the palm of his hand to Madame La Coupole's chin, and the picture of her wailing as she nursed a sore neck tickled his sense of comedy.

"That's no way for a gent to act," I told Sudge.

He looked chagrined and explained. "She tried to catch your arms and was going to hold them behind your back just as that Pole was ready to soak you. He would have, too. He kicked at your privates. That fool woman always sides with newcomers to the Quarter rather than with her regular clients. Why should she have the gendarmes discipline you more than the others?"

I didn't argue to get to the bottom of who started the fracas, and felt relieved that Sudge was a friend in need, to understand that my nature, while independent, is not quarrelsome. The affair wasn't civilized, but agreeing that few people think much of so-called civilization today, we let the matter drop. Though Ross wasn't there, I said to Sudge, "You can't drink, but come up to Bricktop's anyway. She has some grand new songs, and I'll tell her that you're my nephew and not allowed to drink."

Sudge wanted to wait for Ross, but at my suggesting that Ross seldom waited for him, he came along. At Bricktop's we stood at the bar where I wisely drank beer, and Sudge talked of his problems. His father was worth a million, mainly inherited or brought by marriage. Sudge's plaint was that the old man was himself no useful member of society, and therefore couldn't rightly demand too much purpose of an eighteen-year-old son who was to have a fortune of his own at twenty-five. Furthermore, his father made money off the capital which Sudge was to inherit. He was deeply pained that his father permitted him no more than a hundred dollars a month. "Two can't do more than muck along on that," he grieved.

"But your father doesn't know you share it with Ross, does he?"

"Yes, and the family thinks Ross neurotic." Sudge looked dejected and bitter. "They just fester along in the most stupid kind of life. She plays bridge, he plays golf, but they're both bored stiff. I had a letter from Mother telling me not to let Dad know, but she was crazy to have a sea captain she likes get back. She was dying of boredom with Dad."

"She actually tells you of her lovers?"

"She knows I know. Neither of them knows why they are alive. Now my brother's going to be married and they'll give him five hundred a month. It's enough to fester anybody." Sudge was righteously bitter with an infantile sullenness, and I agreed that he was right to be. Dull parents of wealth can be most righteous about the purposes of offspring whose educations they have miserably directed. Why had they let Sudge at seventeen go up against the drabness of a clerk's rooming-house life after being brought up in luxury? And why did they leave him at eighteen loose in Montparnasse? He too obviously was not a type to harden and become full of energetic purpose because of such experiences, particularly when he knew he was to inherit money later.

CHAPTER THREE

MY STUDIO, TOO CHILLY FOR WINTER, WAS cleaned and I moved in with dire intentions of working if I could again conquer Paris. However, too many parties and too many pals made my head ring with that song of gin mornings. Among the worldly, where types and situations are well discussed if not understood, the will to write grows feeble. Why an acted play or a written narration? Dramas are being performed constantly before one's eyes, and we often resent the limited design which most writers inflict upon life. After a week I strongly submitted to my weakness and waited to work until I had gone to some little town on the Mediterranean, where ocean breeze and the lap of the sea would stimulate me.

The studio was large and bare, and because the boys were broke owing to Sudge's doctor bills, I told them to locate a bed, shove it into the studio, and move in. They did, and Sudge worked with chirpy industry on his autobiography. It had the million-year-old irony of life which only a bright child could achieve, because with age experience confuses the realizations. It was supreme for qualities that the super-sophisticated Sudge would have squirmed to know were there. Ross too picked at his typewriter with inept hands. So their lives were quiet, because they were broke and more because of their gentle disdain for the vanities of life as action.

They read *Daisy Miller*. Sudge snorted and said, "Sound," while Ross guffawed and answered, "Stout." Having met a perfect ass of a girl, Ross intended to write the story of Daisy Miller married. They were quite bored when a boy from Montreal came to visit them and was excited over having secured copies of *The Scented Garden* and *The Kama-Sutra*. Such naivete on the part of anyone sufficed to supply the boys with hours of titterings. Who did not know all that these books revealed, and why a surreptitious fuss about a thing so banal as sex? They delighted together in Hawthorne's *The Blithedale Romance*, chuckling with tolerance at me because I didn't understand what they found in it to giggle about. Ronald Firbank's *The Flower Beneath the Foot* overcame them. The gentleman given to tucking his nose-hairs into his nostrils was too priceless. Sudge snorted fifty times over that one.

Many times I mimicked them, but one day I used "stout" and "sound" too often. Ross had a dementia praecox. Certainly if anyone teased me as I did them I'd have had several dementias long before, but my gentle consideration was not equal to theirs. Ross spoke with a strange Scotch-Canadian accent. His mesmeric eyes flashed with rage as he came toward me, saying hotly, "Coom ootside and ay'll fight you."

I fell back in my chair and looked at the fragile, wistful Ross and roared with laughter. Chagrin showed on his face, and I got up to pat his cheek. He looked sheepish and then broke into his beaming smile that forgave me. Sudge helped to save the situation by reading a passage on Elagabalus from Gibbon, and they snorted and tittered. The difficult moment passed. The life of Elagabalus was priceless, and what the old fogies of his time must have said about him delighted the boys. Gibbon's dry and sly mind convulsed Sudge with choked laughter.

Their Eden could not last. Sudge got well and had ideas of stepping out. Ross looked perturbed, with his old man expression, when he informed me that Sudge would sleep with anybody and always would since he was fourteen. Surely enough, Sudge wandered into the Quarter and encountered Dale Burke, who felt that not enough was happening in her life. Sudge wasn't in evidence for two days.

Before I had thought Ross the stronger, deeper, and more sensitive of the two, but such a need as Ross had for Sudge annihilated any sense of his self-sufficiency. He was a mere shadow registering neurotic wistfulness when Sudge did not appear. Given to biting his fingernails and scratching the back of his hand, he did these things for an hour as he sat at a cafe table. Now and then he jumped up, thinking he had seen or heard Sudge. It was impossible to make conversation. He answered questions but didn't listen if one talked. Still, he didn't want to be alone. He liked me well enough, or disliked me little enough, to tolerate more of my company without Sudge than the company of most people about, but he was utterly lost. I wondered if it was the younger, Sudge, who had all the force, wit, capacity to navigate. It occurred to me that Sudge always read and criticized Ross's writing, and offered suggestions as well. He even recalled to Ross incidents in the Campion family as fine material to use. Ross's writings were mainly introspective, flow-of-the-conscious, and delicate. Sudge's writing was young, but objective with a bright wit of cute malice.

"How long have you and Sudge been together?" I asked Ross one night as I was dressing for a dinner party. He was so pathetic that I was sorry to be leaving him alone for dinner.

"Since he was fourteen."

"Were you at school together?"

"Not at a private school. He was too much younger than me. We met in a cafe."

"Didn't you feel rather older boy toward him?"

"Oh, no." Ross's eyes met mine with a startled and condemning look. "I'd seen him around and always wanted to know him. Those filthy people don't understand anything fine, though. They talked about poor little Sudge when we became friends." This he said with gruff, hurt scorn.

Ross was fumbling with manuscripts. "Are those stories you did before coming to Paris? Let's see some of them; do you mind?" I asked.

Ross was timid as he wouldn't have been had Sudge been there. Sudge would have shown them to me saying that they were "sound" and "not as good as he does now." Though Ross showed them to me, I didn't ask again, feeling they were too intimate. His pawlike hands trembled as he handed them to me, but he was often in a nervous state.

There was little to say about the long thing I read. Its revelations were so intimate as to be distressing. They showed that Ross was idealistically and passionately in love with Sudge, and letters between the characters were obviously some which Ross had received from Sudge. I felt sorry for the pain that Ross had suffered because his devotion to Sudge was misunderstood, and had to chuckle at Sudge's letters. At sixteen he had taken a trip to France and what the boy had been up to, without any convention, would have supplied wonderful material for a picaresque novel. It occurred to me then that it was all natural and all right, for Sudge remained untouched, direct, and astoundingly honest about admitting what he did to anybody who had his confidence.

"The story has material you'll use later, but it wouldn't get accepted by any publisher now, and it's just as well. It's a mistake to reveal so much about yourself to the public at your age," I said. "Sudge believes in a full life, I judge from this."

Ross was less pathetically lost without Sudge's presence now that we talked of him to bring up memories of their friendship. He chuckled with overwhelmed mirth. "Last spring we were broke, and ran into a dirty old Englishman who wanted to see a show. We took him to our room and staged a pose for him and he gave us two hundred francs."

"Was he satisfied?" I asked, concealing the jolt of surprise that Ross's information gave me. I realized quickly, however, that the boys could do such a thing and think it a huge joke.

"The old fool," Ross scoffed, "didn't know we were only pretending. We made noises and the idiot pranced around having a great time. Then Sudge and I went out and ate the first meal we'd had in two days, and then to La Noctambule where we picked up a girl."

"The one you shared?"

"Not the one that gave Sudge a disease. I took her first, but just played around till Sudge got excited and wanted me to hurry."

It was probably always "just playing around" for Ross with girls they picked up, I suspected. Both boys struck me as strange little animals, with few emotions or reactions generally associated with people, but Sudge was nearer that fanciful state "normal" which persists in the mind and language. Whatever they did had not marred the clear look of innocence which both possessed.

Soon Sudge came in, and he and Ross were immediately chuckling at Sudge's account. "I bounced about a good deal and enjoyed myself soundly. It was frightfully jolly." They laughed at Dale Burke's idea of herself as a passionate woman. Their laughter wasn't mean; they merely thought she was fooling herself and being pretentious with silly released-romanticism, but Sudge loyally defended her generosity and goodwill. He knew, however, that she understood little of love or passion. Still, her entering their lives, as well as Sudge's being well, let the boys step out into active Paris nightlife. She had her coterie, and incoming boats constantly brought new people to the Quarter. Thus casual minglings made carousing far too easy for them to consider serious work now.

CHAPTER FOUR

FOREST PEMBERTON SHOWED UP AT THE DÔME ONE day. Since I had last seen him he had become a best-seller novelist, acclaimed a stylist of modern writing at its best. I wasn't comfortable because he had been divorced and taken on a new wife, and it remained in my memory how publicly insistent he had been about his love for his former wife. She was always "Muzzie-Cat" to him, and he "Lion-Papa" to her, and the baby was Jumbo while a pet puppy was Waxen-Pup. Before me when his wife talked of their love, Pemberton would beg, "Muzzie-Cat, he isn't interested in our love," and she would answer tearfully, "Why Lion-Papa, you've never spoken like that to me before." My nature could not feel the situation authentic or healthy, and I wished often one of them would let rip with a strong, irritated curse. Pemberton went to prize fights, bullfights, and races, to harden himself by becoming used to blood, pain, brutality, and sudden accidents. In his writing his stereotyped figures were often "swell guys" or "bastards" or beautiful and impossible ladies sacrificing all for the clean-minded young American hero, who in turn was brusque, unready to reveal the real tenderness within him, but truly delicate beneath his brave, war-seared attitude toward grim reality. When Pemberton shadow-boxed, shadow-bullfought, or cauterized scratches with a burning match to prove his stoicism before pain, his self-hardening process left me embarrassed.

A year before he broke with Muzzie-Cat, we went together to the Parnasse bar for a short beer. Lady Mart, always with a brandy at some bar, was there, and "needing just one more to set her up" hailed me. I said to Pemberton, "Do you know Lady Mart?" Pemberton's response rather surprised me. "Oh, Lady Mart, I have heard of you." It was clear at once that he was impressed, and I had remarked before that he had in him an almost awed respect for the English aristocracy, who may or may not hold their liquor like ladies and gentlemen. Long ago I had learned to think of Mart as a desperate and terrified "lady," something of a tramp and a nuisance, but likeable in her pathos. But it appeared that Pemberton was smitten by her, and she put on her lady act, even to the extent of saying that she must be on soon to meet her friend—actually her cousin—Lord Mike, as she called him. But Pemberton had arranged to see her again. He did. For the next two months he was doing the bars and nightclubs as he had never done them before, every night, taking Mike along with Mart who had so obviously infatuated him.

One night at Palermo's his wife had also come along, and later was quietly shedding tears at the end of the bar while Pemberton danced with Mart. I heard him ask Mrs. Hale, iron-gray-haired Kate, if she would take his wife back to the Quarter. With Mart, he no longer called her Muzzie-Cat. Kate looked at him with surprise and said coolly, "Really now. I am with my party. She can take a taxi herself, and if you are breaking with her, why ask a casual acquaintance to help you?" After that rebuff it surprised me that Pemberton also asked me to take his wife home. I was with other people also, but would not have done so in any case. "Don't you expect more service than you rate, Pemb? If you and she are busting up, it's not up to me to console her in her tears. I'm with people too."

It was a fortnight before I ran into Pemberton again, and it appeared Lady Mart had gone south with a Jewish bookdealer.

After a beer at the Dôme we went to a bookshop. In the bookshop was a frightened and slow-witted French girl. She couldn't change one hundred francs when Pemberton wanted to buy a magazine. She spoke no English. Pemberton pointed to a copy of his book and said that he was the author, so her employer would trust him to pay later. Obviously the girl was afraid that her employer would be cross should she take the responsibility of trusting him. Pemberton's loose mouth curled with a hurt snarl, and he left muttering about her dullness. I couldn't play up, and had no intention of knowing him as a good, bad, great, or minor writer. His success as a writer had not changed him humanly or for his apprehension of life, and I see literature as conception rather than as writing. There are many fine writers, and most artists are damn fools for the priorities they assume and the recognition they demand from people not interested in their mediums. Surely the French girl worked in the bookshop because of the miserable salary rather than because of a love of literature. Nor did she read English to know anything about any American writer's standing.

We went to sit in the comfortable Falstaff bar where soon Ross and Sudge arrived, walking cautiously as if on tiptoe. It was their manner when broke or up to mischief. They beamed smiles on me, but instinct kept me from asking them to sit with Pemberton and me. Sudge had snorted because of Pemberton's habit of shadow-boxing when approaching or leaving a group at a cafe table. Sudge was sure that Pemberton now viewed the Quarter divided by two fears: Should he appear too often he might lose prestige; if he did not appear at all he would be thought upstage because of success. It's very difficult to handle fame if one cares about what "they" say, and "they" say it however one acts, whether one has fame or mere publicity.

Pemberton was most conscious of people, and asked often, "Do they like me?" His lips curled with hurt when he said, "They don't like me, do they?" As he was most given to not liking many people, I wondered why he cared, but he suffered even if people he disliked spoke against him. His book revealed that he heartily disliked several people he had treated with declared friendliness when in their presence. He looked now at the boys as they sat at the bar, turning now and then to admit a friendly feeling toward me. Their subdued snickers sounded now and then. "You know them, do you?" Pemberton asked. "I've seen them about. They have great fun giving us all the razz. They're priceless British boys. I'd like to know them."

"They're canny children," I said. "Their manners are mainly perfect. You wouldn't get into them unless they chose to reveal themselves. The British have it on us in reserve."

Pemberton was canny too. "You don't think they'd like me, Kit?"

"Would that matter?" I asked, knowing that my not having had them join us made Pemberton aware that I knew the boys didn't like him. Sudge particularly scorned Pemberton's affected modest directness as a writer, and when Sudge scorned in a certain way, he'd no more consider the person involved than a dogfighting cat would consider a dog.

"The supercilious little runts." Pemberton's lip curled with soft bitterness. "Dutch and I were talking about our writing the other night, not showing off a bit. You know how Dutch has to talk technique because he thinks he's a sloppy writer. I heard them laughing, but didn't know for sure if they were giggling at us."

"They were," I told Pemberton cruelly. "It wasn't the talk of technique they laughed at. When you spoke of Flannagan's boxing and said he imitated your writing style, it tickled them to think of your having a rival boxing-literary man. They heard you say, too, that Flannagan was coming to Paris, and wondered how it would strike him, as they judge from his writing that his world consists of gangsters, broads, boxers, and morons who are dragged sluggishly by fate through situations in which their reflexes and wills never operate."

"What to hell, Kit," Pemberton complained with a hurt-boy tone, "can't a guy ever be himself? I get a swell kick out of putting on the gloves. You know I don't go in for that crap of showing off. You know I know there's so many bastards in the world that I don't want to be one of them."

"They didn't ride you hard," I lied. "They simply wondered if the people you write about ever talk in paragraphs."

Pemberton was not one given to direct reactions. Some code belonging to simple, hard-boiled guys, gruffly modest about their true sensibilities, informed him how to feel, think, and react. The boys, however, bothered him. They were British but not mannered, devilishly mocking but polite, and their irony was contained within a harder shell than Pemberton's. To them a maggot-eaten dog was just that; to Pemberton it was something to gaze at a long time, as if fascinated, to harden himself. To them a prize fight was a prize fight; to him something to study because he might get into a fight himself someday and had to be prepared. Though older than the boys, he was more immature in many of his attitudes about how to think and act than they were. In his stories his characters talked in clipped phrases, muscle-bound emotionally, to reveal the maimed psychology of their author. They too bravely withheld all emotions, wisecracked and joked to conceal any gentle or tender feelings, and seldom spoke more than three- or five-word phrases. The boys were drily as dastardly, ruthless, sentimental, or tricky as they might be. They might fool themselves about their minds and discriminations, but as they battered about they were beginning more and more to admit their bewilderment.

When Pemberton was leaving, he said, "It's good you were around, Kit. I'm damned fond of you. You know how it is. There are so many cheap sonofbitches around I wouldn't come to the Quarter except for you few, and people will say I'm trying to act the great man if I don't come. You know I don't go in for that bunk."

Sudge gave me a quick sparrow glance, but his birdlike face didn't change its expression until Pemberton had left. I sensed that a mirthful snort was in his nostrils, and after Pemberton sparred off and did a few shadow-boxing steps as he went out the door, the snort burst. I joined the boys at the bar. "Does Pemberton ever act natural and say what he thinks without pleading with his voice to be understood as a simple clean young American beneath his brave athletic style?" Sudge said sourly. "I'll bet he's written a war book in which he just won't tell the world how much he really suffered."

"He has," I said, surprised at Sudge's guess or actual understanding. "What makes you think so?"

"Don't be silly," Sudge replied. "They're the books to write now. The public has had enough nymphomaniacs of high society who are desperate-drive ladies, still pure in their ideals. They want ooze about war. I suppose Pemberton's war characters will be choking forth, 'It isn't any fun without war. No, it's no fun if you can't have war. The kick's gone out of life.'" In simple-mindedness, or without reflecting, I might have thought the recent public craze for war books a sign that the world was tired of wars. "Hell," Sudge chortled, "do people who buy best-sellers ever read anything but sentimentality? You'd think the war was fought by schoolboys from *All Quiet on the Western Front.* If they were tired of war, they'd read *War and Peace,* or not read about war at all. Be brave and noble and suffer on through and they will eat up your writing. I'm festered. Father's threatening to reduce my allowance." Sudge's baby face was sour with disgust.

Ross departed to write at his family novel. Sudge and I decided to cross the river, have a looksee into the Ritz bar, oysters at Prunier's, a walk down the Champs Elysées to Footit's bar, and back to the New York bar where I wanted to find Tony Crane. At six o'clock, not having run into anything in the way of adventure which we would have embraced with ready abandon, we returned to sit in front of the Select. Ross came across the street, radiant with a beaming smile. "Jesus, Sudge, I've fallen. Wait, she'll be along," he confessed a miracle.

Before this Ross had been intent upon falling in love. I waited. Along "she" came. She was wan, a true decadent type, fragile, with a delicate air of being lost through knowing too much to bear. Ross beamed at Sudge, and Sudge looked appraisingly to cluck "Sound." The girl had an anemic quality of ash lavender that Poe or Baudelaire might have liked, but with her were two stolid-looking girls, who seemed resentful at things generally. One of them glared sullenly at Ross when he beamed at his ideal. Going over to her with an air of delicate worshipfulness, he said, "I want to know you," and she accepted him. Her companions, however, told him not to butt in. They weren't bothering him. Ross plaintively told them he didn't wish to know them. He saw that they were as mediocre and distrustful as factory girls. There was no scene though. His wistfully confessed love seemed to have struck understanding in the girl he liked. I remembered having seen her about the year before. Her name was Fern Mallow, and some years ago her father had shot himself when caught embezzling. She'd been to Russia, been taken care of by an elderly woman sculptor, and must have known, in bewilderment, the travail of insecure existence. Seeing her vagueness and pallor, I suspected that she was one of those who had found the doubtful solace of drugs. The decadent strain in Ross would respond to such a person. Having little success in his wooing, he went across the street for a pernod. Sudge knew he would get drunk and persist in his passion. Sudge chuckled but was despondent. Ross was a great problem, but it was no use telling him not to muck around like a bloody fool, Sudge knew, and anyway Sudge didn't interfere with others.

I saw Ellery Saunderson approaching, fat, shiny-faced, with an apologetic air for sneaking out to let down on his dignity. Sudge regarded him with amusement, for Ellery looked much like the figure of a fleshy butcher done in blond tones by Rubens. He sat with us and offered drinks. "I say, Kit," he said pompously, "isn't Howard getting a bit too—you know—too strong? A man doesn't mind making a loan to a man less fortunate than himself now and then, but today . . ."

"Howard's incurable," I interjected, stopping Ellery's jovial and pompous sputterings. "You loaned him what he asked for? People do, whatever his spell is. I can't figure it out unless he lies so flagrantly that they feel he'd think them stupid to bother telling him he lies."

Ellery held a position in the journalistic world and had an alert curiosity if not much subtlety. He observed Sudge, but was as ready to impress the child as anyone else. He sputtered with his great manner of kindly tolerance. "A man doesn't like being niggardly, and I must admit, I have had good fortune, as journalists go, not to boast. Some think I have earned my laurels. I won't say. Let us admit that I have had what you Americans call the 'breaks.' But I do think Howard goes a bit far."

Sudge couldn't hold back his snort, and got red because he couldn't control his indelicate mirth that Ellery should fuss about such a well-known cadger as Howard. Ellery laughed while his blue eyes appraised Sudge out of his plump shiny face. Not finding the subject one from which he could elicit sympathy, he asked me what I thought of Philip Danbury's war novel, which he had also seen in script.

"I don't follow it much. He scolds the English for their smugness and hypocrisies as they love to be scolded, from the inside. It may establish him with the conservative press. Are you going to John's party Saturday night? He and Danbury got together and if we go we are each to write a sonnet for a prize. I never did learn what constitutes a sonnet," I said.

"Oh, yes." Ellery was jolly. "John finds the name James Fernley John meaning less in the literary world than it did two seasons back. He wishes to get in touch with the young again, to lead them again, shall we say. Ha, ha, ha, poor John. I must say he gets a bit too much. He writes—I don't wish to be cruel, and the remark isn't mine originally, but as it's a good one I'll pass it on—as though he turned on the faucet to check it at will, and have his weekly, his fortnightly, or his famous style, hot or cold. He overdoes that prose-master business, don't you agree?"

Dear me, yes, I did agree, but Ellery was being indiscreet. He had bought Sudge and me drinks, but he knew too that I am given to outbreaks of frankness with a nasty laugh. Surely he was aware that I knew the water-faucet remark was made originally by James Fernley John about the writings of Ellery Saunderson. He might also have heard that he and John were called sometimes the steady-flowing twins. Newspapermen are heartless about twitting their fellow craftsmen. I didn't twit Ellery, though, and he continued, serious now, not to have Sudge think him trivial-minded. "I say, Kit, don't you find this contemporary tendency in the arts has about run its course—this realism, and playing with language, and the cubes and distortions in painting? I rather think we're swinging back to a sound romanticism. Don't you agree?"

"Ellery, you've written a romantic novel," I asserted.

Ellery fidgeted. "To be truthful, Kit, I have, and it isn't bad if I do say so. Really, not bad."

"Then of course the day of realism is past. I'm glad you gave me the tip. Only I never noticed that the day of romanticism was by. Rather fatalistically I thought the world still supplied us numbers of every sort of thing."

"But, Kit, this psychoanalysis and intentness on sex leaves no room for philosophy, or there is no content to make a man think." Ellery seemed afraid he was being too serious.

"Oh, yes, sex," I answered. "I'd almost forgotten that. If it's something spiritual you're seeking, there are quite a few of the boys in England and America starting higher-thought movements that would bring us back to the beginning of philosophy and religion. You know, Ellery, I'm thinking of writing a book on Paris, as a potboiler. I think I'll put you in it, to return the compliment you paid me by including me in your last book."

Ellery cleared his throat and ordered a round of drinks. "Really, Kit. Well, I trust you won't say anything that my missus . . . you know, we've all had good times together."

"But, Ellery, I wouldn't," I assured him. "You do, when you have an aged story to use for space filler, you do have me relate it at a dinner party, and I hate stock stories. You do have some other characters pull wisecracks on legends about me, but I would reveal you only in your intellectual phases. We're all human and some of our phases look damned comic in print. I could get some fine slapstick comedy out of moments when you're pinching the fannies of *poules*, but a man's a man after all."

Ellery squirmed and forced a hearty laugh. With relief he greeted Reyner, a Jewish bookseller who had recently begun to edit a quarterly, rather fancying himself as a genial patron of the arts. Few editors of other literary reviews bothered to take on the kindly controversies that he would begin. Ellery asked Sudge what he thought of old scoundrels like himself and me. Then he turned to Reyner, who had seated himself. "These youngsters are creeping up on us, Reyner. We have to look out that they don't make back numbers of us. Are the youngsters submitting any good material?"

Reyner looked genially at Sudge and me, sniffed adenoidally, and smiled with what he surely meant to have signify paternal humor. "No, Saunderson, they aren't. They all have too much money to be doing good work. They don't suffer enough."

"You mean to say then, Reyner, that you believe poverty is a good thing for the young artist?" Ellery was gravely considered and duly profound.

"I have decided so." Reyner smiled forgivingly at Sudge and me. Sudge looked pained, and I knew his disgust, for Reyner's income derived mainly from a wife who was a fabulously successful businesswoman. Reyner quickly finished a bock and said he must go on. It was his custom to do the rounds of the terrace a few times daily, but he never lingered long, and as he left he smiled heartily, admitting with broad generosity, "But I have hopes for them, too. Yes, we oldsters mustn't be crotchety." Then he left.

"Always leave the table with a smile," Sudge groaned. "The goodwill editor, that's him."

Ellery looked askance at Sudge, and was quite keen enough to be aware that the boy wasn't apt to be impressed by his type of journalism. He too wanted to leave, and after fussing a bit, managed to escape. As he left he propelled his sizable stomach before him with amazing agile secretiveness. Often he felt that he should be ashamed to be seen in the Quarter. His tale was that his wife disciplined him, but as she came frequently to the Quarter herself and took an ironically amused attitude toward him, one wondered. Cruel people declared that she did much of his better writing, and handled the family money, but this was doubtful. His better writing would probably have been better in that case.

"It festers me to hear two bounders like them talking about writing," Sudge grunted. "Just dear, kind, old men. Reyner promised Ross five hundred francs for a short story, and then handed him an envelope containing two hundred fifty francs. He's the generous patron of the arts. 'The youngsters have too much money!'"

A wave of mirth suddenly struck Sudge, and he snorted until he was red in the face. "Both the old fogies are ready to try impressing anybody, even each other. The way they fidgeted on their chairs trying to think of something bright to say made me wish the chairs really had stoves under them. They might as well have hot pants because their brains couldn't cook a potboiler."

CHAPTER FIVE

COLETTE GODESCARD AND LAURA BRADLEY appeared with recognizing smiles, and it was obvious that the boys would take to them. Laura's look implied that she was in on the huge joke which we all are. In a green velvet suit, topped by a Russian cap, she looked gentle young-boy and appealing. Colette was hatless and her crinkly, gray-black hair flaunted its cowlick. Both girls were decidedly decorative. Sudge seeing that they would join us squirmed with joy. "You know them? Sound, I say."

"Stout," I agreed. "They have the studio down the hall from ours, and fit right in. Laura sculpts and Colette paints, and will they drink! They're bright when it comes to giving parties to round up people to buy their art."

"We were wondering if you were back," Laura said. "There seemed nobody around we wanted to see."

"They're coming back. I have a hunch it's to be a lively season."

"Yes, by Jesus," Colette said rakishly, "I will have a drink and more. I've been a good girl for months and got lots of work done."

Sudge gallantly stood up to place the girls' chairs. Colette was peering around to locate any possible friends who might be in the vicinity. When her glance fell on Sudge she laughed. "Look at this child acting chivalrous to an old bum like me. Where'd you find him?"

Sudge snorted and offered the girls cigarettes, poising expectantly while they took lights from him. Laura beamed on me with an air gently supercilious toward the world, and tolerant as an old roué toward me. I sensed in her smile an appeal. Their finances were low, as usual. "What will you have to drink?" I asked.

Sudge was reserved and took slowly to people generally, but he liked the girls at once. Laura's brownie face was roundly handsome, with kind eyes and a fatherly cherubim expression. Colette was pertly pretty, with cat-green eyes and a boy-gangster cuteness. When Sudge placed her chair, she slumped into it to look drolly surprised at his gallantry. Sudge was so quivering with attentiveness that she was fussed. Laura soon started to mimic "rich old bitches" who might, if played up to, buy their art or help them make valuable connections. "We must give a cocktail party," she said, "to collect some dames who'll buy or help sell what we've done. Are you still in your studio? We could give a combination party."

"Sure, and Sudge and his friend are with me. I go south when the spirit moves me, but I'm ready for anything till then."

Ross swaggered up gay with pernod. His face beamed as he met the girls, and his manner of delicately concerned courtesy made Colette give me a fluttering glance of amazed humor. "These babies, treating old roustabouts like Laura and me like ladies in waiting to the queen. Are they real? They're birds. The mocking bird and the flamingo. They don't miss much, or become tangled up in themselves, I'll wager. At first I thought I'd have to put a napkin around the first baby's neck, but he's a naughtier boy than I gathered."

Seeing Hilaria, Colette hailed her and Hilaria rushed across the street with abandon. After embracing the girls she said to me, "Oh, Kit, I have taken Jan, the Polish boy, home with me last night, and never have I seen so beautiful a body. Marvelous. He was officer in the army, fences, and he has the broad shoulders with a small waist, and the *tendresse.*" She pressed her heart. "Cute! He is the little boy who wants the caress. Why have I not live with him the last six months? He is the good artist, doing the caricature for Polish journals. Tonight later I meet you with him and we go dance. You he likes. For the rest he is *solitaire* and no bothers to speak French, but he finds you *sympathique.* He remembers the 14th of July you and he each drink one tumbler full of whiskey straight down, and he loves you for that recklessness. Oh, he is marvelous."

"Sure, I'll see you later," I told her. "You're picking up in your tastes. Jan's damn beautiful. You wouldn't believe me when I told you. Does he lisp? He and I try German and French on each other, but we're always driven to suggesting another drink as the sole means of communication."

Shortly, I went to La Coupole because the boys were so charmed by the girls it was best to leave them together so the friendship could develop. Dale Burke was sitting at the back corner table in La Coupole bar. "I was looking for you," she said. "Raymond Duncan thinks we all drink too much and wants to give us a party. He says he'll get us drunk with joy, and serve a punch with only spices in it to make you others think it's alcoholic."

"Let's collect our gangs, and we'll bring our own drinks. Raymond will think he's having a wonderful success with his drunk-on-joy idea."

Dale was staying with the Princess of Faraway, doing secretarial work. At first she tried to impress me, until I told her I knew of the lady. Dale then talked of the realities rather than the pretenses of her life. She was a bit off-track in her fear that she was not "living," but inherently she had balance enough to swing back to norm. Slight, flat, and fairly angular, she wasn't suited to the role of passionate woman she now elected to play. She looked too much an aloof and rather bloodless patrician. In Paris she was in the thick of movements for reclaiming art, and was put to various subterfuges to manage existence economically. To encourage herself she tried to believe in whatever she did to make money. When working in a neo-Greek art store, she had wafted about in draperies and sandals, but had been a good diplomat and saleswoman. Now with the Princess she was being a bit social, with a grand manner, but that of a freed woman, too.

A sense of failure and futility was embedded deeply in Dale's soul, and she wrote, not well, but there was some authenticity in the black hysteria and incoherence of her writing. She did drag in Irish twilight, bogs, the smell of peat, rushing into the night, and all for love, but her habit of breaking away from a group to run down the street came from a real enough emotion of pent-up torment. And she was becoming less actressy and arty, having realized that the manner had less success in Paris than in some circles of London and New York.

Dale's background accounted for her artificial qualities. With a groping mother, given to causes, Dale was brought up in an atmosphere of precious rebellions. Her grandfather was an authority on law; her father was the wash-out son of that man and her mother the result of mismarriage and later loss of fortune. In a middle-western city Mrs. Burke had once been a hostess to traveling radical and art lecturers, and there were always those to find Dale a precocious genius. Later there were others to talk of freedom and self-expression, color, rhythm, and beauty. But Dale was discovering that the gesture of self-expressed freedom does not necessarily create or attract the qualities and people that one desires.

At eighteen, after the war, Dale married a young Frenchman who was in America as an honor student to complete his scientific education. His name was André Boissard, and he had then the dark wistfulness and psychic intuition which a man suffering the aftermath of shell-shock can have. Dale thought she loved him, but later confronted with the bourgeois life of a French provincial town and family, she became restless. Because the invalid editor of a new literary magazine praised her writing, she went to give herself to him. He believed that this gesture on her part meant that he wasn't finished, but the romance hadn't been a happy one. She had a child by him who was born after his death from tuberculosis. André wanted her to come back. He liked her, and wasn't of a hopeful enough nature to indulge in the turmoils of accusation and passion. So she went to live in an English factory town where André was employed at a small salary. The middle-class atmosphere there also proved too much for Dale. It was then that she came to Paris to be with the Princess of Faraway while she was writing her memoirs, which Dale had suggested.

The Princess was a dull woman, and had no right to her title except through a distant relative. Dale knew she had no interesting memoirs to write, but hoped to achieve a satirical hoax. The Princess had money, and in the past had met famous people who were entertained by her mother, though the mother never achieved any reputation as a hostess or patron of art. She was merely another wealthy woman to whose entertainments celebrities would go for chance encounters.

The Princess, letting Dale quiz her in the desperate hope of deriving slight material on which she could enlarge, complacently believed Dale a typist writing the memoirs from her dictation. Oscar Wilde, George Meredith, Burne-Jones, and other celebrities of a past generation were making witty remarks long after they reposed in the grave. Whether in life they would have appreciated Dale's version of their wit didn't bother her. She was being paid as a secretary, and should the memoirs place with a publisher she might receive part of the proceeds from the book's sale. Dale knew the racket of the commercial publishing world with an astute business sense.

The Princess had a cousin, Eustace Cross, who also complicated Dale's position. He was tubercular, had a passion for sanitariums, but was feverish about being a poet and also knowing artists. He came as Dale and I were having dinner, and soon grew gay as he told of the delirious amours among patients in sanitariums, who, feeling themselves doomed, want to crowd in as much passionate life as possible. Eustace delighted in their intrigues. Acute, he recalled incidents in the life of the Princess which might be used in the memoirs. The Princess herself had no sense of "copy." Dale was uncomfortable and didn't want Eustace to find out that I knew what a hoax the book was, and she confided later that the Princess and Eustace would surely claim the work as entirely theirs once it was finished, and if placed.

Mrs. Burke joined our party and the atmosphere quavered with pathos. Elderly and unsure of herself, she spoke of what she had missed not to have been more free-minded as a girl. At the moment she seemed to hope that she might still experience a romance or two with some of the lively young men about the Quarter. She had given all she could to help the "girls" while the suffrage movement was still a fighting cause; she had helped labor party movements; had dutifully read writers, now accepted, who had been considered shocking in her day; but for all her ardor about causes existence hadn't much flavor now.

I wished that she were more cynical or ironic, rather than yearning. The women who quest eagerly for beauty, grace, and freedom seem to get less than the harder girls who have a sense of comedy and skeptical awareness. They yearn so much for things to be better or different that they miss what is tolerable.

Eustace wanted to meet many people, and his conversation was animated. For a sick man he could stand a quantity of drink, and was sure that late hours didn't hurt him. He could hardly look more of a cadaver than he did, and the thin, peering alertness of his face was heightened by sideburns. It was impossible to be other than gentle to a man in his condition, but when he began to chant poetry in a holy-holy sing-song, he was trying to let us know how sacred he felt about its beauty.

Others arrived and the party became jovial. We asked ourselves how a later Greek like Raymond Duncan could object to intoxication. I felt heavy-spirited, or resentful. The quality of gaiety about was too deliberate, and everybody found things generally too gaga and funny. I indulged myself by admitting I was depressed and bored. When Jacques, a young French friend of Eustace's came into the bar, I was glad that he sat next to me. He looked grave, with an air of ennui, and as he didn't speak English had no need to pretend being amused at the noisy hilarity.

Jacques also was tubercular, but was a different sort of being than Eustace. His dark eyes looked tiredly out of his waxen face, but there was life in their depths. His dark skin was taut over his cheekbones, and blue veins showed through on his neck and about his eyes. In deep sockets his eyes burned with misery. His gaze fluttered over the group before he began talking to Dale. An hour before he had been examined, and the doctor had told him he must return to the sanitarium at once to have portions of his lungs sealed and thereby stop the infection from spreading. Dale said to me later, "Poor little Jacques. He doesn't want to die. He asks if I think he will, and he will. He hates sanitariums. Eustace loves them, but Jacques has real adventure in him. Take him away from this mob. He must feel ghastly. He's terrified, poor darling."

Jacques told me that when he was seventeen he had worked his way on a boat to Mexico and South America. As soon as he was well he wanted to travel again, and now his mother would give him money. The boy was so frail and near the end that one suffered for him, but it was best to talk as though things were going on. I felt wild rebellion in me. Even in his wan condition he was beautiful with a quality that can't be valued too highly: vitality with a sensitive curiosity. Eustace might quote poetry and speak sacredly of art and artists, but Jacques was the better person.

As Dale was talking I felt Jacques touch my arm with suffering impatience. The forced gaiety bothered him, and he was in a blue funk of terror about dying. "Let's leave this crowd and have fresh air and a drink, in a quieter place," I suggested. Eustace looked startled as Jacques and I left for the Falstaff. "You'll get up in the mountains, Jacques, and feel better," I told him. "Paris and cities are hellish places to be in this kind of weather, whatever one's state of health."

It was a relief when we encountered Jan and Hilaria. In a glance they discerned Jacques's condition and were sympathetic. I loved them for being off-track people. They were much more responsive to qualities in people than conventional beings. At the Falstaff we drank sherry, for Jacques couldn't stand stronger drink.

"He is to die. The doctor has told him so today," Hilaria said, in horror. "Poor baby. He is alive too. He is funny. See, *le pauvre enfant*, already the drinks affect him and he plays not to show that he is frightened." She put her arm around his shoulder and said brightly, "Jacques, you are a beautiful boy. Do you know how much a beautiful boy you are? When you come to the Quarter always you look up Hilaria."

He drank more and became *fou.* He got up to dance with Hilaria. She fancied herself a dancer. When he became tired he didn't bother to mount his stool again. Instead, he sat on the floor and asked that his drink be handed down to him. Jan sat on one side of him, and Hilaria on the other. Jacques swayed as if to indicate that his head still danced. Feeling dizzy, he leaned his head on Hilaria's shoulder. "Oh, the sweet baby," she crooned.

"*Oui, oui,*" Jan said, grimacing in mock jealousy and speaking some of the little French he knew. "*Je suis jaloux.* Hilaria is my girl. Instead of taking her from you, I will take you from her." He cuddled Jacques against his shoulder. Jacques liked the feeling of health and strength from the contact.

"In six months, when I am back, we will have a party for just us four," Jacques boasted, and wouldn't be serious. He finally allowed us to take him to a taxi. Once in he climbed out and Hilaria kissed him good night. Again he got out of the taxi to kiss Jan and me goodbye. We petted him, and Hilaria got into the car with him to escort him home, saying that she would be back shortly. Jan, not speaking well any language he and I had in common, said he'd see me later. I knew. He was depressed by Jacques's condition and needed a quick shot of whiskey before joining our party of foreigners.

When I returned to La Coupole, Eustace Cross had disappeared. "He was furious at you. You took his friend away, and Jacques wanted to go," Dale explained.

"Why didn't he come along? We just left because Jacques couldn't stand the noise, and couldn't understand what was being said."

"Eustace can't stand the idea that he not Jacques's best friend, or that Jacques doesn't prefer to be with him than anyone else."

"Why doesn't he go to one of his beloved sanitariums with the boy then? That's where they both belong. Jacques fights frantically against admitting he's finished, and he's a vital, healthy-minded youngster, not able to get a kick out of sanitarium intrigues as Eustace does. Hilaria and I were ready to pawn what souls we have to give the boy health, but he did get silly and gay anyway."

CHAPTER SIX

COLETTE AND I HAD QUANTITIES OF BAGGAGE IN each of our studios, our own, or left there by friends who used the places for storage. Some of them had occupied my studio; others had merely dumped baggage into their spaces when they left for England or America. Among the baggage were various oddments of costume: a rose canvas suit such as Bretagne workingmen wear, a beautiful red shirt, bell-bottomed trousers of blue velour, and Spanish, Egyptian, Greek, and Czechoslovakian things. Some of them would never be reclaimed since they belonged to their owners' younger days of vanity and display. Such costumes as I had I'd hardly wear again. Having seen years of Quarts Arts and other costume balls, one comes to doubt looking so romantically dashing in costume as one may hope. It isn't costumes that make beautiful bodies.

Sudge and Ross had no world-weary attitude, however, so when Laura Bradley suggested going to the studios to devise costumes for Raymond Duncan's party, they were excited. Because about forty people were ready to descend on Raymond, only two taxis full came to our studios. The others went on to warn of our approach.

Time didn't permit Sudge to comb luster into his locks as he was wont to do for hours. Dumping my trunk on the floor, I let the boys select what they would. Sudge's eye fell on the red shirt and blue velvet trousers. He adored them and uttered merry little confidences about what a dashing figure he would cut. But he stayed primping at the mirror too long, so Ross donned them. Sudge's face fell, but he said resignedly, "All right. You wear them if you like."

Ross beamed rosily. "I look sound in them, don't I?"

"Stout," Sudge said, brave but dismal.

"Hell, Ross, where do you get your old-man contempts if you're taking those colored things away from Sudge? I said he could have them. You're breaking his palpitating heart." But Ross kept the shirt and trousers on. It was only when Laura discovered a beautiful Arab costume for Sudge that Ross doubted his choice.

When passing the Select Ross saw his love, Fern Mallow, and wanted to have her join us. Her companions told him to go away and stop boring them. "I want to know you," he exclaimed to Fern. "I don't give a damn about these sour-faced broads with you. Can't you appreciate it when a man has a real emotion about you?" As he harangued his body swayed, scarecrow forlorn. He had no luck but lingered, so we drove on without him. Sudge was sad at first, but at Raymond's, after a drink, he snorted about Ross's sudden capitulation to love. "He's been festering inside for two years, wanting to be in love. She looks battered; that's why he thinks he loves her."

Before we had arrived at Raymond's, Sudge became affectionate toward Colette. She tittered as she got out of the taxi. "That baby wants me to kiss him. Fancy that. By Jesus, I won't. I'm not an old lady yet, to be getting little boys excited. If I woke up with him in my bed, I'd be scared I'd gotten careless and given birth to an infant."

Raymond and his clan were there to greet us dressed in Greek robes. Raymond's hair was coiled about his head, interbraided with silver cords. Several children scurried about the room. We went into the garden where there was goat cheese, sandwiches, and much hardy Greek fare as Raymond conceived it. I was polite and tried a glass of his punch. Five minutes later I threw it up, and from then on stuck to the gin we had brought. Raymond looked blissful, and we all were gay. True, none of us went often to the punch bowl, but we did go frequently to the hallway where bottles of gin rested beneath a table in the darkness. I danced but found the bottles more seductive on a warm night. Jan came and sat on the floor beside me. Even without a common language we felt *sympathique.* After Colette dragged me away for a dance, I returned to encounter Ross, melancholy with disgust because Fern wouldn't come with him. "Those fat-faced typists thought I wanted to make trouble for her. They don't understand anything about nice emotions. I go to see her tomorrow, though. She says I can."

The phonograph was playing Beethoven when a vision occurred. A woman certainly neither young nor graceful wafted across the room in black tights, her ample hips bulging. I thought this was to be a comedy number, because I'm incapable of believing a woman could so get herself up all for art. When she suddenly twinkled her feet and gave three leaps across the room, I saw her face expiring with rhapsody. Then she subsided, the momentary inspiration over. I looked at Jan; he looked at me as if hurt to have to be satiric, and whispered drolly, "*Oui*, Kit."

"Strike me dead, Beauty," I said, and pushed him. We got up simultaneously and pranced into the room, Jan dancing Tartar-Cossack, and I true Harlem. He had a wonderful physique, but I had misgivings when he grabbed me to swing recklessly through the air. The Duncanites, particularly the children, giggled, not at all offended at our teasing them. We knew that in drink we grew more released than these people who made a cult of self-expression. Afterwards, we retreated back to the bottle, where Hilaria joined us to sit on the floor.

Some of the others had poured bottles of gin or cognac into Raymond's spiced punch, which was not my dish. Hilaria, Jan, and I stuck to cognac, planning to shift to gin if need be later. Jerry Gladwin came over to us, but his stomach ulcers were acting up and he couldn't hold drink well. As he was trying to write a novel with social content, I suggested that he too get into the movement and have his characters talk about "revolution is eternal and in constant flux." He became petulant when I added, "But Jerry, your revolution seems to be internal, so attack the ulcers of society." He left us knowing that we were futile and trivial, but Raymond Duncan's devotees didn't sell themselves to him, either. He told Dale Burke that he—all of us—ought to go back to America and face our responsibilities. But it still being speakeasy days there, I wondered if we wouldn't do night-life and drink as much as in Europe.

Although the light was poor, Jan took a sketch pad out of his pocket and started to do caricatures or sketches of members of the party in pencil. Later, if they came out well, he'd send them to a Warsaw paper. He did one of Hilaria that made her look gaunt with dramatic hair and eyes. She was pleased. Then he started one of me. "Kit is beautiful man, isn't he, Jan?" Hilaria said, in her cups, wishing us to believe her a woman of heart with great affection for both of us.

"*Mais oui, beau, beau*, with a warped face to one side," Jan said, his French and few English words like the grunts of a deaf man. To show his goodwill he patted my cheeks, and Hilaria said, "Jan is a beautiful man too, Kit?"

"Hell yes, we're all beautiful, but don't try starting things, Hi-lo. We have lively enough ideas on our own." I got up to join another group, but

Jan stopped me. "No, stay while I draw you. You don't care for the people much, either, except to have around when you don't wish to be alone."

I went anyway and ran into Ross. "How can you stand that brute-faced Pole?" he said disgustedly, very much the superior English boy.

"I like him. He travels on his own without pouring out some sob story. He drinks hilariously too."

"See his common face. He's vulgar as hell."

"Are we surrounded by higher beings? His caricatures and paintings aren't dumb," I said, wondering why Ross chose to be antagonized by anyone so amiable as Jan.

"You and he are in love with each other," Ross scoffed.

"That's fine. But we're such damn fools we don't do anything about it," I answered, observing that Ross had nagging jealousy in him. When Jan told me that I was neurasthenic, I understood him to mean that he too couldn't stand much intimacy with any one person. Mannerisms, habits, and attitudes too insistently revealing themselves got on his nerves rather than deepened his intimate fondness for that person.

"I suppose you're taking Sudge to Bricktop's with you tonight," Ross pursued grumpily.

"Come along. It may be good fun."

"I thought you wanted to be alone together," he said.

As he spoke it struck me how completely I thought of the boys as one. Alone with either my talk was mechanical. I didn't understand what went on in the mind of either of them, and one away from the other always created the sense of waiting for his other half. Ross assumed that others easily felt toward Sudge as I did. I did intend to go to Bricktop's because there I could be noisy and careless without being disciplined, much, since few clients came to her rendezvous these days.

"Rats, I'm barging about the town until I get fed up enough to head south and work and lay off the booze. All I want is company I can stand. It's good you two are in the studio to look after it while I'm gone, which will be soon, so you two will be as alone as you like."

"How do you know what we want?" Ross blurted fiercely.

"I don't. But I guess you and Sudge want each other more than you want anybody else. You get on well and are more considerate of each other than most people. It's nice to regard."

"How do you know?" Ross was blunt, and challengingly sullen.

"Hell, I'm not a blind man."

"Come ootside and ay'll fight you," Ross shouted in sudden fury. I laughed in wonder, then patted his face.

"Now Ross, calm that wild Irish temper. A bull moose of a man might take you up someday and go outside to fight with you. It's a passionate lad ye air, me boy. Don't make things complicated."

"You fester me with your brute-faced Pole," Ross said, and swung back into the room belligerently. When I went there too, he was talking to Laura, who handed me a glass of gin.

"Ross, come ootside and ay'll fight you," I teased, but Ross beamed his open smile, all joy and good will now. In or out of temper, he was far too fragile a person to be treated any way but gently, but with drink I facetiously thought his tormented young soul might need the outlet of temper.

The party was merry, but without the kick we had anticipated. Raymond's idea of getting us drunk with joy was naive rather than interfering. The disposition some had to think him a poseur didn't mean much, since he was sweet and desired to see people happy. It was a painful moment when a young Frenchman assured Raymond that he would murder Cocteau on the spot on sight when Raymond complimented French literature by praising Cocteau's books. How could Raymond know how violently a young surrealist would posture his savage disdain.

As his place was far out Raymond telephoned for taxis. Ross was right; Sudge and I did go to Bricktop's. Ross refused to come along. He was disgusted at the way Sudge and I would want to hear a Negress sing sentimental songs while we grew maudlin. Sudge had heard Evangelina Washington sing "Lover, Come Back to Me" with full-throated nostalgic passion, and he wanted his emotions stirred. We had a fine time talking about Sophie Tucker, Norah Bayes, Lee Morris, and other women who sing heavy sob songs with great conviction, but who can be wisecracking, hard-boiled, and comic ladies, very aware of reality, the moment the song is finished. Ross was too intellectual and critical. Sudge wanted his low moments, too. Why not have all the rip-and-tear of life to regard? Ross could go back to his flour-skinned little decadent girls, whose common friends would rebuff him.

Brick was seated at her cashier's desk looking matronly and competent. She didn't bother to use her elegant cabaret-hostess glide when greeting us. I was just one of the old drunks who was a good client, and she rushed across to embrace me. Toward Sudge she was humorously maternal.

"You's adopting babes now, Kit. What's all come over you? You used to bring around swells and rich people. I'd have starved my first year in Paris if you hadn't brought me rich customers and told everybody I was Duse or one of them great dames."

"I know. But one needs variety, and they didn't respond to my enthusiasms nor I to theirs. They wanted to be shown sights that long ago bored me. Do you want me to land in the poorhouse? One might as well go there when vitality departs rather than be a doddering old fool who people wish would pop off, but I'm not that way yet, and the rich have a great habit of departing before I do. They always think it's all right to let me settle the bill."

Brick had a whiskey and sang "Lover, Come Back to Me" for Sudge. She had the pianist break its rhythm into joy after she rendered it huskily, for Brick never cared much whether any one lover came back to her or not. She danced, and in spite of her bulky body she had amazingly neat legs and trim ankles. As she sang with her feet better than with her voice, she didn't even want to make her body behave, and neither did we.

"Sure, I was feeling blue tonight," Brick said, rejoining us at the table. "My mammy's coming to Paris and I ought to be happy 'cause there ain't nobody means to me what she does. She's a better woman than her daughter now. She hasn't hung around the boozehounds, or had so many lovers. You'd love mammy. She's a card. No more idea about money than a kitten. If she saw an ermine coat she liked, she'd try to buy it if she had only five dollars. You'd die laughing at her. Once she used to work as a sorta policewoman for Jane Addams in Chicago, and she shoulda seen tough life, but mammy thinks everybody's sweet and good, and they don't let her know different. I started doing cabaret work when I was twelve, but she don't know nothing about the kind of life I lead, and she ain't going to." Brick was part Irish and could have passed for white when her hair was sleek with oil. Now she ran her hands through it and it snapped into crinkles that revealed the dark red that had given her her name.

"Me and Louis had a scrap last night," she confided gleefully. "Just one of those nights. I felt lowdown blue and didn't want no man messing round my room and told him so. I always wanted a baby, but Louis told me I'd never have one if I used them there French basins too often. I can't help it. I gotta be clean. I suppose I won't have a baby. I wash 'em all away." Sudge snorted. Bricktop looked at him and then at me. "I guess I'd better get back to my desk. I always forget I'm a businesswoman when bums like you come in, Kit."

Sudge sat looking pink and white and childish. Brick didn't know how naughtily he appraised her as he murmured "Sound." It was just as well. Brick wouldn't mind having Sudge appreciate her charms, but she was no cradle snatcher, and did have a healthy, well-built man of her own race deeply devoted to her.

Soon after three, Joe and Bobbie, from the Palermo orchestra, came in and sat with us. They greeted us with warm hilarity and insisted on buying us drinks. Sudge pleased me by recognizing the genial fondliness which nice colored people emanate with a cordiality that whites withhold or don't possess. Joe was worried because I didn't appear at the Palermo anymore.

"What's the matter, Mister Kit? Don't you like us anymore?"

"You're one of the best, Joe, but the Palermo's too crowded and expensive, with its flock of *poules* making you pay for their drinks when they see you're lit up. They discipline you there too if you get too gay. What to hell, Joe? We've had gin at the bistro across the way several nights within the last ten days. Where do you get that 'not looking you up' business?"

"That's right. I just wanted you not to forget us. We get bored seeing them faces at the Palermo every night, and most of them don't talk to us. You folks from Montparnasse are pets of ours. You talk to us right, and you're one of the best boys in Paris, Kit. I never do forget what you said about my having children, and I been thinking it over. My wife don't mind, and what you said has sense. People get it in the neck one way or the other, and it's as interesting being mixed blood as not if you're going to amount to anything. I'd educate a boy if I had one, so he could play jazz, if he had to, but I'd put money aside and he could be one of them intellectuals, like that colored writer you brought along one night, if he wanted to be."

"Why didn't you like him, Joe? He was a bit self-important, but he's all right."

"Oh, I liked him, Kit," Joe defended himself. "I liked him, but you know, among us folks we call them Jamaicans 'monkey-chasers' or 'banana-climbers.' One of them is in our orchestra, and he's a good man, but we just don't look at things their way, somehow. I thought maybe because I was a jazz player he sized me up as not able to understand his high talk. I liked him, Kit. You know I always likes people you bring along. Your friends are mine."

"I'll take you and Bobbie to Montparnasse after we leave here. You say you want to have a look at it," I told Joe.

"Sure, Kit. I been hearing about the place so long I got a curiosity, but I don't want to seem butting in, and like you say, there might be some of those boys round who don't like us, and I don't want no trouble. You know I like my people and your people, and I got no time for colored folks who have a hate on whites, any more than I got time for your people who think we ain't got feelings."

"The people in the Quarter are a good sort, now. No crap, Joe. You'll run into lots of your friends."

Jimmie, a Montparnasse barman, came in, his plump face grinning enigmatic mirth. Jimmie was born with a snicker. "Hello, Mister Kit and Sudge," he greeted us. "Jimmie's getting drunk again. Have all you want to drink. To hell with high blood pressure. If my nose bleeds I can cut the lobe of my ear and bleed off enough till I see the doctor like I always do."

I'm not one to be giving sane advice, but I nobly warned Jimmie to look out for high blood pressure, kidney, bladder, and stomach trouble. Jimmie hadn't for three years suffered much because of love, since Quarter life had made his heart less excitably romantic. A Liverpool Irishman, he had at one time been a prizefighter, and when drunk still had joyous moments of wanting to show his prowess. The Paris police knew him and took him somewhat as a comedy. His dumpy little figure gave little indication of the knock-out blow he packed once he started sparring like an overfed battling cock. Lately he had been behaving, but he was still capable of going on drinking bouts that lasted from two days to a month. Jimmie was a pet of the Quarter, because he was polite, full of snickers, knew the inside lives of his clients, and was discreet. If experience and knowing things signify that one is educated and cultured, Jimmie qualified.

Jimmie told us how it felt to be inside the ring, and how he had conquered stage fright. He recounted his arrival in Paris, drunk. Seeing a fire-alarm, he had sounded it, simply to discover what it was. This resulted in three weeks in jail for him, but that didn't quell his spirits. As he talked about boxing I remarked that I was getting more nervous in my old age. I hated barroom brawls among types who might readily be yellow or vicious. "That's all right, Kit," Jimmie solaced. "I'll handle them. If they start anything on you, I'll take them on."

I didn't anticipate that anything would be started on me and squirmed because Jimmie had the fixed idea that I needed to be taken care of. Brick joined us, and we were a happy, confiding party. Nevertheless, I found myself some time later confronting a police judge. My beautiful nose was battered, and I didn't know who had hit me or why. Jimmie and I were consoling each other with human sympathy when I realized the judge was waving my colored handkerchief while gendarmes snickered.

It enraged me. I regarded the judge with fury, grabbed the handkerchief, and said, "Why is the man who hit me not arrested rather than me? Give me my handkerchief. My nose is bleeding. It's no comedy. You are here for justice and not to ridicule a man. Is it a French custom to forget courtesy and turn offensive on a man arrested for no cause?"

My courtesy remark was a fine point, evidently, because they laughed and were chagrined rather than offended by my arrogance. Nevertheless, they put me in a cell and locked the barred gate. I shook the gate for a time but had relaxed and fallen asleep on the stone bench when Jimmie was shoved into the cell. He shook the gate, but I had become philosophical and was sleepy as well. "Hell, Jimmie, give up. We're in till they let us out. How did we get here?"

Jimmie snickered but did not know. "I think you took such good care of me that we both got into a fight," I grunted. Jimmie tittered again, not wounded by my lack of belief in his nobly protective intentions. We both rolled over on our benches and went to sleep.

It was after nine the next morning when we were taken before the judge. There were no charges, but we had been drunk, so they had let us sleep off our jags. I was still drunk and insisted that whoever had hit me should have been arrested. At my side were Bricktop and Sudge. She tried to calm me, and assured the judge she'd see that the address on my *carte d'identité* was corrected. I swore I wouldn't bother, but the judge and gendarmes were disposed to find me comic. Outside I tried to learn what had caused the fight and where it had occurred. Brick said a Negro hit me because he thought I was trying to force my way into her cabaret when I was only leaning against the wall to try and think. Sudge had come along toward the end, to find my nose bloody and Jimmie slugging at various Negroes who disappeared when the gendarmes hove into sight. Clearly, I wasn't going to get a definite explanation of the battle. I felt injustice, remembering that Joe had spoken the night before of Negroes who cherish deep resentment against whites. Why should a colored man hit me when I always insist that color, class, family, wealth don't count, that nothing counts with people except personality and talent? The world was getting too much for me to bear. Brick comforted me by taking me to a bar where she forced soft-boiled eggs into me. Only then would she permit a brandy. I felt grateful to her and Sudge, who had stayed up all night at her apartment to get me out of jail in the morning. Sudge was a loyal child. He couldn't do much, but he did his best.

Taking a taxi I dropped Sudge off at the Dôme and went on to the studio. Deep grief was welling from my depths. I was still very drunk, but remembered. They had laughed at my handkerchief, and my ring was missing, and they had both come from Fritzi of Vienna. After living with her for a winter I still thought her beautiful, but an older man, a former lover, offered her marriage. Now keenly I regretted Fritzi. In the days with her I could still boast of never passing out drunk, and with her I'd have no bloody nose. I condemned myself for not having offered marriage, but felt in sorrow that she loved the older man more anyway. She was ten years older than I, but we got on magnificently, and now life was all an unsatisfactory attempt to avoid things I don't like, rather than participating in anything actually satisfying.

She had given me the ring and the handkerchief when we parted in all tenderness. The handkerchief was a sublimated bandanna of fine material and glorious colors, basically red, and dear to my eyes and heart. It had daring and elegance and subtlety as had Fritzi. It was my kind of handkerchief, and it is only in handkerchiefs that a man can soothe his taste for color, because stores don't sell garments which are colorful and also distinguished. My nose was broken or the cartilage very sore, and I had done nothing that was not amiable. Nobody would understand that the loss of the handkerchief was a major tragedy, for the handkerchief itself, let alone because Fritzi had given it to me. There are people and friends, but never could I replace the handkerchief. The ring, too, had been of strange design, a primitive African ring of silver. When I returned to the studio, I flopped on the bed, too broken to moan my despair.

Ross came over to me chirpily, thinking I'd tell him a merry tale of the night's activities. I covered my head and moaned, "I'm bored. Christ, I'm bored, bored!" He saw my face and went to the water faucet. I noted his fumbling awkwardness, his inept hands like animal paws wetting a very dirty towel, which he wanted to lay on my eyes. I thrust him away moaning. He meant to be gentle, but his nervous hands were nervously fumbling and awkward.

"To hell with you, if you can't appreciate when a fellow's sympathetic," he blurted out. I didn't mind. I rolled over and buried my aching head in a pillow, feeling disintegrated and ruined. My stomach was going back on me. I didn't hold my drink well any longer. I had a nose and a smile that sometimes got me things I didn't have to work for, but the nose was broken and the smile wouldn't operate. The world was coming to an end, and the sooner it crashed, the better I'd like it.

Sleep came to solace my agony, however, and when I awoke I thought I might live. I looked across the room. Sudge, seeing me awake, tiptoed gently to me. "See, Kit, I got your handkerchief and ring. Ross said you were griped as hell that you'd lost them, so I went to the gendarmerie and told them you were too ill to come for them. I also took your *carte d'identité* and got the address changed."

Appreciation flooded through me for Sudge's boy kindness. But I felt sour toward Ross. He'd never have gone to the trouble Sudge had. Going down the hall, Sudge told Colette and Laura that I was awake and inclined to live. I had dozed off again when they entered the studio to find me naked. That fazed none of us. I grabbed the bottle of beer Colette brought to solace me, and when Laura came with lamb chops, green beans, and another bottle of beer, I felt in better humor, thinking what to hell's a scrap or two in Montmartre. Still, I wanted to know who had hit me. Jimmie, drunk and brawling, would even hit himself in the nose to bleed off his high blood pressure. Whoever hit me had done it well. Now, four friends were with me, and the girls talked of helping us make the studio look less like an empty barn loft. They were the sort of people I liked. Things were nice, after all.

"Hey Sudge," I said, "stick your head out the window and see if Gaylord is in his studio. If he is, go get a dozen bottles of cold beer and some whiskey and gin. We might as well have beer to drink, and the rest in stock for the party Saturday. Laura, have you asked any people yet?"

"Sure, we'll give a party that rocks the building," Colette said. "Your nose will be all right in two days. The lavender around your eyes makes you look delicate, but we're all decadent beauties these days. I'm going back and watch Belinda have another kitten. We've been watching her give birth to kittens since eight this morning, and she has about the same kind of worried look on her face as you have on yours. Come over and see the show when you're ready."

CHAPTER SEVEN

THE QUARTER HAD A PERIOD WHICH WAS COMparable to the days shortly after the war. It was not all past-day sentimentality when old-timers bewailed the present trend of Quarter types and events. Once people of wit, promise, and achievement had congregated in such cafes as Vavin, Rotonde, L'Escargot, and Rendezvous des Chauffeurs after all the other cafes had closed. Now, however, it had become a rare event to find people concerned with intelligence or production. Few people made even the pretense of producing. There were drinkers about, but they were types who had drifted in from racetracks, drifters from anywhere, or salesmen cutting loose more noisily and openly than they could at home. They were inclined to resent artists as supercilious, conceited, snobbish, effeminate, or whatever term they chose to express their resentment.

For a few weeks, however, the Quarter had a rebirth. An Oxford-Irishman who had written a book on Einstein and another on Beethoven talked most intellectually over beer. His books had been published to the approval of conservative London critics. A famed English sculptor, and a famed English painter and lover, lingered in the region too. Several boys from Oxford, not Rhodes scholars, they insisted, took so readily to Quarter habits that one of them was on the water diet a week after arriving. All of these English imports drank and were ready companions. Of the younger men Mat Powers was most in evidence. He had translated Rimbaud and hoped to get his translation published.

Mat was not primarily literary, however. His father was a well-known judge in Utah, and Mat confided that his old man was balmy, so that he came by his own cuckoo streak naturally. At birth there had been a twin for Mat, but when the twin died, Mat felt himself doomed to live incomplete and without an affinity. He drank and concentrated much love on a girl who lived with another boy. Consequently, Mat, within the course of his six-week sojourn, managed to sleep with every *poule* in the Quarter. After he had returned to Oxford, he bombarded several of us with letters to wire him a doctor's certificate stating that he had overstayed his vacation in Paris because of legitimate sickness. Often he talked of writing articles for *The New Yorker*, and when he showed his masterpieces they proved to be almost verbatim renditions of articles he had seen in print.

Mat was quick to take a hate on faces. He would sit in a restaurant clucking obscene noises and making faces at whomever he picked to resent. If the people objected, he turned polite and comic, letting them think him slightly touched and prone to talk to creatures of his cracked imagination. Sudge and Ross delighted in Mat's ability to disconcert types of whom they too were scornful. Mat and his colleagues had that knowing cynicism which youngsters affect to prove their lack of illusions. Nevertheless, the gravity emerged at sentimental moments. But not any of this lot went in for the hard-boiled attitude so much as they cultivated comedy and nonchalance. They were too lively for the barren leaves of wasteland resignation, and rejected brave reserve as hurt-boy pretension.

It wasn't surprising a year later to see Mat Powers launched upon a diplomatic career, and he was rather uncomfortable when Quarterites encountered him with his diplomatic acquaintances. Mat had something to learn about how diplomats relax, but then he wouldn't be a novice long.

Ellery Saunderson was also much about. He had several up on his literary twin, James Fernley John. John had, it is true, written a book on Provence, one on America, and was to have two novels out before the end of the year. Ellery, on the other hand, had written a book on France, another on Italy and Mussolini, a third on the European political situation, was planning a trip to America to do a book on the state of that country, had a novel out, one in press, and two in preparation. Besides these efforts, which he brushed aside with modest comment, he had a book that was selling very well indeed. In it he modestly told how artists and celebrities in Paris had for the last fifteen years sought him out for advice about economic, emotional, or artistic problems beyond their ability to solve. Ellery's book revealed him as a kind, tolerant, discreet man, always ready with sane suggestions and a helping hand financially. He wasn't always, he confessed, able to aid the most complicated cases, but he gave solacing sympathy. Anyway, Ellery had earned a right to relax, and came nights to sit on the terraces before glasses of ale, stout, or black velvet. There, the many struggling artists and promising youngsters, who knew how to value his opinion, could find him and sit quietly over drinks that he paid for while intelligent conversation was listened to by all.

Arrived writers, who away from each other declared each other's work rotten, were prone to congregate. Philip Danbury's war book was out, and a success. He scolded English hypocrisies with such nagging garrulity that the *London Times* and the *Observer* could only recognize him as a sound English literary man. Saunderson, John, Pemberton, Danbury, and an Armenian who didn't quite belong, gathered together, were facetious, complimentary, and generally careful about what they said. Pemberton talked modestly, telling the Armenian that their books were neither as good nor as bad as critics found them. "We know the racket," he said, "and what crap goes on. They won't have it that a fellow only wants to be himself. I never knew how good I was until some of them wrote about me, but now others or the same guys are saying how rotten I am."

James Fernley John was protected because his mutterings could not be understood through his walrus beard. He still retained his reputation as a master of prose style, and that prose-style-master reputation is formidable, even for the man who possesses it. Among so many writers, one might pursue the phantom—intellect—but encounter mere shop talk and the diplomacies of writers pretending to be awed by the others' successes.

Tony Crane's wife had departed for a watering resort, so Tony came nightly to the cafes. He had been my standby for years, and we got together by six o'clock, to wander through the night until one wanted to go home. Tony generally went first, not because he wanted to, but he had work to do, kept office hours, was over forty, and didn't want his wife to come back and find him a nervous wreck.

Tony was a competent journalist, but not capable of turning out columns of printed matter as Ellery Saunderson did. There were a variety of things he couldn't explain or analyze with specialized acumen, but few attained the breadth of analytic comprehension which was Ellery's. Tony was also a romantic, about people and about his own store of energy and wealth. In the Quarter he seemed to believe it his duty to pay all drink bills at the table where he sat. Others might remonstrate, but in the end agreed, "I'll get you later, Crane." Tony must have felt himself responsible and paternal, and he was perennially hopeful of discovering new talent. Hilaria particularly charmed him.

Hilaria and I guessed that she was a bum and would remain one, but Tony believed that she should become a famous *poule-de-luxe*. Hilaria knew very well the effort it takes to become a grand courtesan; moreover, her heart fluttered readily at the sight of any passable young man. As young men aren't often wealthy, Hilaria would not help support them, but she would pool her problems with theirs and live with them cooperatively. Tony wished to convince Hilaria that she might have her young men, but do better by herself also. Hilaria's vanity was pleased. She became romantic about Tony's chivalry but decided to keep him as a friend. He was *un homme serieux*, kindly, and not given to trivial ideas about women. He was one beautiful man with the fine heart.

Tony Crane came into the College Inn one Sunday when a lot had collected with that Sunday feeling. Gaylord Showman thrummed at the piano. He knew a variety of songs: sea chanties, cowboy ballads, blues, Trinidad Negro things. With a talent for argots, dialects, and the mimicking of types, Gaylord might loosen to gaiety and give us good comedy. He belonged to circus-clown or burlesque lineage. His face was a landscape, bounded by huge flapping ears. His mouth was large and loose and his eyes floated with dark dolor in a face prone to disintegration. Today, however, he was sour about what the Quarter and his life had become. Steve Rath was there, and sullen too, because Hilaria acted skittish with Gaylord, Sudge, and me. Gaylord didn't respond, because in the years before Steve had taken to women, he had been romantic about her. Steve was resentfully friendly toward me, because she didn't believe I respected sufficiently her right to Chloe, Hilaria, or whatever girl she chose to adore.

Tony's entry was therefore a relief, for Steve considered him a perfect gentleman, normal, and not inclined to flirt with Chloe Andrews. He at once offered drinks, and everybody accepted, though we had agreed not to have a drink till six o'clock. Tony bought drinks, and more drinks. He looked upon the boys as bright children, but they were, as usual, reticent. Steve and Hilaria were whispering confidences to each other, so Tony and I talked. He spoke of a newspaper story that might break and make a fine special article. It was reported that the Spanish heir was a hemophiliac, and the king thought of asking the pope to annul his present marriage so that he might remarry and produce a sound heir. Tony said that John's last book was a flop in America. He had overdone his writing of essays and blurbs for young authors. Somebody had written a savage review of Saunderson's book, and poor Ellery was distressed, but remarked, "I will ignore the attack. It's obviously done in malice, though I have never wronged the man. It's beneath one's dignity to answer such attacks, don't you agree, Crane?"

Tony had probably come to that dangerous age, just beyond forty, because he was alert for adventure and had an Indian-summer hopefulness. For others it was a good state since Tony was ready to step out, to drive his car into the country with a load of Quarterites. There we could sample fine food and vintage wine, as Tony was a wine and food expert. This night he was ready to take a full car to wherever they could best taste the tranquil joys of small-town life around Paris. Having a visit to make first, he left saying he would be back soon.

"Is that the great Tony Crane you talk about?" Ross said, implying that my discrimination was of a low order. "He's just another common commercial-minded type. He looks you up because he thinks you can give him news."

I was irritated when Sudge agreed with Ross. The boys got too persnickety. Possibly I'd oversold Tony. He was a direct, intelligent, generous person, and had done me many a good turn. Why did they expect a brilliant, forceful being? Tony worked too hard and had suffered too many bad breaks not to be reserved and matter-of-fact. Forgetting that Tony was to return, and feeling it a strain to keep understanding the snootiness of youth, I left. I saw Mat Powers and thought he'd be company for me, but Mat had recently met a young lady fashion designer who was in the process of deciding that she might do the Quarter now and then on a slumming tour. I realized that Mat was afraid I'd shock her or flirt with her if he introduced her when she arrived. His was an understandable sentiment.

Later I found Hilaria free, and we went to the Right Bank. At the Boeuf sur le Toit she deserted me and picked up a Serbian boy she thought beautiful. They had been playing for each other for the last month, so I found three French boys to drink with. We went to the markets after doing a few bistros and dives. In the morning I woke up in Le Père Tranquille and rested my head on the table as two of the French boys were arguing passionately about the deadness of conservative French art. After we had onion soup and beer we walked through the markets and then wended our way back to the Dôme for another night-after beer. Ross and Sudge were there, fresh from a night's sleep after having had dinner in the country with Tony. In spite of their disdain for him the day before, they were telling each other what a sound, stout, decent, and unpretentious person he was. Ross thought he might even tolerate doing newspaper work if more men in the profession were Tony's sort.

CHAPTER EIGHT

HARD-UP AS THE BOYS WERE THEY MANAGED TO life-save a variety of people. To a Dutch boy who finally found a job but had no decent shoes, Sudge gave shoes. A Danish cartoonist confessed to not having eaten much for several days, and Ross loaned him money. Even when Hilaria mourned not having francs to buy a drink, Sudge or Ross aided. They had a tremendous but concealed ability to scent authentic down-and-outness, with merit, and beneath their scornful assertions lay quickness of sympathy. They made me aware of how one can become calloused and unresponsive without noting the process in oneself.

In their young brightness the boys kept one aware that age has little advantage. They continually exchanged glances and bird-twittering comments to verify each other's conclusions, and when they quarreled they did so as twins. Gradually their presence made me realize the race and age difference in outlook between them and me. The longer I knew them, the less I understood them. Sudge declared that Ross's fine eyebrows signified delicacy of perception, but Ross never returned the compliment. Sudge believed Ross already a fine artist. He saw himself as more ordinary, and while he had moods, he gave his money to Ross when things were so dull that Ross needed to forget. I knew at least that Sudge was the kinder, with more imagination to understand the plights and sufferings of people. What had seemed Sudge's sly malice now struck me as protection. He was youthfully tormented and groping, and not quick to damn people unless Ross was with him. His enthusiasms were not rare and quibbling unlike Ross's. He tried one day to assure me that he wanted to know me. When I assured him that he did, he would not have it so.

"You patronize me. You joke about Ross and me, and fool people are always asking where your adopted children are. You don't say what you think to me."

It was a difficult situation. Time and experience stamp much into a person which one is ready enough to reveal, but not to explain. But Sudge couldn't see that on-a-par-of-realization conversation with people, my age doesn't necessarily mean intimacy. He was confused and brooded because he felt himself given belittling appreciation. "Hell, Sudge," I evaded, "we show phases of ourselves to different people. The older people I know are married, or settled on their bottoms, comforts, or jobs. I want a livelier existence than that, but I understand why they submit. I'd have submitted myself had the war not caught me at adolescence to jar me out of adjustment until it was too late to want to turn back. You're good for trying anything that might furnish amusement, and certainly you don't value that thing called 'growing up' as most people do it."

"Ross and I can't go on always like this," Sudge mourned, giving me the strong feeling that he felt himself bound. "I don't care about being a great writer. I just want to be a rakish old man, enjoying myself soundly." He snorted lusciously at the idea. I saw his funny baby profile, and his eyes, which regarded me sidewise, analyzed me to discern whether I disapproved of his lack of ambition. It struck me that Sudge had stated the kind of older man he'd be: a good sort for easy companionship in many situations. Morals and conventions wouldn't disturb him, but he'd have a doggy idea of fastidiousness.

As yet, Sudge appealed to the sympathies more than that sort of older man. He still had perplexity, restlessness, and curiosity. Youth is not inherently interesting. It is often dull. But it has wonder and alertness, the drive of vitality, and impressions which aren't jaded. These are a fair substitute for imagination and energy. The emotions of youth are livelier, too, whether tender, ribald, tragic, or furious. A dull or mediocre young person is less trying and hardened than a dull older person, and one can still hope, for youth, that the faculties are not yet awakened.

The boys didn't care much for drink, but indulged because others did. Sudge liked going to Bricktop's because she was a good rough-and-ready showwoman and felt fondly toward him now. Ross's disdain had not dampened his delight in Argentina's dancing. Sudge, however, would feel young and shy batting around Paris with me. I knew the town for years and was ready to drink with tarts, gendarmes, taxi drivers, or whatever nightlife type I encountered. Sudge had little fear in him, but had not undergone the anesthesia of experience sufficiently to reject the grim or tiresome aspects of many people and events, while searching for human, comic, or acceptable qualities. Scorn and intolerance are not bad qualities in youth, but they narrow one's capacity for enjoyment if they are carried in excess into maturity. It wouldn't have done to let Sudge know how little I found the run of events wonderful. He sensed awfulness too well without my expert aid.

Sudge had a renewed siege of working on his autobiography, into which he poured all the characters he had recently met. Across the room Ross wrote at his family novel. They would each do a page and show the other the result, whereupon they emitted a series of snorts and snickers. While Ross gave Sudge no suggestions, Sudge actually told Ross what to write. Still, they agreed that Ross was the great man who would be known to the world as such someday. Sudge was sure of Ross's delicacy of perception; Ross assured me that Sudge was a common little bourgeois who'd be hopeless if he hadn't been rescued from that boob family of his. Ross suffered when Sudge was away, or was interested in somebody else, while Sudge had tried to aid Ross in his romance with the decadent waif, Fern Mallow. That the romance never congealed was not her or Ross's fault: She was too surrounded by other girls, stenographers on a fling, and they were all trying dope. Ross finally decided that she was not his real love anyway.

Doing nightlife, I saw little of them, but they showed me their writings now and then. Sudge was putting every person he knew into his autobiography with sharp, concise sketches. They didn't sum up the persons, but their cute and wicked wit achieved bright caricature.

Their writings and chatter acquainted me with their native city and its inhabitants. Ross talked of his mother, Tina, who was canny and did not bother because her sons drank heavily. One was inclined to marry his whore. "No," Tina chuckled, "she thinks she'll get money through marrying Ralph. She'll be fooled. There is none. Her profession might take Ralph's support off my hands if she's foolish enough to marry him."

That one always drew a ripple of merriment from Sudge, as did the tale about the dog that smelled of stale fish which could start a fight in the Campion family at any time. When Ross told with choked mirth of his father, Sudge doubled up. Old man Campion had a quiet way of not being where the family rows occurred. Though a minister, he couldn't concern himself with his family's morals. "The old crutch," Ross rumbled, "can't stand my sisters, particularly when they tell him to discipline the boys. He just sneaks to his library, pretending absent-mindedness."

Ross laughed helplessly when he told of Tina's fear that her aged brother might appear and expect her to look after him. This uncle had drunk himself into a half-wit stage and was a beachcomber in some out-of-the-way place. Tina's family had been wealthy and fast, and it was a great joke with the Campions that their father should be a Presbyterian minister. Tina said often that none of her children were as passionate as their parents, and Ross was amused at the idea of his father being a hot old boy. "He must have been, though, and both of them careless, to have six of us."

The boys paired off well with Laura and Colette, who worked in their studio down the hall. They went to the Quarter together, matily, and when hard-up ate at a bistro to sit over cheap wine of a heady variety. The arrangement was fine, because the girls chuckled over the boys, the boys chuckled over the girls, and I was a comic subject to talk about. As I was generally about with other people, they had to drum up old news in my life. They had their comedy nevertheless.

The memoirs of the Princess of Faraway were finished, but needed revision and retyping. Because Dale Burke was bored, and the boys strapped, the Princess employed Sudge to type the script. At once Sudge saw that the manuscript wasn't very bright. For one thing, there were no letters from various celebrities the Princess mentioned as dear and intimate friends. She had, moreover, few anecdotes, and said little about how they looked or acted. Sudge sniffed out immediately that any wit in the book was Dale's, and let Dale know he understood. They laughed together over that. Money was the one thing the Princess had a devastatingly clear memory about. Sums she knew exactly. Otherwise, she was empty, and as little entitled to fame as an art patron as she was to the title of Princess.

Nevertheless, Sudge was glad for the chance to earn money, but his suspicion that the Princess wouldn't pay him much proved correct. He had meals with her. But since she was on a diet to reduce, he had to eat the same fare, and she didn't allow much wine. Sudge liked to play her phonograph, for Eustace Cross saw that she had the newest records. Sudge took to slipping a record under his coat nights as he departed. These he gave to Laura. The Princess was too excited about her memoirs to notice the missing records.

The new script of the memoirs was beautiful, for Sudge typed well and got the manuscript up with professional competence. Later, when the book appeared, it had a slight success, but everyone knowing the Princess understood that all the dainty wit and bright malice were Sudge's. Dale had furnished Irish gaiety and witticisms here and there, but she admitted that Sudge had slipped in the best cracks. He had a talent for drawing old dames and gents with cruel caricature, and though his contributions to the book were trivial, the memoirs were so trivial that Sudge's insertions took on profundity. The Princess, however, stolidly believed the book entirely her creation. She didn't understand, for instance, my remark that "You didn't know you had such a full and interesting life, did you?" The memoirs were reviewed by the *London Times* and the *Observer* as the gracious record of a patron of the arts, a woman of force, magnetism, with a genius for drawing out the brightest aspects of a great man.

With the memoirs done, the Princess believed that she must investigate Quarter life. Eustace Cross was back from a sanitarium, where his friend Jacques had died, and Eustace was still intent on knowing artists and having his poetry published. Had he been able, he surely would have persuaded the Princess to subsidize one of the dying mushroom magazines so that his poetry could have someplace to appear. The Princess, however, was wily about the use of money. Both she and Eustace intended to have it and her title impress people as much as possible. She would be loved for herself, not because she spent money. It is quite the habit among wealthy people, whether their riches be new or inherited, to think that others exist to entertain them, and often they are annoyed that people are not entertaining enough.

The great event in the Princess's recent life had been an operation on her tiny bitch, which was nicknamed the Nightingale. The Nightingale would reject strangers' advances with all the haughtiness of her five pounds, but if the Princess tickled her chin, she lifted her head to sing a series of yipes which constituted her "bird thou never wert" contribution. At one time, however, the Nightingale had so forgotten hauteur as to become intimate with a gentleman hound many times her size. To avoid dying attempting to give birth to puppies larger than herself, the Nightingale had a delicate operation performed on her. The Princess believed proudly that she had advanced science by having the Nightingale endure this bit of surgery. She kept the tiny beast with her constantly, sympathizing no doubt with its female trials.

Sudge had little conscience as regards the Princess. He knew she was stupid, but she was middle-aged, stolid, and moved ponderously. Sudge was slightly afraid of her. One night she came to the Quarter with Eustace, drank and ate with a group of us, and left without paying her or Eustace's bill. Immediately there was conspiracy. The next night I handed the Princess the bill, saying, "Your share is—," hoping that Sudge or Dale would remind her that she had forgotten last night's account. When they didn't, I dared further and told her to pay tonight as my finances were short.

I was surprised that the Princess was fussed. She was then diffident rather than haughty and reserved. She came and went with a frigate-bearing manner, and wore many pearls. They were imitation, but Dale, to impress others, insisted that they had cost a fortune. Vaguely the Princess began to understand the Quarter spirit. For now whenever a bill was presented at her table, she grabbed it with an air of panic, saying, "I will take it." That was as it should be. Some of the millions her father had made on ale might as well be spent, especially as she wished to meet new celebrities to put into her later memoirs. Upon being presented to them, she maintained a silence which they believed meant arrogance, but knowing now that she was timid, I tried to make them trot out anecdotes or parlor tricks to break the ice. She found the Irish tenor voice of a famous writer "quaint" when he sang old come-all-yous dear to his Irish-twilight heart. He couldn't be persuaded to be around the Princess after that. She had no soul to understand his soul. He'd seen his family through the war, and his wife said, "To the divvil with Jim's genius. I want a little life of my own." With family troubles he had enough to bear without taking on the Princess with her lack of understanding.

The Nightingale I was fond of enough to woo, so that she at last let me hold her without quivering in terror, and yiping at me as soon as the Princess took her back. She showed real dog signs by having a lively interest in smells and gentlemen hounds. The sight of a police dog sent her into hysterics of rage. Really she was a nervous lady dog, small and delicate, covering her timidity with hauteur. The Princess, however, didn't appeal to me much. Now and then she had Dale invite me to dinner at her place, and we all had to eat her diet food. After dinner I had to be blatant and ask if the maid had forgotten to bring in the liquor. The Princess didn't try to discipline me as she did Sudge, and she thoroughly disapproved of Ross, thinking him lazy and a leech.

Still, the Princess proved helpful and a good sort. I found Dale Burke in La Coupole one night. She was nervously gay and said she was going to get drunk. It seems that one night she felt sorry for the English Jew, Simon, and let him come home with her. Simon boasted of his enormous virility. No man ever believed his fifteen-times-a-night tales, but girls were curious, and Simon was sullenly gentle and pathetic. He had touched Dale's heart, but now she was caught and wanted no child of whom he would be the father. The Princess was sporting and offered to pay Dale's expenses until she was out of this jam.

Dale felt tormentedly worried about money and the care of her two-year-old daughter. Things struck her as messy, complicated, and futile, and she felt herself acting idiotic. She heard much loose talk and believed that people were as free as they spoke when in a ribald humor. The older women were not by a fraction. They didn't show disapproval, but were careful not to—well, not often—get themselves into such a situation as Dale's.

Laura and Colette came in looking bored. Laura said that she must get down South to work. She was fed up entertaining rich old dames who accepted her hospitality and bought no pictures. "They don't calculate to give anything. They think we're here to entertain them," she complained, then whispered, "Can you lend me a thousand francs? I can return it in a month."

"Sure, I'll give you a check later," I told her, feeling that my days in Paris were numbered, too. Things had been nicely casual, but such periods always come to an end, and tiresome things happen en masse. I was running short of money as well, but could live economically in a cheaper place. "Where will you go?"

"Not Saint-Tropez," Laura said. "Give me the address of that town where you lived for twenty-five francs a day. We don't mind not having conveniences in the country. Lady Mart's back. Did you hear?"

"Hell," I ejaculated, remembering Mart's custom of fainting off the barstool when she was penniless. If I happened to be in the same bar, upon coming to, she confessed to having no place to stay. And at my studio later she would sob all night that she wished she had the guts to kill herself. After several years of realizing that Mart didn't want to pull herself together and snap out of the routines she found so tragically boring, I felt little sympathy for her. "I'm heading south tomorrow then. It's come. Things will be grimy from now on. I can't stay to listen to any more sob stories."

"Chloe Andrews is looking for you," Laura said. "I suppose you know. She goes so far to say she'll kick Steve out if she doesn't give up Hilaria. She knows that Steve had always wandered, but . . ."

"I know," I said curtly. "Chloe overdoes her maternal, who-will-take-care-of-her-if-I-don't line. She could discipline Steve or kick her out. Hilaria doesn't give a damn about Steve. She likes men, but Steve's easy to barge around with. Poor Chloe. After her years of newspaper work, and variety of lovers, how can she pull that 'Do you think Steve's really promiscuous?' line? Steve would get chummy with a crippled street beggar if she had liquor in her. She's broad-minded and loves to talk about life and humanity. I understand why she gets fed up having Chloe idealize about her being something no lively human being wants to be anyway."

I went to the Dôme bar for a change of air. As I sat reflectively, somebody put a hand on my shoulder. It was Jan, the Polish boy. "Kit, *kommen, bitte*," he said pathetically. At first, as I walked down the street with him, I didn't understand what he wanted. Finally he said huskily, "*Je suis malade.*"

"That's it," I said impatient at the idea. "I'll give you the address of a good doctor. How long have you been sick?" He grimaced and looked sallow, with circles around his eyes. "*Avec qui?*" I asked.

"Betty."

"That's hell," I said, feeling a twinge of remorse. A month back he had come into the Select one early morning, feeling joyful and saying he wanted a woman. Only Betty was there. If I had considered the matter, I'd have thought that he knew Betty was little apt to be safe. Jan wanted to talk more, but we couldn't understand each other. He went to find Hilaria, who had once lived with a Polish lover and also spoke better German than I did. Later she came up to me busily.

"It is awful, *pauvre* Jan. He is foolish boy. For one month he has been ill and has not seen the doctor, and today the doctor tell him he may become tubercular. He must have a change of climate. It is silly, the beautiful young man like Jan, not to see a doctor if he goes with *une sale grue* like Betty. He make the scene with me one night because I no go with him, and said he would take the cheap Quarter girl. It was to me nothing. Because I sleep with the man does not give him the right to make the jealous scene. But now I look after him. Tomorrow I take him to the doctor. Oh, it is difficult, the life among such fool people. Now Chloe thinks I take Steve from her, and what I want with Steve. I am woman with the serious idea, and not for the silly *scandale.* Chloe is very beautiful woman, but one tamn fool with her intelligence about Steve. She should know that with love one must never show that one cares enough to stand for anything the other does, and Steve is one crazee fool, with the weak heart, when she has been drinking."

"It's hell, Hilaria. Are you becoming a teaser? Why get Jan all upset and then leave him when he's drunk? He looks sick as the devil."

"The Jan is a leetla boy. He no eats good food. He won't learn French and orders only silly food, and doesn't drink for days, and then drinks two bottles of whiskey in one night. If I was not busy studying for my acting, I should take care of him, but it is all complicated." Hilaria felt competent and important.

"Hilaria," I said, "you and I aren't very naive or simple, not very. Jan is both, and Chloe's worse—old-fashioned and a sentimental liar to herself. She wails, 'Why should Steve be faithful to me? I'm an old woman, and anybody gets tired of seeing the same face too much.' What Steve needs is a good kick in the pants. Who wouldn't get bored with Chloe's clutching motherliness? She knows Steve's an old soak and roustabout. Hell, I head south tomorrow."

"It's no good for a woman of intellect and the beauty, like Chloe, to act one tamn fool. Everybody takes all they can have for nothing. I too, ha, ha, ha, but I'm the clever girl," Hilaria said and bustled away.

"To hell with you, Hilaria," I called out as she retreated. "You and I just have the luck not to let anyone disturb us much. We don't know the disease of being in love. You fool Chloe, but you can't spoof me. You and Steve are sneaking off somewhere tonight. Chloe's looking for me. If she finds me, I'll take her to the Boeuf to make her feel a little gay with drink. Tell Steve. It always gripes Steve when Chloe's with me, and I cuss back if she tries to curse me out. I don't respect her hands-off attitude toward anybody she thinks her conquest. That's a warning. So don't appear at the Boeuf unless you want to run into Chloe."

"Kit, you are the bright boy. Ha, ha, ha. For you I come to the Boeuf and we go dancing and leave Steve with Chloe. Steve makes me mad. She thinks the other night I stand for her making scenes because I talk to Jan. For me it does not do that anyone makes the jealous scenes. I giff one tamn if Steve loves me. I was beautiful girl for many when she was one tamn fool baby. What is the love, to go with the 'orrible people like she do?"

Lady Mart came in and time dropped away. She was not in a game state such as let her arrive at the Ritz without luggage, take a suite saying that her trunks would be delivered later, stay three days, and disappear without paying the bill. Instead, she felt too low to hope that she could trade much longer on her title. She was at her lowest moment in my casual knowing of her for ten years, in London and Paris. In her panic of desperation, she did quaver that "We don't do that sort of thing" about such things as she had been doing for years: that British righteous attitude she employed to keep others usable by implying the "we" who are "one of us" are always sporting and never let each other down.

"I say, I'm stony-broke," she said. "It's good you're here to offer a chap a drink. I am nervy. They tell me Pemberton's in town. It was crummy of him to write about me that way in his book, wasn't it?" Mart didn't disapprove really. His portrait flattered her, and gave her a romantic glamour she didn't possess in life. "I say," she laughed with nervous and forced gaiety, "he did love me after all. I must look him up. I'm stony-broke. Have you his address? Do you know his new wife? I fancied the boy. He'd come back if I wanted him, and no tosh, but of course I don't mess into people's lives."

I didn't have his address, and this affair didn't involve me anyway. "His present girl was at one of John's parties with her sister," I told her. "I just met them and they seemed prim and prissyish. Pemb said he thought so too, then. It's not possible to keep up with such quick changes of passionate emotions."

"Yes." Mart was sharply bright. "I did feel a rotter. I didn't want him. It was me he cared about at first, and that broke up his marriage, and when I was occupied elsewhere he took the other woman. It's rather a good yarn, isn't it? If I see him I must demand my share of the royalties from his book. After all, I am the heroine."

"You're not the only one," I said. "There's the Jew and the blond villainess who'll also be after their shares, and a few other characters as well. He's having a difficult time now. Having made himself the hero, a man of maimed virility, he brings his son about the cafes so that sightseers will know that he is really a father. Some cruel woman asked him how he could be sure the child is his. Elsie Mime says she'll crack a bottle over his head if he ever tries to sit at a cafe table where she is. It burns her up that he drew her as a gold-digger. Reportorial realism has its trials."

"He was hard on that Jew, wasn't he? And really, the Jew was rather a good lover."

"My heart doesn't bleed for that boy, but Pemb did play tennis with him as a swell-guy chum. The book sold, and that's what Pemb meant it to do."

"I do feel seedy," Mart said. "What's a fellow to do? I wish I had the guts to suicide, but the idea terrifies me. What's to become of me? I haven't a bloody sou, or the chance of getting one. Mike was rotten to leave me after my divorce, when I'd stuck by him for four years. They want me to be a saleswoman at one of the best dress shops. Fancy me, ha, ha, ha," Mart laughed boisterously, without mirth. "If I could ever get there mornings. I say, you will give a fellow another brandy, won't you?"

Time had altered Mart. She was more nerve-brokenly desperate and on the verge of hysteria than ever. She sounded her boisterous, mirthless laugh more, and made painful-to-hear attempts to be a ribald lady with a hearty humor. She appeared to bother little about mere cleanliness now. Her breath, her whole being, emitted an odor of stale cognac. She drank not to forget or to become hilarious, but to break down what feeble reserves she had so that she might weep because of her panicky desperation. Perhaps she drank hoping that soon drink would kill her, but perhaps she had not even calculated that. Life had been muckish on her, not only because of the war, but because it had given her no apparent capacity to rebound and readjust. Bored as she was with her present mode of existence, she couldn't hope to attempt such work as she could get. It was fortunate for her that she still believed a lover would come along and rescue her. I wanted to get away and started to get up.

"You won't leave me like this?" she said. "Do buck a fellow up. We don't let each other down."

How to buck Mart up was beyond my imagination, but I stayed. The constancy of her tragic state of desperation acted like a narcotic on one's sense of despair and pity for her. She had been wailing her boredom and terror for years in London, in Paris, and even when she went to the seaside, she rejected swimming or any form of exercise to nurse the brandy bottle. If hers was dipsomania, it was a form beyond my comprehension, for she certainly didn't have her panicky emotions numbed, and her gaiety was so forced that it screamed with desperation. Possibly if she hadn't accustomed herself to leaning so hard on her title, she could face the fact that she had to depend upon her own abilities. With innumerable creditors pursuing her, there was slight chance she could go on tricking hotelkeepers, bars, and restaurants.

We went to dinner, where Mart nibbled at her food, her stomach in no shape for digestion. A hunch, she said, told her to go to the Select, and as we sat there Pemberton did come along with two women. They sat outside. Pemberton, looking into the bar, saw Mart and me, and beckoned to us to join them on the terrace.

"I'm in a blue funk," Mart said, her hands trembling as she played with her brandy glass. "What will I say to the woman? She knows about me. Be a dear and talk to her and come back to tell me what she's like."

"Rats, Mart, I won't feel comfortable with her, either. The last I saw of Pemb he was solicitously in love with Olive, who staged weeping scenes because of his devotion to you. What am I expected to think? If he's using any form of lovey-duck terminology on this girl, I'll bust."

"She will hate me. I can feel iced arrows in my spine from her eyes now," Mart said.

"Why? He married her after his infatuation with you."

"You saying that! Do you fancy the woman doesn't know I can still have him if I make the sign?"

"I give a damn, Mart. It's your situation. He's asked you to join them, and you will surely run into them sometime. I'll go to the table with you until the ice is broken."

"Give a chap time, will you?" Mart said. "I must have a brandy. I'll see it through. It does make a chap nervous, and I didn't bother to clean up after the auto trip. I do look muckish. Come on then."

Yes, time had wrought changes in even Mart's weak morale and reserve. Once she had poise and manner of a sort, but when Pemberton presented her to his new wife, she was limp with nerves and her laughter hadn't any energy behind its hollowness. The new Mrs. Pemberton didn't look prim and prissyish as I had first thought. She was tailored and as efficient looking as any competent businesswoman. Surely she was older than Pemberton. Neither her nor her sister's manner showed anything, approval or disapproval. They were polite but made no great effort to ease the tension. Mart could not know what they thought of her, but I, aware that Mrs. Pemberton belonged to the fashion-design world, knew she couldn't fail to spot the sort of broken-morale lady Mart was. There was little chance, too, that Pemberton and this wife would use cuddly baby talk to each other.

Pemberton didn't know what attitude to take, either. He had known he was in for it, and had asked Mart to meet his new wife to have it over with. He tried being facetious and wisecracking, and Mart responded, but both their efforts quivered with nerves and discomfiture. The scene was grim, so I escaped, avoiding Mart's gaze while realizing that she controlled an involuntary gesture to hold me there. Mart had been wrong. She couldn't have Pemberton back, however hard she tried. He'd recovered from his infatuation with her as the lost and desperate Lady Mart. His cold look showed that he realized that she was a shattered wreck. Perhaps the rather grim, efficient, well-groomed simplicity of his wife had attracted him in reaction from his crush on Mart.

Later that evening Mart came into La Coupole looking easier-minded. She offered me a drink and accused me with gay irony of being a bad sport. "You might have stayed to see me through," she said.

"What could I do? If I'd had known Mrs. Pemberton, my presence might have helped."

"Anyway, he was sporting. He took his wife home and came back to have a drink with me, and see, one thousand francs. You know, that boy could still be mine. His depiction of me in that book was rather complimentary. He did love me, I gather."

Pemberton's thousand francs were making Mart feel momentarily secure and gay. That was about as it should be. He had claimed to love her, and the story of his romance had made thousands of American college boys' hearts quiver. A thousand francs was a reasonable price to pay, if she didn't get at him for more. On Mart's side, she would be pointed out to tourists and romantic young men as the heroine of his book. There was no knowing what that might do for Mart's life.

I had the feeling that the war had been over several years. Things were brightening up. It was silly to let despondency clutch the brain because of cases like Mart's, especially when one wasn't fond of the person. Before I left La Coupole Mart was deep in conversation with three college boys from America. One was thrilled to discover that she was the original of Pemberton's frail heroine. Mart was being gay, feeling capable of making more conquests, and what do boys come to Paris for if not to have romance?

CHAPTER NINE

Hearing the bang of a trunk lid, Ross sat up in bed and surveyed me brightly. Sudge was sleepy-eyed, afraid of being awakened by the smell of coffee. That would mean another long day ahead of him which he preferred to pass in sleep till well past noon.

"What's up?" Ross asked eagerly.

"I go south tonight. Fed up with Paris, want to work, and feel right now that places are a damned sight more important than people."

Sudge came actively to life. "Where to? Monte Carlo? I wish we could get away instead of festering in Paris. We've been here eight months without a change, the same muckish routine. I'd like to be by the sea."

"Come along. I go third-class. You have the fare and can find a *pension* in Nice or some little town where you can live for little."

The boys consulted each other with birdlike exclamations, and decided to come. Sudge packed his bag neatly; Ross took up a bundle of his clothes in his clawlike hands and dropped them into the suitcase. It was but a matter of time before Sudge would express mild disgust and dutifully do the packing for Ross as well. Ross moved in a strange finicky way, handling his limbs and body like a wild animal whose sense are not active. "The train goes at 8:55. I'm going out and drink beer all day to be foggy on the train. It's easier to sleep that way. See you later," I said and went out, leaving the boys twittering with excitement as they fussed about the studio.

Chloe Andrews was seated in front of the Dôme looking tired and dismal. "Hello, Kit," she greeted, "I hoped you'd come along to curse everybody and everything with me. I may have to go back to New York and make money. Christ, how I hate it. What does a woman do when she's particular about who she likes and has no business sense?"

"Why limit it to women. It's too late for you to become a scientist or a philosopher, and you're so romantic anything you might invent would be dangerous to use except by somebody with an imaginary sense beyond the sixth. Hell, you won't tolerate resignation. You like commotion, obviously."

"But I'm getting old, Kit," Chloe croaked. "And I will still have to live in Greenwich Village, or some dump. And Steve's gone. I told her this morning to go, that I knew she went with other people, lied to me, and I couldn't stand it anymore."

Poor Chloe. Steve had been drunk last night and told her she was sick of being mothered, had gone, would go off with other people, and wanted to be away. "Maybe you should have done that several years ago," I responded, hoping Chloe didn't know I had heard that Steve had given her the gate.

"I know. It's hell, not only to be damn fool, but to know you're one and can't do anything about it."

"Have a drink, Chloe, and snap out of it. Steve's not the world, and things do happen. You concentrated too many starved emotions on Steve. Now you might use your impulses and debonair imagination."

"Have I any? Hell, Kit, I've been trembling in terror that sooner or later I'd ask Steve back, on her own terms, and stand whatever she does. Do you realize the kind of people that girl thinks she can love? And I a proud woman."

"You knew and asked whoever liked you to pretend with you we didn't know. Hilaria won't be serious about her. She's giving Steve the kind of treatment Steve gave you. Now Steve's up against a younger person who goes out and gets her prey, and takes Steve's conquests away from her. Isn't life well organized?"

"Hilaria's cute. She's the only one of Steve's dear friends I can stand. I scream to think of most of them, but I'm beyond pride now. Maybe I am a tired, hideous, old woman. How could Steve? But she's a baby, too," Chloe's husky voice crooned. "She thinks everybody means well. It isn't because of Hilaria I sent her away. I talked to one woman. She looks like an old hag, but she treated me decently. She told me of herself and ten others, and I believe the poor old thing thought that she and I would hold hands and weep together how each of us stood for whatever Steve did. Steve's a poor baby. Everybody loves her and wants to take care of her. It isn't her fault she's so beautiful that everyone who sees her must have her at once."

"Rot! That line of yours spoiled Steve for you. Here's one in whom she didn't arouse a quiver, except when she swore at me because I was friendly with somebody she wanted. Be as hard-boiled as you try to act. She's no world-beater. It's easy to sleep anywhere with anybody without being a person who sets the world on fire. You know. Enough have tried to make you, but you would be haughty and exclusive."

"Kit, I can't stand people. How do you?"

"Do I? That's news. I drink and try to think I'm satirical. But you and I don't fool each other. You would be faithful to a lost cause like Steve."

"Kit, are you propositioning me," Chloe mocked.

"No, no, our sentimentalities don't click. You'd kill me with your protective approach. I understand why Steve goes balmy because you pet and fuss over her. I'm not even that last straw for you to grasp. You'd better have a chamberry-fraise. I head south tonight, and will set you up to a lunch. Forget your lacerated pride and your wounded mother heart. After all, you have a kitten."

After a drink Chloe was less dejectedly intent on the sorrows of life. A gleam came into her green eyes that were placed unevenly in her Celtic-Slavic face. She slashed plum-colored lipstick across her crooked mouth. Running a hand down her slim waist, she sat arrogantly erect. "I still have my figure. Some think I'm a beautiful woman. Why can't I be less exclusive?" It wasn't so much that she was beautiful but that she represented beauty. Her head sat nicely jaunty upon her neck, and she carried herself with a manner. Her tannish, slightly freckled face, with a droll nose, was of the kind modern painters do.

"Change your style, Chloe. You've used that getting-old line too long. I'll set you up to a haircut and you can go the limit and make yourself the latest model female. Let Steve think you're stepping into high gear. Let's have another drink and by then I'll offer you a dress. You give me the willies letting Steve muck up your energies."

"Why, Kit, imagine your talking like that to me," Chloe said weakly, becoming a bit austere.

"Yes, you've done your cape-throwing gesture of haughtiness with me, while talking of faith and truth, too long. There's nothing inherently noble about your idea of faithfulness. It's passion and possessiveness in you, too. Steve makes the brotherhood of man her playground and is most Christly in giving her flesh to mankind. Now that she's made the break from you there's no use my helping you pretend to yourself you're not aware of what's happening."

"Can't a girl have ideals?" Chloe grimaced feebly.

"Yes, but why make them an imposition on other people who don't want to live up to your ideals for them. You aren't without the capacity to play a few tricks yourself when it comes to having things as you want them."

"Now, Kit, I am a good woman. When have I ever let anyone down?" Chloe became defensive but tried to seem facetious.

"Whenever you ceased hero-worshipping some elected idol you got sour because he or she wasn't what you imagined, which they'd have been damn fools to be. Because that hack-reviewer husband of yours pretended to be erudite and acclaimed Dostoyevsky as the mode in 1915, you adored Dostoyevsky, and your husband, till somebody showed him up as a windbag. Then you adored Jinks and swore he had a brilliant intelligence because he could spout weird ideas, related to no reality or observation. When you discovered he was merely shouting ideas from books he read, you turned on him, and worshipped Margot Train because she bullied you as an inferior by saying that you knew nothing of art and literature, and were simply a near-illiterate country girl. Someone pricked her balloon and you realized she was crooked, but you couldn't bother to admire or be amused by the fact that she was rather smart at stage-setting her charlatanism. Anybody in love with you wouldn't dare to be himself. You are sentimental, but you're hard as nails with people who don't attract you, and you always inflict some slushy literary qualities on the characters of those you choose to accept. More than anything else Steve is a roustabout who likes making tender confidences with other bums over booze. That's how she makes love, but it's doubtful that anybody really matters to her. If there isn't one drunk to talk with, there's another, for her. She doesn't lie to me or to other people. She is outright and hopes we're sports enough not to break your heart by telling you that we all know what you know: that Steve likes to wander."

"*Garçon,*" Chloe called feebly, "bring me an amer-picon. Yes, I will have my hair cut. You silly boy, Kit, throwing away money on an old woman. But my hair . . ." She removed her hat to reveal hair the color of dark bronze. "If my mother saw it short, it would break her heart."

"Break a few hearts and hasten progress, particularly your own. Lay off your growing-old line. You make me think of old dames who douse themselves with patent medicines and tell each other their female ailments over back fences. Suffer for the world at large if you must, but don't be a wailing mother. That Jesus-Christ attitude in you is a damn lie. You'd use Steve to have her, and you'd use other people more rockily and without conscience to help you.

"You know whose salvation you want. Everybody doesn't mean well, wish for nobility, intelligence, and the nice things of life as you claim you see them. Why not try using your honest capacity to know what's what in regard to your obsessed desire for Steve exclusively? You believe in fidelity, that hoax, as little as anybody when someone heaves in sight who appeals to you. Drink up and let's start shopping. There's a kick to be had out of decorating you as you ought to look, and my decorating impulses have been inhibited long enough. You've cramped your own style and blamed Steve too long. I refuse to submit to solacing lies any longer."

Chloe was pent-up with remarks she wanted to make, but they had not yet formed themselves into words. As she got up she assumed some of her old swagger, defiantly resenting my comments. She threw her coat over her arm and walked haughtily, as though aware of being stunningly elegant. She nearly stumbled into a man, who lifted his hat and started to speak. Chloe looked at him coldly and walked on.

"That bastard," she said. "I heard he was in town, looking for me now that a book of mine started to have a success if only it had been marketed properly. I'm feeling young again. He's the head of a publishing house. One time he thought they might publish a book of my short stories, so he asked me to dinner at the Lafayette. He's the type who would try to get familiar. I waited, but he suggested nothing for my best story, a darling. When I felt him pressing my knee, I let go. I threw my cape over my arm, got up, and said so the entire room could hear, 'Mista—, you think I'm a woman of talent, do you? Well, there are mirrors in the world, and if looking into one you can stand what you see, you're too lacking in taste for me to talk with. You think you can buy the stories of a talented woman you find beautiful and have a few free feels as well. Waiter, bring me the bill—my portion. I don't let any sonofabitch like this person pay for my dinner.'"

"That made him happy, I judge," I said, liking to see Chloe feel herself a dramatic and tough woman who could put people where they belong and let them hang there limp.

She was a bit dour now. "Maybe it ruined my chances of getting published then, but nobody who looks like that man can be familiar with me if I did want to be a literary woman, and I will be literary. He nearly collapsed before he got out of the dining room, but I have to tell those goddamned he-men that what they have to dangle before the world isn't irresistible, publishers or no publishers. Imagine. What do men think? If I wanted him, I'd want the matter treated a little delicately. How can they think any intelligent woman wants her knee fondled? I don't think much of the world, but I don't think so little of it as to believe even a whore likes such treatment."

The incident enlivened Chloe, and during lunch she recounted her experiences interviewing boxers, actresses, society women, a murderess, and other celebrities. It was difficult to hear her challenging the world, ribald and snooty, and to remember that actually she was a soft, sentimental mother-woman, given to incoherent and vague remarks about truth and standards and ideals. But analytical intelligence wasn't one of Chloe's points, and certainly any she had was never directed at herself.

When we went to the Dôme for coffee, Ross and Sudge were there to look up expectantly as we approached. Seeing that we would join them, she said, "They're babies. Where did you find them? I can't believe that such things are anymore. I must behave like a woman of dignity now."

"After coffee, go and get yourself done over," I said. "Then meet me at six for a few drinks, and we'll have an early dinner before I catch the train. They go with me. We may see each other in America before long."

"You'll go there too, Kit? Why? Don't tell me you have to earn money."

"Before long. But that's not the main reason. What goes on there is more of our time than what goes on here, where it becomes agonizingly grimy. Oh, New York and London are that, but they both force one out a bit more. Here we all understand and sympathize with each other's ennui too much. The cafes and bars let us congregate for that purpose. New York has a cocaine stimulus, even if it does drive one gradually crazy. Certainly France doesn't supply us any of that culture we once were made to fancy we sought."

"You're adopting children?" she hedged.

"Yes, for companionship, to avoid being lonely when I don't want to be alone. Real parenthood has too many pangs and responsibilities, with results hanging in dire doubt. Adopted ones can be sent back to the orphanage if disappointing."

Chloe was genteel before the boys, very gently the older woman, not interested but duly considerate. Sudge regarded her with a twinkle in his eyes, but he was reticent. As she went away I kissed her, saying, "Come back being hearty, Chloe."

"Sound," Sudge said chirpily. "She excites me."

Ross was scornful. "She's a schoolteacher. She should be a governess or headmistress of a girl's school." He was right, but he didn't know how right, to detect the Victorian-female righteousness of conventional emotion there was in Chloe. Ross simply would not be impressed by people who impressed Sudge, or whom I praised.

When Chloe arrived at five-thirty, her hair shone sleekly in a cut which took several years off her age, and she was wearing a smart gown of modern style, rather than a refined middle-aged woman's get-up. She didn't dine with me, though, because across the river she had met up with other women who were feeling gay. They thought, too, that Chloe had been a home-body long enough and were all for leading her into night gaieties. Knowing that the girls had comedy and confidences among themselves that we couldn't share, Sudge, Ross, and I went to dine ourselves. Chloe was thus the center of the party, and her manner was such that she would not suffer pangs because of the lost or strayed Steve this night.

CHAPTER TEN

IN NICE, IT WAS SUDGE WHO DISCOVERED POGGI'S, which looked from the outside like a mediocre and dingy tea place. Sudge tried the fare, and divulged the information that Poggi's food was excellent, as Mrs. Poggi, a Cockney woman, did the cooking and knew English, French, and Italian cuisine. At the first meal Mr. Poggi was speedily named Andy Gump by Sudge. He revealed that he had two vacant rooms above the restaurant, in an apartment from which the landlord wanted to dispossess him. We moved in, unaware of the hall-room boy's boardinghouse delights awaiting Ross and Sudge. Existence arranged itself beautifully.

The boys arose at any hour from ten to twelve, long after I had sunned on the beach and swam. Going in bathrobes to the beach, they sat sunning themselves, forever hopeful of adventure. Sudge was proud of his quickly attained tan; Ross became lobster red all over his thin white body, and that color he remained. Sudge plunged into the water and swam far out; Ross pranced in dainty agony upon the hot beach rocks, wincing and complaining. His feet wouldn't toughen and he had no stoic's intention to accept discomfort without wailing. Once in the water he didn't swim badly, but one day he fainted in the water and Sudge had to rescue him. It was so with him, whenever anybody made a quick gesture in his direction, that he winced but made no effort to protect himself. When asked if he had been beaten as a child, he declared he had not been. His tendency to cringe before physical attack was apparently inherent.

Days when the boys' monthly allowance was overdue or when Ross received bad news, he ate mincingly, fussing at his food like a nervous, blue-blood old woman, or rather like a sick marmoset, for his gestures were dainty animal nervous.

Usually, however, they were nonchalant and carefree, with few moments of sourness such as had come to them often in Paris. Sudge particularly had a merry time watching girls bathing from the beach. He and Ross tittered over the possibilities of getting acquainted with various girls who "excited" Sudge. They did pick up two English girls, one of whom was lovely, with a slight, young-girl body. I saw the boys only at mealtimes to hear of their excitations. Then they talked much of schoolday friends, their families, or of trivial glances from people seen on the boardwalk. It was not much use to them to meet various older people I knew who lived along the Riviera, nor did they want to. Surely they chuckled at how simply I could be amused and taken in by people who were to them dull, mediocre, and hardly worth a snicker. As they didn't care for drink except to escape depression, which didn't bother them now, it was understandable that they shunned the types encountered in the barrooms of Nice. To them a whiskey-soda among just plain people didn't mean companionship. Whoever one knew the other had to know to make either's acquaintanceship complete, and each was scornful of the other's discoveries.

It was Ross who latched onto the Mowbray sisters, Gwen and Olive. It wasn't difficult, for the girls went frequently to the library, too, in hopes of encounters. Ross managed to reach for the same book as Olive; they confided—what both knew—that they lived in the same direction, so the boys took up with the girls.

Olive was seventeen, and lovely with an open manner of childish brusqueness. Gwen was nineteen and pretty, but her skin was not clear, and she was very Anglo-Colonial in her prudish snobberies. Sudge elected to admire Olive, which caused scrappy moments between him and Ross, who declared it was always he who found girls only to have Sudge take them. They called on the girls one night and returned to tell of Mrs. Mowbray. She was another worried, fussy, army widow, from South Africa. Though understanding that her daughters needed friends and entertainment, she was nevertheless fussily afraid that they might do something improper. Finally she decided that the boys were really "nayce" even if they were Canadians rather than truly English. She permitted the girls to go dancing with them at the Blue Pavillon without her chaperonage.

Each morning the four met on the beach, but soon Sudge began to feel festered. Things weren't developing, and the romance was empty after all. The girls read nothing but crummy books and didn't know what they were about once they had read them. It was Mrs. Mowbray actually who desired indiscreet romance, vicariously. She had a real devotion to novels about dashing men disguised as bandits, who with ruthless passion kidnap beautiful ladies. As the bandits always proved to be titled Englishmen in disguise, Mrs. Mowbray's sense of propriety was placated. Olive gallantly defended her mother's finicky neuroticism, while Gwen was waspishly discontented. What chance had they to meet the right people in Nice, guarded by such a mother?

Sudge borrowed an old phonograph from Olive, who beneath her cryptic youth was a generous and rather shy child. Nightly after Sudge returned from visiting her—Ross had decided that Gwen was too dull to bother with—he had with him one or two of Olive's favorite new records. He loved the blues, and jazz in general. Olive was either too kind or too timid to ask that her records be returned so that she might also enjoy listening to them. With dire intentions Sudge plotted to lure Olive to the apartment alone to hear her own records, and should he contrive to do this, Ross and I were to make ourselves scarce. He wasn't faithful to Olive either, because now a full-blown woman had come to sun herself on the beach, and she excited him, particularly when she stepped into the water, her hands caressing her mature contours.

The region was a community in itself, and the boys had great talent for discovering the life stories of the people about. Undoubtedly the Mombrays, aided by a gangly South African girl, helped supply the histories, but Sudge had a talent peculiarly his own. The full-blown lady was a Russian countess named Margot Lindstrom. She was married to a Finnish diplomat, had a six-year-old daughter, and her husband being in a "sanitarium," her child stayed with his parents. Madame Lindstrom's amorous life was now taken care of by a young Chilean, Anatolio Grijalva, who also "excited" Sudge. He had the habit, Sudge learned, of making scenes on Madame Lindstrom. One night he had broken down the door to her room, and the resulting scandal forced her to seek other quarters. Anatolio also came to sun himself on the beach, and he was a comely young man, with a handsome body. Dark, and generally gay, he looked most amiable until Madame Lindstrom appeared to disport herself to the public gaze. Then Anatolio showed signs of tormented jealousy. He and I spoke to each other because we both patronized a homey rope and wine shop where heady Corsican wine could be had for little. Passing each other several times a day in the wine shop, it became our custom to recognize each other's need for an occasional snifter. Finally we talked to each other, and planned to get drunk together some rainy day, or when one or the other felt the need for such an outlet.

The rope and wine shop was distinctive. Coils and balls of rope and twine of all sizes were in the windows, hung on the walls, or reposed about the room. Also on the walls were some forty mandolins, violins, and banjos, because the Corsican patron fancied himself not only a musician but a collector of musical curios. Refugees from various countries had pawned instruments with him through the years and never reclaimed them. Feeling sure that his place was my kind of hang-out, I got chummy with him, certain that gala nights were destined to break out here.

Anatolio learned from me that Poggi's served fine food of great variety, so he and Madame Lindstrom became clients there, too. Naturally the first night Anatolio offered our table drinks, and we responded, to soon adjourn to the Corsican wine shop. Margot revealed that she could sing well, with much style. She had a clear soprano, a gay lilt of voice, and knew songs which had witty naughtiness. Anatolio too, with drink, wheezed out some South American gaucho songs, and I became raucous-voiced while rendering Negro spirituals, barroom ballads, or cowboy songs. Ross and Sudge coyly tittered and thought us all huge jokes, but they would not perform.

Another night the patron relaxed, took down a mandolin, while a Corsican client took a violin, another an accordion, and the intimate concert was on. A few old soaks of the neighborhood drifted in, listened, croaked their contributions, and drank. The atmosphere was cordial and old-timey, with bronchial, gin-broken, and sea-blasted voices croaking noisily.

Anatolio got excited easily, and the drink made him passionate tonight. He was not inclined to be jealous of the boys or me, but he did think that Margot was too interested in a jolly, virile, handsome captain of a fishing fleet. No, he would not believe that the Corsican looked upon Margot as a lady who was merely being gracious. He saw her as a woman, and Margot was leading him on with coquetry.

Margot laughed. There was a gay-bright taunt of voluptuousness in her voice which revealed that Margot was no conventional woman. Her gaze did appraise the sea captain, with a challenge. She'd known Moscow during the Revolution, Constantinople and Berlin in their reckless postwar days, and she had no refugee attitude. She wanted gaiety and wildness, she said after her sixth glass of wine. She teased Anatolio for having become English and proper during his schooldays in England and Switzerland. He did look very young and petulant, and unable to cope with Margot. He was temperamental, perhaps, but he wasn't toughened enough. Margot's abandon confused him, and he let her see that he knew himself as an inexperienced youth who thought her a woman of the world. Obviously she had scolded him for becoming so easily jealous, and for denying her freedom, which was the only reason she continued her romance with him. Margot was a fine example of the modern woman who steps higher and faster than the once-vaunted polygamous male. Anatolio wasn't old enough to control her, and he was a paragon of fidelity compared to her. Evidently, only now was he realizing that Margot actually would do the things she said she did, which he accused her of doing, hoping to shame her. He couldn't believe that she didn't value the standards he had been taught to respect, and yet he was infatuated with her.

Margot's luscious violet eyes gazed at Anatolio with mockery. Upset, he banged out of the place in a rage of torment. The boys looked uncomfortable when Margot continued being coquettish. Soon they too slipped away. It was raining outside, but drink made the remaining people in the wine shop reckless. As three Corsicans sang a savage song, another got up to dance. He pushed me off my ball of twine in rough good humor, to indicate that I should dance too. That was all I needed to put me in a hell-raising mood. I slammed a glass on the floor, let out a long yodel, and jumped up to leap around. The group shouted and yelled, and more bottles of wine were brought. When the shop closed Margot and I went to the cafe on the corner for a last drink. She confessed surprise that I had a wild streak in me. "Before I thought you were quiet and talked ideas only."

"Hell no! Let's go to Maxim's in that taxi outside. Let's have some excitement tonight."

"Anatolio might run into us," Margot laughed.

"What of it? I don't think he'd be jealous of me anyway."

"You think not?" Margot warned. "You are not afraid?"

"Of Anatolio? He's an excitable boy, that's all. The Chilean temper has nothing on the Irish. But it won't come to a scene. He and I like each other. He'd understand we drank and felt like stepping out."

"Are you afraid to come home with me?" she taunted.

"So you're a tantalizer. If it comes to that we'll go to my room. If you want to give him the gate, go ahead, but it'd be lousy to let him come to your place unaware I was there. Don't you want him anymore?"

"I am not in love with him. He has a nice body, and is gentle. He is lithe and firm. I like the feel of him. He goes a little crazy when he makes love, but like a boy. He and I are not long for each other. He wants to be petted and looked after. Always he wants to be consoled whenever he's slightly unhappy. I have seen too much to have feeling for these little emotions. Maybe he has passion enough that he might sometime kill me when I am a devil. But he too placidly thinks it enough to tell me what he wants. What is that? I want a strong man, a brute, someone to arouse and excite me. I know deeply that there is no dangerous passion in Anatolio, and he will bore me in the end. It is all very sweet, but he is too delicately boyish, a baby for tenderness, except when he is in passion. Then he is unaware, but that is for so short a time. No, no, I must try a brute who takes me roughly and cares nothing for what I feel." Margot laughed wildly, with a reckless taunt in her voice. "What can it mean to a woman like me that Anatolio wants to own me?"

"I guess you and he haven't any overpowering love for each other."

"Yes." Margot became wickedly confidential. "It is too much, letting time pass. I have had excitement in life and won't live to accept life without excitement. He doesn't know me. He thinks I am a nice woman with temperament and intelligence, ready to live calmly with her lover. No, no, if there were brilliant people with audacity to make a spectacle, dramas, around me, I might stay with one man, if he was beautiful or attractive enough to draw the bright world around us. There is for me only pleasure. I understand how fast women have become nuns, an excess of another kind after wickedness, for such as believe in wickedness. But to be a good woman? That is banal. They are not generous or good. They have no spirit or imagination. Did the little boys who have a nose for learning things tell you that my husband is insane? My little girl is silly, not an idiot, but not bright. That is my contribution. I married a diplomat and was to lead a conventional, honest woman's life."

It drizzled steadily, with an autumn chill in the air. The dankness heightened our wish to be in a cozy bar, among lights, the voices of people, and the warmth of alcohol and company. At the English bar we found no other clients when we arrived. Jake, the proprietor, looked dismal, and was glad that we came in. An officer wounded during the war, he had put his capital into this bar, but he was given to off-track obsessions and didn't like not having a quantity of people about. In the manner of Englishmen his class, he acted elaborately the gentleman of the upper classes with his clients. However, the very cut of his clothes and body—his starched linen collar, his manner—revealed him as city-clerk stratum. He was pleased that Margot treated him archly, and didn't detect that she was laughing at his gallant efforts. He offered us drinks after our first round, and stood at the table, timid of sitting down without being asked.

"Leave him to me," Margot laughed drily when Jake went behind the bar to get the whiskey bottle. "He will supply us our drinks tonight. I don't like his coming to talk to us without being asked, but he has seen me here with a Polish friend, Natalie, who was ready to flirt with him. I will call her. She will flirt with him seriously. She needs money. Once she was the governess to my sister's children, but here she is useful to me when I have no money. Ha, ha, I have no love for the English people. Jake believes himself a great man with the women. We will keep the whole bottle of whiskey he's bringing."

Natalie did join us, and appeared to imitate Margot's abandoned quality. But it didn't sit well on her. She grew silly and her coquetry with Jake was that of a giggling governess. He played with her, but wanted to hold Margot's attention. She had turned indifferent, and looked weary. Natalie and Jake were getting on my nerves, too. They were needlessly voluble to create an air of hilarity, when ennui was decidedly in the atmosphere.

As we sat drinking, Jan, the Polish boy from Paris, came in with a middle-aged woman who was probably a relative. Margot overheard them speaking Polish, which she understood. When she saw Jan nod to me, she laughed and said, "He is bored with that woman, a sister, or an aunt. Have him join us. I like him. Maybe I will take him, or you, or I may find somebody at Maxim's who makes me more curious. Whatever I do, do not tell Anatolio. Say that you took me home at three."

Jake was again at the back of the bar as more clients had come in. I went there to have a whiskey and Jan came up to drink a greeting with me. He tossed off his whiskey with a gulp, and indicated he would be back after seeing his sister-in-law home. He was now, he said, cured of his illness.

Jan was back soon, and a competition began among him, Margot, and me as to who could hold the most whiskey well. But all northern race people, we quit that game and drank because we wanted to. Natalie got increasingly maudlin, so we took her home and started toward Maxim's. Margot was not going to take Jan home with her easily if she wanted him. They were of the same class. He knew Russia and Scandinavia, as she knew Poland, and her type didn't impress him unusually. Smiling at her, he touched his heart, indicating Margot. "*Non, rien là.* She mocks men and plays to get much money."

Margot wasn't beautiful, but when she returned from the ladies' room her eyes and lips glistened. She had a soothing contralto voice and laugh, and she registered grace and charm, suggestively. Obviously *poules* in the place knew her and she nodded to them. From their manner I judged they thought her an *honest woman* who was gay and indiscreet. Their manner toward her erected a barrier between them.

Observing various men who came and went from the bar, Margot made comments. She didn't want the old French gallant, or the racetrack American. She said she wanted money, or to be curious, and neither of them would satisfy either desire. As she spoke, however, she showed that she actually didn't give a damn. She was desperate. She was born not caring. When she mentioned Copenhagen, I asked after people I know there. She looked at me in surprise. "But Karen, you know Karen. She was my friend at school. She is *une idiote.* She is almost on the street, for the love of a man. Her family has not the money they had and he wished to delay the marriage, but Karen went to him anyway. He will never marry her. I told her last spring to take a rich lover, now, while she is still beautiful and has position in society. If she will be silly, why does she not come to France? When they think her *déclassé* in Denmark and Sweden she will be finished. But she makes scenes on the man. Poor Karen. If I cared I would pity her, but she is foolish. She retains ideas about a society that once meant something, but it will not help her. She can't disapprove of me now that she lets sentiment wreck her. That is too lower class. I thought she was gay and indifferent within herself. I thought she would come to Paris and we would be *un grand succès.* Neither of us is beautiful, but I understand men—to get money. Someday one of them may choke me dead, but. . . . Barman, give me a whiskey."

Margot started a conversation with an American who owned a yacht in the harbor, but he didn't know she recognized him. He was courteously interested, and began to be more so, but Margot's rakish talk evidently put him off. When he left she said, "It's tedious making love to a gentleman who takes me thinking I am a lady who is lost, perhaps because of a scandal. Where is a prizefighter, a savage man? I think now I might love a man who would beat me for fighting him. Anatolio is a schoolboy with his jealous scenes. I suffer ennui." She had stopped paying attention to Jan, who grimaced as though he didn't like seeing a woman of his own class acting loose. Her taunt bothered him.

Margot leaned across me and put her hand on the arm of a man, saying, "You are *très sympathique*. I like you. Drink with me."

I moved from between them and looked at the man she had picked up. He was her great brutal he-man type, all right. But his suave manners were surprising, and a bit menacing. His face was corrugated, and quite that of a thug or gangster. Still, he included me in his invitation when he offered drinks, and his speech belied his tough looks. I danced with various *poules* to let Margot talk to her man. After a while she suggested that the three of us go back to her room. There it proved that Margot had nothing to drink, and the situation wasn't the sort for my sitting down and conversing. The man obviously assumed he was to stay with Margot, for he was attempting to embrace her. When she repulsed him and he moved to leave, she recalled him. When I started for the door, she said, "You must not go! You must not go!" A little of that sufficed, however, and I left, feeling rather ashamed and perplexed. But surely Margot had enough experience to take care of herself, and she wasn't at all so drunk as to be unable to decide things for herself.

The next day it was Sudge who knew how the affair ended. Margot and Anatolio came no more to Poggi's. After I left the man had suddenly become so angry at her playing with him that he slugged her. She cried out for help from her landlady, who had to be awakened. As this scene was happening Anatolio appeared. In spite of his Chilean blood, he hadn't attacked the man. Seeing his rival with clear eyes, he sulked and went away, as did the man, but Margot and Anatolio had definitely broken. "She's furious at you," Sudge said.

"And Anatolio?"

"He doesn't know you were with her last night."

"What was I to do when Margot picked up a man she said she wanted?"

"She wanted to make you jealous," Ross said scornfully.

"Why didn't she give me a chance to show interest first? I couldn't fight for her when she selected the man herself. Margot just likes to think she's a destroyer. I'm glad Anatolio didn't find me with her."

"Would you be scared?" Sudge was brightly interested.

"No, I don't think he'd have made a scene. Anyway I'd have felt sheepish. What could he do under those circumstances? Margot likes scenes and intrigues, and liked Anatolio because he supplied them for her until she thought his scenes too mild."

Anatolio appeared one night at the Excelsior Cabaret and was perturbed about the Margot affair. He didn't want to see her anymore, but felt that he should have attacked the man. I was glad for him that he hadn't, because the man was a bruiser half again Anatolio's size, and it was too bad Anatolio felt embarrassed for being no braver than I'd have been.

Nice is very cosmopolitan in its way, and because it's easy to lead a drifting life there without feeling that one is necessarily enjoying oneself, I decided to go to a small town, to be away from any incentive to lead a nightlife with its fictitious amusements. Sudge's parents were in London and expected him to visit them, so I agreed to stay on in Nice till he returned in ten days.

CHAPTER ELEVEN

ROSS ADMITTED THAT HE WAS A PROBLEM, AND the boys had it worked out that he was Sudge's peculiar problem. Through the weeks as Ross talked of members of his family they emerged as individuals. Whenever Ross read a novel about a decaying family, he was sure to find prototypes of his own relatives. Saltykov, Dostoyevsky, Strindberg, Couperus, Thomas Mann—all proved for Ross that those imaginary figures, "the fittest to survive" and the "competent," are no more persistent than decadent types. It was in the difference between the responses of Sudge and Ross to books of this sort that made one think Ross the deeper. He read and was amused by intimate family-study books, because he always related these studies to his own life. Sudge found little to snicker at in Mann or Couperus, and was heartily scornful of Dostoyevsky's epileptic soul-searching. It didn't amuse him to read about a lot of dull people festering their lives away.

The member of the Campion family for whom Ross had the most sympathy was his drunken brother, Angus, who until Ross came of age had been the family's greatest problem. In fact, he still remained so as Sudge had taken on Ross. Angus could not hold any position long. He was forever involved with some girl of lower class, and staggered home often to be sick on the family rugs. Mrs. Campion felt protective pity and affection for him, and managed to get him to his room before his irate sisters discovered that he had disgraced them all again.

It was the daughters who gave Tina uncomfortable moments. They blamed her and their father for extravagance in the past that had left the family in poor circumstances, and they blamed them more bitterly for not disciplining the boys. Tina drily informed her daughters that the vices of their brothers did not constitute their lack of ability to attract marriageable men. She disliked having the easy, sardonic tranquility of her resignation jarred. She had known more gay impulse and abandon in her youth, and had she not married Mr. Campion might have married a fast young man who now reclined in prison because of embezzlement. Moreover, she hadn't married their father because he was a minister, but because, for her taste, he was a desirable physical specimen. She understood why he wasn't strong on the dutiful parent side of his nature. When children arrived they did, but he didn't think much about their futures. So far as his ministry was concerned, he had a manner, charm, and preached easily, but when Tina's money permitted him to retire, he did so and helped spend her not great fortune.

As the boys grew so mirthful over the fortunes of the Campions, it was not surprising that they gloried in the Poggi establishment. It was the center of a variety of characters, all of whom the boys gave nicknames. There was a retired English major who liked betting at the races, talked big money, and dressed shabbily while asking Poggi to wait for board payments. Another Englishman with his wife expected de-luxe service, and told his wife to "shut up, you're being hysterical" whenever she spoke. A former music-hall star lived in the room next to the boys. Mrs. Stout lived up to her name, for now she had trouble getting through the doorway, but this did not dampen the robustness of her Cockney humor. An elderly woman from India lived on the other side of the boys' room, and she, Mrs. Stout, and the Englishman and his wife constituted the boys' trials and mirths. Any of these people was apt to go into the washroom to remain a long time. One day Sudge learned the trick of snapping the lock from the outside, and the Indian woman was most upset to discover that she couldn't get out of the bathroom when she wished. There was no bell to summon help. After a time Sudge relented and let her out. He was all consideration, and wondered earnestly how she could have been locked in. His ambition then was to get Mrs. Stout or the puffy Englishman in the same situation, because Mrs. Stout, Sudge declared, either did not bathe or had a fearful odor. The bathroom smelled for an hour after she left it. The Englishman roused Sudge's ire because he nagged and scolded and seemed to think the company bathroom was his privately.

When Sudge learned from Poggi that the Princess of Faraway had occupied this apartment the previous year, his joy was perfect. It was here that her little dog had been indiscreet with a male dog several times her size. It was here that Dale Burke had convalesced after having given birth to a child. Sudge could not write to Dale soon enough to inform her of this coincidence.

At mealtimes Sudge and Ross watched a French party who came often and appraised the food as though Poggi's were a gourmet's establishment. He noted with glee that an antagonism existed between Mrs. Stout and the English major, and that Poggi couldn't stand the fussy Indian woman. Mrs. Poggi's mother was about, vaguely simple-minded and prying, and Poggi confided to the boys that she was a nuisance.

Poggi was a most human soul, and given to lurking jollity himself. He didn't know why he was called Andy Gump as he had never seen the cartoon, but he felt that the boys meant well by him. He had great ideas of gambling in Monte Carlo, with small sums, and someday having great luck. He expressed his delight when he managed to smuggle a shipment of Italian wine across the border. Little did he know how the boys appreciated his crookeries and smuggling, to justify little tricks of their own. He confided in them as friends, with a chuckle, and aware that any sensible person has little patience with this red-tape law business.

For all their hall-room joys the boys had moments of depression, for Sudge was a problem to himself while Ross was problem enough for any boy so given to brooding as Sudge. Little had happened in their lives to give them high ideas about people or purposes. When Ross left college Sudge left too as a gesture of loyalty. Ross had an older brother who managed a lumber company office, and he gave both boys clerical work. This brother, Theron, was no man with a go-getter attitude, however. When he talked to Ross he sympathized about what a hellish period youth is, and let Ross understand that he was miserable with his wife. Hating his work, and nagged by a wife, he was apathetic. He had been in the war, suffered shell-shock, seen college chums killed, and was generally resigned into the attitude that a man might as well take what comes. His attitude toward Ross was that the boy might as well follow vagrant impulses, and as Theron was the only semi-balanced member of the Campion family, Ross found that Theron's attitude was fine. Theron talked of having adventure while one was still young, and Ross listened, but Sudge knew that Ross was his problem. Ross hadn't the hope, readiness to put up with hardship, or physique to make an adventurous type. He was a fragile, neurasthenic, wistful type, and somehow Sudge believed himself strong.

He would not at any rate desert Ross. He wouldn't have visited his family in England if I hadn't agreed to stay in Nice until he returned.

When Sudge was away Ross and I went one night to Maxim's. Ross, possibly ill at ease with me, was talking wistfully of his need to be in love. But unlike Sudge he wasn't easily "excited" to find a girl "stout" or "sound." He had spiritual standards.

The season was dull and the house *poules* loitered at the bar mourning the lack of business: few good clients were about town now. What men left were not *délicat* or generous, and though it may be a girl's *métier* to be a *poule*, such men make the profession a boring one, but what would you? Business was slow also in the shops and for hotels.

Sporty, a large, handsome girl, with more spirit than the others, and a tendency to hearty comedy, decided she found Ross delicate, a nice young man. She knew he was poor, but she felt the need of affection and nice emotions. She would take him home with her. The next night Ross wanted to go again to Maxim's to find Sporty. He wasn't in love, but he was sure Sporty had something fine in her.

Dancing with me, Sporty revealed that her experienced heart was touched; she was bored with having to stay with a party of wealthy men this night. They were common and vulgar, and could not understand that a girl gets tired of having to play her *poule* role for them. "They do me no honor, and they bargain. I think I may become serious, if I can find honest employment. But your friend Ross, the little boy, how he is innocent and naive. He understands nothing of making love, but loves. One needs to be tender with one of his kind. It makes me sick of the gross lumps of flesh who don't make love well, have no feeling, and think I am always ready to laugh at stupid jokes. Nothing occurred between Ross and me. I understood that it does not do for a woman of my experience to frighten such a boy. Tell him I have real affection for him. He is *sensible*, but one must live, and I would make no nice love experience for him. He touches my heart. He is such a sad little boy."

Ross was somewhat hurt that Sporty appeared indifferent to him, having decided that she must not play with his romantic emotions, so she sat with a group of older Frenchmen, though she did come to the bar to share companionable drinks with us. Ross thus had his desire to fall in love satisfied.

As we sat at the bar an aluminum car passed the door, and it could be nobody's but Felix Lutyen's Rolls Royce. He lived about 80 kilometers from Nice, and probably was feeling the need of change from beach-country quiet. When he entered his dyed-looking yellow hair flopped about his loose face in which watery blue eyes floated. Exhibitionistic generally, he now wore an orange and green tricot, plum colored trousers, and no coat. Had the place not been nearly empty, they would not have served him in such a get-up. When he started talking he was excited to run into someone he knew. His voice broke into a crackling falsetto at times, when his laugh sounded with a hysterical break. With him were his sister, Consuela, his wife, Sally, and a cousin, Hortense Waters.

"This is luck," Consuela said, warmly gay. "We hadn't your address to look you up. Meet my cousin Hortense, and flirt with her. She's a nice woman but too well-behaved, aren't you, Hortense? That does not do. She was married and got divorced eight years ago, and hasn't had a lover since, I'm sure. We can't allow life to stay dead on her that way. She doesn't get much kick out of things, do you, Hortense?" Consuela's talk and laugh was kind but mocking too. She jerked off her hat, tossed her tawny hair, took off her coat, and was ready to drink. French-American, but brought up entirely on the continent, she cared little for her mother's social atmosphere, and alternated between staid and free circles.

Sally Lutyens was a Jewess with a great fortune, and try as she did to adjust to the Lutyens' mode of life, she appeared bewildered and out of things. Felix wrote; Consuela had studied opera since she was fourteen; and Sally had ideas that she might subsidize artists. As none of the three achieved their ambitions well, it had been said of them: "Felix, a writer who writes badly; Consuela, a singer with no voice; and Sally, a philanthropist who can't give away money." Of the three Consuela had the most force and self-assurance. Her voice was not strong or remarkable, but she sang intelligently, and had she forgotten opera and the conventional concert type of song might have had success, by creating a type of witty song which she could sing with authority and stage presence. Stockily made, blond, with a healthily nervous intensity, she gave a primitive impression of worldly spontaneity. Unlike Felix she had no need for weird costumes. Usually she was elegant. Felix perhaps was driven to eccentricities to avoid being known merely as the husband of a rich woman.

Consuela felt well disposed to the boys, because they had attended a concert she had given in Paris whereas many of her well-known friends had not. She asked Ross where Sudge was, and was moved by Ross's reticent and considerate manner. He was one of the few people of the other sex whom Consuela was not inclined to challenge coquettishly, but his shy reserve and courtesy made her see him at once as a boy she could talk to seriously rather than facetiously.

Mrs. Waters talked earnestly to me about this life in France, declaring that she didn't want to be reactionary, but that many things puzzled her. She didn't want to be a mere romantic, but wished to retain her ideals and adjust to the times. I couldn't keep up the facetious tone that Consuela advocated, because Mrs. Waters was a serious groper in life. To regain breath for a second lap of earnest inquiry, I danced with Consuela.

"Tell me something. I'm pent-up and restless. I made the others bring me here tonight. The atmosphere was getting threatening at Cavaliere."

"Because of Sally, again?" I asked.

"Yes." Consuela was curtly reflective. "Of course she doesn't like me. No woman would, under the circumstances, but I don't see how things can be different. Felix and I have always understood each other as neither of us understands other people. We want to see each other frequently, to be together. Sally feels cut off. Two nights back some of us wanted a ride after midnight. Sally said she didn't want to go, and when we came back she wasn't in the house. We looked around but couldn't find her. She didn't answer our calls. Felix was in a horrible state. Her sister died a few months ago, and I must say she does extract all the Jewish drama possible out of that death. She and that sister hadn't seen much of each other for years, and didn't seem to adore each other when they did meet. But Sally's strange. Of course we were worried. Sally has moods, and there's that rock cliff just before the villa. After two in the morning she appeared, saying she'd gone to sit in a nook beyond the beach—to think. She had heard us calling but didn't answer. That made me angry. She must have known how worried Felix would be. The next day he made a scene. I suppose I should stay away from them, but he always asks me not to. Maybe she wants scenes; maybe he does. I'm losing my ability to understand him. Between them there are too many scenes. I ought to marry, I guess. A girl has to marry once, even if she doesn't stay by the marriage. I haven't the hold I had on Felix to quiet him when he gets hysterical."

It was possible that Consuela would never be satisfied as long as Sally and Felix were together. Apart from having married Felix, Sally was antipathetic to Consuela, who thought her calculating about money, and a bad influence on Felix because of her strange psychological quirks. Sally in turn thought Consuela rakish, or worse, vulgar, and apt to delight in her ability to take other women's men.

"Sally's money messes things up for them both more than they admit," I said.

"You don't know the things that Sally observes to comment on. Every franc Felix spends she keeps track of. If she's alone for any time, she has obsessions and imagines that she will lose her fortune, and then, because nobody likes her for herself, she will be helpless."

"There are freakish strains in all of her family. It's cruel to say, but Felix isn't so balanced, either. You don't know, Consuela. Maybe they want scenes. Look at them now. When they're with a group they get together and chatter confidences. They want each other. It's too bad you feel as you do about Felix. It's hard on Sally as a wife, and on you and Felix as well. The situation is strained. Are you still putting off your marriage?"

"I can't decide. I will someday, but Pierre hasn't much money, and once I'm married mother can't give me so much allowance. I'll have to give up a good deal, and Pierre, being a Frenchman, may think he has to be less serious about making money since we have it in the family. And there's my singing. I may go next year to do a concert tour in the States. But to hell with it. I want to be gay tonight. Who's somebody to play with? I know you too well. We talk seriously, and tell each other our problems. I want somebody to flirt with."

"Take on Ross. The poor child yearns to be in love. Possibly he believes he's less appealing than Sudge. Anyway flirt with him. He's all who's available right now."

"That wistful little boy," Consuela chortled. "He is full of ideals, as we all are at that age. He's not to be flirted with. He wouldn't respond, or he'd be serious and write pathetic letters. Come now, Kit. This is too much. Fun is fun, but . . ."

"No, he's seen you enough about Paris not to be heavily serious. He's not as innocent as he looks, quite. It's smoky in here. Take him down the seafront for a chat. Be young and girlish. I don't want to dance, and Hortense aches to finish our talk about finding ourselves in life. She's not a bad egg. Evidently among the people she knows in Boston there has been convention, and there's nobody around she would want to play with."

Hortense invited us all to dinner with her the next night as their party was to stay in Nice till the morning after. Ross did not arrive home until three in the morning, and then he was quivering with ecstasy. Consuela had kissed him once or twice, and they had sat talking on a bench on the boardwalk for two hours. Before he had thought Consuela merely flighty, but evidently she had been serious and sympathetic and delicately understanding. Ross was and remained for some days in a state of excitement about her.

"Be careful," I warned, with some seriousness back of my facetious tone. "Felix gets jealous as hell if Consuela seems actually interested in any man. When he makes a hysterical scene he goes wild. Once he threw a full bottle of wine at a man in a restaurant because he thought the man was trying to flirt with Sally or Consuela. He broke four thousand francs worth of glasses and dishes. It took several more thousands of Sally's francs to keep him out of jail. He scared Consuela that night, because he didn't pay attention when she reasoned with him. Instead he thrust her aside, and three gendarmes had a hard time controlling him. Since then, Consuela's rather decided she hasn't the influence on him she believed."

At dinner the next night Consuela was very gently nice to Ross, but shy too. Later she said, "He's too wistful and serious. I can't play with a boy like him. He told me about his family, and that other little boy. Of course he's really in love with Sudge and wants to be free. The other child isn't attractive. I don't know why. There's something mean in his chinless baby face. No, I can't tease Ross. He's sweet, poor child, but what will become of him I can't think."

The Lutyens left early to drive back to their villa. Ross was sad, but had received a letter from Sudge which gave him some happiness, and also made him comment bitterly on Mr. Galbraith. "The old fool has made nearly a million on the stock market in the last six months. Why can't he give us more money? He inherited everything himself, and gets graft money off his job and directorships."

"What does Sudge's father do?"

"He's secretary-treasurer of a university and director on various boards. His wife's relatives have money and that puts him on the inside of investments. Both he and Mrs. Galbraith are so thick-witted they don't know they're alive. The money they spend on clothes for their nasty five-year-old girl is more than they give Sudge. She'll have a fortune when she's twenty-five, and it's accumulating. The old man uses Sudge's capital to make investments, and you can know he takes any excess earnings. Why they think they have to do England and Scotland every year I don't know. They don't know anybody or go anywhere, and don't belong. After parking themselves in a de-luxe hotel, she shops a little and plays solitaire, while the old man grumbles about how bored he is till the whiskey comes up after dinner."

Sitting in bed reading the letters of William James, I thought Ross had gone to bed and was sleeping. James as he revealed himself in his letters wasn't that rather imaginary thing, a "great man," but he made one feel fondly toward him. His philosophy was an apology rather than an explanation, but I don't rate philosophy high. Various philosophers command one's admiration or supply intellectual enjoyment by the simplicity or intricacy of their logic and reasoning. They don't, however, allay the rigors of what we must put up with. As an art philosophy does, but its utility is dubious. James doesn't dazzle, but he commands sympathy.

I was into letters written during his youth when he was bothered by futility and suicidal thoughts. When Ross came into the room and stood by the bed, I thought that surely he was one to like these letters. He stood hesitatingly. Thinking that he was so used to sleeping with Sudge that he didn't like sleeping alone, I asked, "Do you want to stay in here tonight?"

He crawled into bed, but didn't speak for a time. Speech was choked in him. Finally he said, "I was thinking of Consuela. I have to see her. You said you might visit them, or go to the little town near them. Let's go there tomorrow. We can wire Sudge and have him join us there."

"Oh hell, Ross, I didn't really intend to visit them. They're all right, but I can't work when they're around, and I'm in the middle of a book and don't want to be thrown out of gear. Wait for Sudge and you two go together. I'll go to Theoule, to be alone in a room above the sea and rocks. Nice is getting on my nerves, and the little towns near where the Lutyens live are all swept by the mistral. When it blows it depresses one wildly."

"I have to see her. Do you think if I went there that brother of hers would make scenes?"

"No, not on you. They'd invite you to stay with them. They have two small shacks on their property. But Consuela's engaged. She doesn't take it too seriously, but she can't take you too seriously, either."

"Come on," Ross said, looking at me with luminous, pleading eyes. He took my hand to play with the fingers. "I'd feel shy there alone, and you're an old friend of theirs. You always say you can stop work and take it up whenever you will without being thrown off track."

"Rot, I won't," I objected, willing to take him there if I hadn't known Consuela would be uncomfortable. "If anything was to come of it, I would, but you're not in love with her. You're just dotty about the idea of being in love. She likes you, but she's thirty-four and thinks of you as a child."

Ross coaxed and was wistfully dejected at my cruelty. The mention of five hours on jerkwater trains, with two changes necessary, didn't dampen his ardor. He stopped persuading and looked appealingly hopeful, sure that I, always ready for anything, would accommodate him in such a crisis. Finally we agreed that he should write to Consuela and wait for her reply. If she wouldn't be embarrassed by our arrival, we would go to her. He wrote the next day, and after tearing up several drafts mailed the letter.

A day later Consuela's reply came; it was kind but not enthusiastic about his coming to visit her. Her fiancé had arrived from Paris for over the weekend, and then she was going to Toulon for a few days, and possibly back to Paris to study for a concert. Later she hoped to see him, in Paris. She let him down tenderly, but Consuela wasn't having complications in her life that could be avoided, and a wistful boy, talking idealistically about love, is decidedly a complication in any free, worldly woman's life unless she is so old as to come into a second girlhood. For Consuela love still had as many comic and rakish aspects as it had profundities. Her days for trifling with delicate boy adorations were not upon her.

In the short time between letters, however, Ross's passion had somewhat subsided. He worried because he had not heard from Sudge for two days, and was afraid that Mr. Galbraith had cut off the small allowance. That would mean both Ross and Sudge must return to Montreal and work. "I gave father a scare, though," Sudge wrote in letter that came the next day. "I told him I could be kept, and would be staying in France if he didn't go on giving me money. He came through, and even admitted that I had grown more mature and was generally improved."

Sudge wrote me, too. His letter depicted how dull his parents were, how he hated London, dressing for dinner and waiting till the whiskey was brought up evenings. His last sentence was, "Of course I love papa and mamma very dearly, but they don't understand things." Possibly he loved them dearly, bored as his letter sounded, but that sentence revealed more what a little boy Sudge still was emotionally than it indicated affection. However Sudge felt toward his father, he pictured him as a pompous and mediocre man who, because of age alone, assumed a patronizing and dictatorial attitude toward a younger male, his son. The boys' tale was that Mr. Galbraith had accomplished nothing but to become older, while fitting into various offices and positions which inherited wealth and a few well-placed funerals left open for him.

After Sudge returned, I went to my small town. The boys remained at Poggi's, leading quiet lives, to get unholy joy out of beating the Englishman to the washroom mornings, "accidentally" locking fussy women in the bathroom when they took undue time with their toilette, and chuckling over Poggi's tales of his minor grafts.

CHAPTER TWELVE

IT SNOWED SEVERAL TIMES DURING THE WINTER, AND with snow inches on the ground the Riviera weather was miserable. But it was equally so elsewhere, and having a beautiful room overlooking the sea and turbulent landscape, I stayed on at Theoule as the Alsatian landlady, having no other winter guests, was careful to keep a fire in my grate. Liking to cook, she took every occasion to serve fete-day cuisine. The fishermen, the town's doctor, mayor, and passing tourists congregated often in the small bistro, and there with drink I could soothe unrest when the wind and the little-varied social life brought that useless emotion in their train.

Sudge wrote that he wished to leave Nice, but being in debt to Poggi, could not. In Paris he might pick up extra money as a typist. Betraying as cities and quantities of social contacts can be, the desire to test them reincarnates in bosoms more disillusioned than Sudge's. The fantasy of being in the center of things persisted in me as well, so I went to Nice intending to take the boys out of hock if they did not owe too much money. We then could go on to Paris together.

During lunch the boys revealed merrily what had been happening in their lives, in Poggi's ménage, and in their families. Poggi, tired of the Indian woman's fussiness, tried to get rid of her by saying that as she had arranged to stay only one month, her room was promised to another party. She remained nevertheless, meekly asserting she would go if he insisted, but her health was feeble. Poggi also wished Mrs. Stout away. Her appetite was equal to her elephantine size; she pained the sensibilities of other clients; and she constantly put the water closet out of order. During the chilling winter Poggi believed one pail of coal enough to keep the stove in shape to supply heat, but his coal bin was kept in the kitchen of the apartment. One day he discovered the Indian lady putting more coal on the fire, as he later detected Mrs. Stout at the same trick. A Turkish woman who called herself a princess had eaten with him for a month, then departed, her bill unpaid. The British officer contrived to borrow one thousand francs from Poggi, to gamble for him at Monte Carlo. The money had been lost, and the officer couldn't pay his bills.

Evenings, over Chianti, Poggi liked to confide his troubles, which made him chuckle, to the boys. The landlord wanted to get him out of the apartment, to raise the rent, but Poggi had a lease and declared he was putting the apartment to home use as his contract demanded. He had been successful in getting several shipments of wine from Italy without paying duty. Mrs. Poggi too had given the boys special meals on fete days. It had been very homey, with the added joys of boarding-house intrigue.

Sudge felt sour about his brother Pinky, who was to marry. The girl's family had found out that Pinky and their daughter were enjoying each other, and because Mr. Galbraith had wealth, clinched the occasion to bring about a marriage. Sudge simmered to think that his brother would now be granted three hundred dollars a month additional money and would also enjoy marriage. When Ross snorted that there'd probably be a baby shortly to cramp the groom's style, Sudge beamed and gurgled. Pinky had earned sixty dollars a month as a clerk for an insurance company, but because of marriage and influence was now to get a hundred dollars. "He couldn't earn fifteen dollars if they paid what he was worth," Sudge was sure. "But Dad's making more money on the stock market. He'll buy Pinky a directorship here and there, and soon Pinky will be one of the bright young commercial lights of Montreal, a brilliant, self-made go-getter. He doesn't know what anything's about, but neither does father. I nearly passed out in London, they were so boring."

Ross was worrying about what would become of him. Sudge seemed more prone to be "excited" by various girls than formerly, and his brother's marriage put ideas into his head. Should he marry, his father would also give him a much larger allowance. Ross admitted that his own family had influence. He might get diplomatic employment, and the university had granted him a degree as he had passed a special examination. It was therefore possible for him to get employment as a professor of English. Evidently his easy life in Nice had not caused his literary aspirations to flower into production. His interests would not awaken, however. He admitted that one shouldn't give in to a sense of futility, but remained scornful of decision and purpose.

Ross, who looked generally a fragile boy, had moments of suggesting a nerve-shattered old man, and less and less could he be away from Sudge without suffering desolately. He knew the rounds of cadging drinks. Sudge's money gave him leisure. Set adrift on his own, there was much chance he'd indulge the process of self-destruction through dissipation, and Sudge dolefully recognized this fact. Sudge was dismal about Ross's chances of ever arriving as a money-making writer. His stories would never interest a large public. They had an intimacy of revelation, the fuzzy, incoherent and inconsequential designlessness of introspective existence. They were held together merely by his neurasthenic irony. It wasn't intelligence he lacked, and many a good man in youth has been as directionless as Ross, but he pampered his emotions of despair. If action was suggested, he recalled the lives of Gibbon, de Maupassant, Stendhal, Van Gogh, intent on the wreckage which occurs in the lives of achieving beings. Ross had disdain and cynicism that might have hardened him, but it was all mental. He was another Hamlet, and all in Sudge that wasn't Hamlet Ross spoke scathingly of as vulgar or insensitive. During lunch several times I nearly asked Ross bluntly if he believed that his sentimentality about himself constituted sensibility, since his range of intellectual interests was small. Given Sudge and money to live on, Ross appeared to demand nothing more, imaginatively. Sudge realized that Ross could not and did not want to cope with any problem unless made to, and if forced he might crumple up and have nothing but sourness.

At tea time we sauntered to town and peeked into the English bar, little knowing what awaited us. There sat Laura Bradley, and surprisingly, with her, Rose Morgan. No sooner had we greeted and joined them than we realized that they were properly oiled and resentful about a variety of things. Rose's husband, Frank Penryn, had gone once too often to Vienna to be psychoanalyzed by Freud. For three years she had permitted him to return from these trips and try his hand at psychoanalyzing her, but now, she swore, she was being driven crazy and would stand no more of it. He accused her of having a grandfather complex, a father complex, a motherless child complex, an aristocratic communist complex. He told her that she was a drunkard, that she was unfaithful, intent upon sleeping with all the famous men of her time. He was furious whenever she failed to make this or that famous man, and now, so Rose declared, he was wanting her to take on the famous women of the day, too. If his own life couldn't be complete, that of his wife might as well be. It infuriated him that she wouldn't go to Vienna to have herself psychoanalyzed.

Knowing Rose, I wasn't impressed with the necessary truth of her story; but Sudge was sympathetic and understanding at once. Later, when she had told him that she was the granddaughter of a French marquise, the niece of Oscar Wilde, and showed him an emblem ring which was the last relic of her ancestors' former greatness, he looked a bit perplexed. She talked of Russia and communism and freedom; she cursed Frank's snobbish pretenses and demanded democratic simplicity; and she reverted to telling of the titled people she entertained in Paris. She was a revelation to me, and I wondered if Rose was actually going balmy. Always before a great woman with men, it was soon evident that she was sentimentally interested in Laura Bradley. One arrives at a state when it is difficult to be surprised. Still, Rose, while near forty, wasn't yet so aged or unattractive that she'd be driven to that sort of change of life.

Before we left the bar Rose had started an altercation with the owner. He tried to keep her from whispering something to Laura. Rose objected and backed the owner against the wall behind the bar. On her finger was a huge amethyst ring, and had she hit him, he would have certainly passed out. Her complaint was that he was a lower-middle-class bully, with lousy ideas about women. She hadn't liked his face from the moment she entered the bar. Sudge caught Laura's arm, and I Rose's, and we persuaded them to leave the bar. Rose, however, still shook a ringed fist at the bar owner, and mumbled her rage. I caught Laura's eye, and she grimaced helplessly, indicating, I guessed, that she would explain later how Rose had gotten into her present intoxicated condition. Before there had been rumors that Rose was a secret drinker, but never had I seen her so publicly drunk.

For years Rose had been known as beautiful, or pretty, with that extra *it* which made her appeal to men in general. Married to a man idealistic about social causes, she had gone in for them too, but after his death her own ideas and convictions were not strong. Then she married Frank Penryn, a millionaire and social figure, who fancied himself also as democratic and communistic in his ideas. So long as the ideas didn't affect his income, and Rose was ready to be dressily social at times, all went well. But Rose, having tasted bohemian life, found her taste for relaxation stronger than her love for social show. She wasn't a good hostess, and collected people most unsympathetic to each other when she did entertain, and her friends blatantly informed her of this fact. In all, since her radical-idealist husband's death, she felt herself a failure, and Frank Penryn hadn't the magnetism to attract people necessary to keep Rose among vital beings. Once, by following where her communist husband led, she had a name and reputation as a dramatic and adventurous person. She participated in labor fights, went to jail, and was pleased at the attention and flattery of men who often stood for everything she thought she resented. Being feminine and coquettish, she didn't reveal any hard cause-fighting aspects to men who flirted with her, whether they were capitalists or not. Finally, it was impossible to believe in her as a "great personality," but now that, apparently, Frank Penryn realized this, Rose was tormented, and believed that she must run amuck to make Frank understand that she was a liberated woman.

Outside, Rose seemed suddenly to become sober, and said that we must all have dinner with her at a de-luxe place. The idea wasn't pleasant, if she was going in for making scenes; nevertheless, Rose might act the grand lady if she was dressed for dining out in elegance. When she and Laura rejoined us, they looked expensive if not elegant. Laura's mink coat, and Rose's white fur cape, were disconcertingly expensive for what we might do in prosaic Nice. Rose wore a variety of jewelry which would make it unsafe to visit such dives as she was apt to insist upon seeing later in the evening.

"Call me Rose," she told Sudge when he called her Mrs. Penryn. "I want to forget Mrs. Penryn. You saw it coming long ago, Kit. He persuaded me at last to see Freud, and don't tell me that senile old idiot is a genius. He told me everything Frank had said, and didn't analyze me at all. How could he or Frank know what my grandfather was like? He died when I was five years old. Decent people don't talk that way or do such things. We just don't. And Frank decided later I'd love him more if he beat me. When he came in one morning with a switch and struck me, it was the finish. I called him a goddamned Boston banker, with low-class Jew blood. He got pale. His mother was a Jewess, so that he was never quite a real Penryn. Not one of them. That's the only reason he tried to deviate from his silly snobberies. I told him to get the hell out and go down to the butler who might appreciate his damn silliness. When I ran out of the house, I found Laura and said, 'Let's take a trip. I must be way.' And here we are. Let me have your drink."

Rose had not used to drink much, but now she took one straight brandy after another. She spilled cigarette ashes on her dress, but didn't care. When she put the cigarette to her lips, she smeared lipstick on her face and let it remain. Laura, worried, wiped the color from Rose's cheeks. Rose was in a state, and headed for a nervous breakdown, but would not stop drinking. Soon every remark brought giggles from her. "You don't like brandy, Kit? How funny. Ha, ha, ha. He doesn't like brandy. Kit's getting moral."

Laura was in a state, too. She revealed that her friendship with Colette was ended, and looked tragic. "She said I got jealous and tried to mastermind her. Imagine that," Laura drawled, and tittered. It came out later that Rose was going to Baden-Baden for a rest cure until her divorce was over. Possibly Frank was divorcing her, and might not be sporting enough to settle money on her. In that case it would be hard for her to readjust as a money-making journalist. New journalists were on the scene; her name meant little now, and she had hated journalism before. To return after escape and luxury made the horror of doing so multiply.

Rose ate only spaghetti which she fumbled with her fork, but Laura finally got her to take onion soup, part of a small steak, and green beans. Again she regained some poise, but felt recklessly gay. By saying that we could enjoy ourselves longer on gin and ginger ale, we kept Rose from pouring straight liquor into herself. Now the idea of playing with Sudge amused her. He looked so babyishly concerned and earnest, and Rose believed that he was "falling in love" with her. She believed this readily of any man.

In the washroom Sudge looked painfully concerned, realizing that both women were unhappy. "Can't we do something to keep them from getting into a muckish mess? Laura's so decent when she's sensible. She says they drove from Paris and raised hell. Rose takes a bottle of brandy to bed with her, and it's empty every morning. Her heart is weak, and she'll pass out."

"Let's take them to the Excelsior," I suggested. "We'll tip the Madame there to give Rose small portions of brandy if she won't drink beer. Maybe because I belong to the sort of world she knew of old she'll snap out of it. I hope her husband is not leaving her penniless."

"Would he?" Sudge asked.

"His vanity is wounded, and he is a snob. Hell, in Paris he always wanted to discover places where one could see vice elegantly stage-set, where aristocrats go. He wouldn't have it that vice joints are as dull as Christian

Endeavor meetings once one loses the idea that vice is thrilling. The bigoted, snobbish-puritan strain in him would demand something sumptuous and exotic once he decided he wasn't enjoying life without naughtiness. Rose earned this. Her Irish would rebel at his routine and she can't go on living with a person who bores her. Maybe she thought she loved him, but it was money and security that attracted her. She married him when things were shot to hell, with no lover there to bolster up what she thought were her convictions. When these emotional radicals lose their ideals, they go flatter than deflated bladders. Frank Penryn was always a playboy. At these times my skepticism has a positive value."

"Your what?" Sudge looked whimsical and snorted, but said no more.

The Excelsior was a dance cabaret for people of the groomed working classes. Entering, Rose bore herself as a gracious lady being democratic. However, she would not become maudlin before these people. A girl called to her merrily, "What a beautiful gown, and woman. You are charming, madame." Whereupon Rose, pleased, insisted on buying drinks for everybody seated in the small barroom leading into the dance hall.

The Madame of the Excelsior was a type; she was warped-faced, frailly decadent, and wore unique costumes. One shoulder blade was higher than the other, and she concealed a scar on her neck with a scarf wound about and thrown over the lower shoulder. Her face was an Odilon Redon sort. Her hair was natural gray, her eyes large and wanly pale-violet. In her emaciation she had distinction and elegance that have nothing to do with period fashion, a wraith-like quality. Clearly she was a woman of breeding. Her elegance was not the accidental chic of a common person. Sometimes she recited poetry and tales, and well. I had given her a book of Laforgue's poetry, and tonight she recited something of his. Her voice was wind-broken and rasped with febrile huskiness. Her thin-veined, attentuated hands made strange awkward-graceful gestures, which reminded one of Sarah Bernhardt's performances in her crippled old age: particularly when Sarah was carried onto the stage to stand on her wooden leg, eyes turned upward, as she quavered a passage from *L'Aiglon* in her penetrating insect wail.

Rose capriciously scoffed at my interest in *Madame la Patronne*, with whom I had talked frequently. She was a world-worn, world-knowing person, who first pleased me by laughing that I should think she ran this cabaret because she liked it. No, she needed money, and wished only to have enough to be lazily leisurely. Read she might, but any more active form of energy she valued not at all. Seeing that Rose was upset, she started her drinking beer by making our party her guests for the first round. "Madame is perplexed about situations in her life," she said as I stood handing beer from the bar to our table. "*Elle est une femme sentimentale.* Such women are difficult to cope with when they have riches, as she has, I see. She will always suffer emotions about the same kind of thing, never learning by experience, never knowing that ennui and resignation have their satisfactions."

Our party was happy. Others in the cabaret were working boys and girls who felt no feverish or hysterical need to appear needlessly gay. Some of the girls were dressed with that amazing style that French girls of their class achieve. One of them, dark and slender, danced beautifully, and had a dashing insolence. Rose tried to attract her attention, but she cut our table with her cold glance, resenting perhaps what she felt was our patronizing in coming to this place. The boys and me she knew and danced with, but she ignored Rose.

When Sudge was dancing with Rose, she caught my glance and smiled, patting his shoulder. Sudge had tried to be amorous and kiss her, and was disgruntled that she did not take his attentions profoundly. He was nearly six feet tall and well-proportioned, but his small chin, peering brown eyes, and baby skin made him look childish, as he would appear for some years. Try as he might he could not look the seasoned rake, or even an experienced young blood. That did not necessarily interfere with his success, as several older women had at times taken him home, tickled by his young boyness, and prone to believe him a virgin.

Rose stuck to beer, and later agreed to return to her hotel early, without protest. If she took a bottle of brandy to bed with her, she got it from the hotel. Anyway Ross and Sudge told each other that to take on worries about another's drinking habit helps nobody. They found Rose a nice woman, but were more worried about their old friend Laura. Things were perplexing and complicated. They were sure Laura and Colette had made a mistake to break up. Neither would find more satisfying relationships. The boys might have periods of dissipation, but they were most British in their unwillingness to be romantically hysterical.

CHAPTER THIRTEEN

THE BOYS WERE TOO MUCH IN DEBT TO POGGI FOR my help, and couldn't come on to Paris. Montparnasse, which always has gossip to supply, was swarming with histories and intrigues. At the moment no Quarterite's existence was complete unless he or she was playing a major or minor role in some history. Colette Godescard appeared to offer her version of events. Her catlike eyes revealed no torment. Colette took things as they came, and had few emotions or ideals to be displaced.

Laura had thought, Colette explained, that she was the original roaring girl and master-mind of their organization. In a volatile way Colette went one night with another girl, and two days later Laura retaliated by taking the same girl away from Colette. Rose Morgan had horned into the drama by wanting not to be alone after she left Frank Penryn. Colette then decided that she wanted a flier in men anyway, and took up with a young Frenchman. Naturally Hilaria was not to be left out of so much drama, and because Colette's young man had once been Hilaria's lover, Hilaria and Colette became very thick friends. Hilaria now had another young French lover, who upon meeting Colette became flirtatious. Hilaria didn't care, as she had spotted a Serbian boy who appealed to her. Finally, Colette, the two French boys, and an older doctor decided that Paris bored them. They were going to ship to Tahiti on a cargo boat, for adventure, and third class, but Colette was sure she could vamp the captain and be allowed to travel first class.

In Tahiti they might paint, do short stories and special articles, and surely have romance. Already Colette was sure the two French boys would have a duel over her sooner or later. She wasn't going to choose one or the other, and might throw them both over once aboard the ship, certainly if they cramped her style. Just now she was having regretful emotions over leaving Hilaria, who was a better roustabout and trouper than the men.

They got too serious about love. With Philippe Colette acted coy, talked baby-talk, and conducted herself as a helpless, clinging person, but with Hilaria she had more laughs in common. Few men could hope to understand their comedy so intimately and robustly as they understood it.

"Hell, I haven't had a man in three years," Colette confessed. "Hilaria's right. The girls make too many scandals and fuss over little things. They're all off me now because I'm not loyal to their sect. To hell with them. I'm myself, and want what I want when I want it. Why do they insist on a limited idea of what a person is? I don't give a damn about the bloody masculine or the bloody feminine. Things have to be different in my life. Every time I try to settle down and be a good girl things happen wrong, and I won't try anymore."

Hilaria hove into sight to greet me gaily, but soon she and Colette disappeared. When they reappeared, Hilaria presented Colette with a rubber bag and a set of instructions as to how to be careful in Tahiti and en route, but Colette knew that it would take more than Tahiti to get her into trouble. She planned to arrive there a rich woman, since she was doubtless to be the only passable woman on a boat full of lonely men. As long as she was going to sea she would be a sailor, and sailors don't care.

Some weeks before, Felix Lutyens had returned to Paris, alone, having kissed Sally goodbye, with the understanding that she would join him in a few days. Instead, trunks, suitcases, boxes of books, and wires demanding a divorce arrived for him. Sally had painstakingly packed all his belongings, even worn-out tennis shoes, underwear, and rubbish. If he did not submit to the divorce, she threatened to mention in court various fights and jails he had been in, as well as scenes he had made on her. Felix submitted, however, and solaced himself quickly by starting to live with Dale Burke; and Kate, Dale's sister, married Hal Meng. A great siege of mating took place in the Quarter, either first-mate affairs or rearrangements. The situation drove the celibate to other portions of town.

Gaylord Showman's kidneys were in a state so that he wasn't drinking and didn't appear on the scene. His mental condition was such that he found Paris too lousy to tolerate and even considered returning to New York, which he hated. Having been away from Paris for months, I soon saw his viewpoint. Nightly brawls occurred in each of the several bars, and the fights were not comic. They were witless, the result of antagonism nursed between various drunks over a long period. The presence of Jimmie at the Falstaff bar started a feud between its clients and those of a small smelly bar where Jimmie had once worked. Its patrons still wanted Jimmie as a barman, because where he was the trade went, and during the last two years their bar had lost caste. Both the *patron* and *patronne* were given to bad disposition, he because of stomach trouble from drink, and she because he bored her and she was sick of sitting at the cashier's desk to see that dull people didn't get away without paying their bills. She played bridge with a few regulars most of the time, and looked annoyed when clients came in for a drink and diverted her attention from the game.

Steve Rath had departed for America, and whenever Chloe Andrews appeared it was to wonder if she was going to be weak enough to follow Steve and take up with her again. She was in no shape to write articles for money; her apartment had yet to be paid for; her last book had been so poorly advertised that she got little from it; and she agreed with Colette: There were too many histories among the girls. The split between Colette and Laura had caused a clatter among all the ladies of that set. "Why must they make a cult of what they are or do? Why can't people do or not do things, as they want, without raising a hullabaloo?" Chloe moaned. "I daren't stick my nose out of my apartment, but when Tony Crane said you were in town, I decided I must see what that young one is up to. I'm fit for nothing but an old ladies' home, with a cat and a parrot to console me. I have the cat, but now it proves to be a male. I will have to have him altered. He smells. Poor darling. I would have to tamper with the love life of a cat in my old age. He has fleas. What is a woman to do? And I'm such a good, hardworking woman, too, but people won't believe I'm not fast. With my reputation I have to depend solely on character."

Chloe's woes were not new, and the English-speaking element of the Quarter was in a general uproar, so I cultivated French, Swedish, German, Serbian, and Russian comrades, so much that without improving my French accent, I gained hundreds of new words with which to disregard French grammar.

Whatever complications Tony Crane was sure to have in his life, he was a man with reserve, and not given to wailing for sympathy and advice. Meeting him at the New York bar I discovered he had plunged. For years he had talked of buying a place in the country, and tonight was driving out to look over an old mill which he had purchased. I went along, having talked romantically myself of finding a cozy place in the country where one could retire and become pastoral, away from the frenzies of city life.

Tony was remarkable in his ability to retain hope and trust in people. It was a rare week that did not bring him an idea for an invention, the combination of talents among various people, a movement to free artists and individuals, the original marketing of art wares, or the finding of subsidies to aid members of the advance guard. This night he was intent upon the possibilities of his mill home.

"It's wonderful, nothing less, that mill, Kit," Tony said. "I paid fifty thousand francs and it won't cost more than that again to get it into beautiful shape. Then we'll have a fine country château. There's a mill wheel, and the engineer says we can make it supply power for electricity, heat, and other things. I did think of raising geese, but hear that their droppings are so large they're a nuisance. I can't stand chickens. They're stupid fowls. Maybe I'll go in for bees, or ducks. There are just two acres, but as prettily placed as you could find. Two streams cut the property, with a waterfall, and the mill-stream is always deep with water."

Tony's mill was situated behind walls on the outskirts of a sleepy town which had changed little in fifty years. All its inhabitants appeared to have well passed the fifty-year mark. Where three seldom-used roads met, the L-shaped mill stood, two stories high, with sheds and barns of stone. "We can make rooms above the sheds and barns, if we need them," Tony said hopefully. "If necessary, we could entertain twenty to thirty guests at a time, or make it a community center for that group of selected civilized souls that Elihu Law wishes to collect."

"You're not going to start civil war and manslaughter in this mill by any chance, Tony. Most of Elihu's selected group aren't so chummy toward each other."

Two streams converged at the boundary line of Tony's property and a waterfall with a ten-foot drop led into the mill-stream. The water was clear and plentiful, but in the quiet upstream masses of water-weeds were thickly entangled. "Hell," I said spontaneously, not intending to blast Tony's hopes, "ten men couldn't lift this weed, it's so thick. You could have it cleared out every month and it would be back by the next month. This place will be ravaged by insects and mosquitoes in warm weather."

Tony gave me a pained look. We sauntered to the storage room where the mill-wheel was. It was old and large, but made of sound, enduring timber, though some of the wings were broken. Tony released the lever to let the wheel down and it started churning while tons of water rolled over it into the basin below. We watched mesmerized by the spectacle of water in motion. "There's power enough in that wheel to keep the weeds out of the stream," Tony said cheerfully. The mill had several rooms of good sizes. At the front, one was a large oblong, with high ceilings. Tony planned on building a huge fireplace to burn whole logs. We discussed the charm of sitting before a bright log fire. Outside the weather might be damp and miserable, but the room would be comfortably furnished, with rugs, a bearskin before the fireplace, with calvados or other sound liquor in a barrel at the side. It would be fine, too, to have a barrel of apples in the corner of the room, and a few pictures by various painter friends in whose talents one believed. Along one side of the room any number of books on shelves reaching to the ceiling would add atmosphere. The place would exist for sound hospitality, redolent with aroma and the ripe hostly emotions which this generation tends to disregard. We went finally to the village bistro to share a bottle of *vin de pays.* An octogenarian peasant hobbled in. Tony talked to the Madame of finding a peasant to plow his acres. We were among the really simple people, of the soil. One was detached from the chaos of cities and the inhumanities of a machine-industrial world where standardization reigns. We drove back to town in a glow, while I pondered the idea of getting a cot and table in the village and retreating to work in Tony's mill. The situation was ideal for tranquility, and the village bistro was my sort of place.

Two weeks later Tony said they had concluded that it wasn't practical to use the mill-wheel for power. The engineer advised putting in a turbine which might utilize water power. Tony further found out that already repairs on his property were to cost one hundred thousand francs. His enthusiasm had abated somewhat, and his wife said she couldn't see herself buried in the country yet. They still had to think of their little girl. She needed to go to school in the city, to meet people. Tony's vision of the mill now was as a summer vacation and weekend place. He had decided he wasn't a country man to the extent of wishing to bother with bees, ducks, or stock. To raise any of them would necessitate employing caretakers, and he still needed what salary he made for contemporary family expenses. I concluded too that the tranquilities of a secluded life in the country were for later years, when ardor pulsed less leapingly in a restless bosom. Before long Tony mentioned his mill no more, and did not believe they could spend even weekends there until the next spring. The mosquitoes were thick now, and oil poured on the water all flowed over the falls at once while the insects swarmed heartily voracious.

Rose Morgan returned to Paris and appeared calmly satisfied that freed from Frank she could take up sculpting. The first few times she appeared she drank little and went home early. One night, however, she did sufficient giggling to make one aware that she had been drinking again. As she came into La Coupole I was sitting at the bar alongside three *poules* who were old-timers of the Quarter. Since we were having drinks together I stayed with them. Laura Bradley came in and sat with Rose. Soon they asked me to sit with them, and tittered. When I joined them Rose said, "Kit and his whores. He gets on very well with his whores. They seem to like him."

"What have you against the whores, Rose?" I asked. "They merely get paid for what others often make an effort to give away, and you do believe in equal rights for women. They don't bother me with their problems, and they're not as dumb as lots of others about."

"Kit and his whores, he, he, he," Rose tittered, and Laura joined in. Shortly Rose was telling her repetitious troubles; when or if she and Frank wished to divorce each other they could do so, as others have done. My thoughts flew southwards. It was summer. I wanted the ocean waves soothing me as I swam far out, with the sun beating tan into my skin as I reclined lazily on the sand, unconscious of the problems of people who meant little to me, as I did to them. Rose was too experienced a person to be feline about the *poules*, and started immediately talking of her complications. No one but she and Frank was involved. Dear old friends as we might all be, we didn't so love each other that boredom was out of the question. One of the three *poules* who sat at the bar was a more detachedly intelligent and witty person than either Rose or Laura, and perhaps more moral than either. Frankly commercial sex is straight enough a business among the selective and fastidious *poules*.

Laura told Rose she had forgotten to take the key from her studio door, but nobody would be apt to go in. "You haven't the key, how funny," Rose giggled.

"No, I left it in the door. If the concierge takes it and I get in late, I'll be locked out," Laura responded, tittering. Rose wanted to know if I'd rather be with my whores, and tittered, as did Laura. The girls were in a state to find everything too ridiculously funny; their giggling made me aware that they were upset and being silly in an attempt to seem gay and uncaring.

Laura gave me a sheepish look after her giggles, admitting she saw I knew she felt bad. She had been having bad breaks lately. Her warm brown eyes looked sadly out of her gentle, boyish face. Hurt and dumbfounded, she could not understand why Colette and she were not together. She tried to seem indifferent when Colette was mentioned, or disdainful when Rose scoffed at Colette, but her face was too mobile to conceal her hurt. She was essentially an affectionate person, and grave. Inclined to make a habit of her fondness, it struck her as ruthless, and not real, that Colette was really away, and perhaps disliking her. They had been together four years, exchanging all confidences and problems, and within two days that changed, and they would not even speak to each other. Laura was sure Colette was acting abandoned out of bravado, to show her that she didn't care. She was not hard or gregarious as was Colette, whose rakish street-boy spirit had not been damaged by the break. Laura had, I knew, attempted suicide recently. Her attempt, of course, wouldn't have been successful. She didn't want death, but made the gesture in a hurt-child moment of despondency, thinking it would bring Colette back. Instead, Colette had been angry, and swore Laura would do some fool thing. It was little use trying to get Laura to act as she had a few months previously. Then she'd been able to take things as they come, with a sense of comedy and satire. She might respond with irony for a moment, but reverted to tittering her silly giggle, while Rose laughed inanely at every remark or incident.

Tony Crane came into the bar, preoccupied. As Rose was in the corner he did not at first see her, but sat at the table alongside me. Two newspaper editors to whom his syndicate supplied news were in town and wanted to be shown around. The weather was hot. Tony hated showing these men the obvious places which are designed for boob tourists, and he didn't know what at the moment were the popular hang-outs for old-time Quarter inhabitants. He asked about the Jungle, and a new Russian place, and wanted to avoid cabarets sweltering with either French students or American tourist mobs.

Tony and Rose had known each other for years, since their days in

Washington when both were new to journalism. Rouge was spread unevenly on Rose's cheeks. She had her hat pulled low on her forehead, and made no sign of speaking to Tony. When he at last recognized her, she glowered at him.

"What's the trouble, Rose?" Tony asked.

"Don't speak to me. You are not a loyal friend. I once thought you were, but you turn against me too. Imagine, Kit, Tony is siding with Frank and they want to put me in a sanitarium, to be cured. I know what that means. I am not insane. He's no friend of yours either, Kit. He just thinks he can use you."

"Rot, he has genius if he can find me very useful for either news or money. Don't be silly. How did Tony know that Frank had anything to do with the matter when your friend asked for the name of a good sanitarium at which you could rest?"

"He's no friend," Rose insisted savagely. "He stood and let Frank insult Laura and me in front of Laura's father."

"Rose," Tony argued, "how do I know what goes on between you and your husband? When I went that day to interview Mr. Bradley, Frank was there making a hysterical scene. I did know Miss Bradley was of age, and not under the control of her father. I knew nothing till then of any break between you and Frank. What was I to do?"

"You told Mr. Bradley that he was not to mind Frank. He was so much in love with his wife that he didn't know what he was saying," Rose replied.

"Yes, Mr. Bradley was so upset I thought he would faint."

"Don't believe him, Kit. He's no friend to anybody," Rose said.

"Rose, please! Why this passionate talk about friendship to Tony and me who know only your side of the affair with Frank? How did Tony know whether what Frank said to Mr. Bradley was so or not? You, Tony, and I know each other. We all know many people, and like many people, in passing. Why demand that others mess into your entanglements in the name of friendship? You aren't loyal to marriage and love. Why so intense in your belief that Tony should have knocked Frank down for creating a scene about his wife?"

"He sides with Frank, who takes the most impossible attitude toward me," Rose said, still glowering at Tony.

"I do agree with Frank that you are difficult, Rose," Tony said.

"Go away, at once," Rose commanded. "I won't have you near me."

"After all, Rose, this is a bar, and I came to see Kit."

"Go away. I order you. You should be treated like a servant." Rose was vehement.

"Please, Rose," I intervened, "Tony's at this table drinking with me and stays until we've finished. Don't be the haughty lady of the manor. I'd have acted as he did about Frank's scene making, and I suspect you didn't give him any better breaks than he gave you. At any rate it's yours and his marriage and entanglement, nobody else's."

"That from you, Kit. I thought you were my friend."

"I like you when you're not boring, but our knowing each other is casual enough. It's best that neither demand too much."

Tony and I went to the Falstaff as Rose was unbalanced. "Is she really going out of her head?" Tony asked, perplexed and irritated. "She always had a mythomaniac tendency. The other morning she told Molly she'd been riding in the Bois since six A.M., when her breath showed she'd ridden the bottle since the night before. She gave me a start, turning on me."

"Laura says she stows away two bottles of brandy a day. That would make her fancy things. It's too bad. She's a good sort when mildly reasonable."

"The affairs of her and Frank are all too passionately involved and impulsive for me. I guess I'm simple or normal. It may be a distinction these days. Maybe Rose remembers her first husband as a hero, and Frank doesn't suffice," Tony surmised.

"And maybe not. She claims not, and wandered a bit when he was still alive. She disclaims all the causes he fought for. I can't solve her. Jesus, is everybody going nuts? I'll be glad to go with you to show the visiting journalists the town . . . any part of town but this part. I'll be having delirium tremens if I go on seeing some of the things that are about here."

CHAPTER FOURTEEN

GAYLORD SHOWMAN NATURALLY COULD NOT quell his bibulous tastes and explorative impulses indefinitely. Without the urge of leaping spermatazoa his soul was adventurous and romantic, so when he appeared one night telling of a new Corsican restaurant in a neighborhood untouched by foreigners, his regained enthusiasm infected me. Through the days we explored strange parts of Paris and surrounding villages: Arabian, Persian, Algerian, Chinese, Turkish, and Greek restaurants and hang-outs. Gaylord had a genius for patois, argots, mimicry of types, and soon after appearing in a strange place, his loose mouth wabbling, dog-eyes floating dark fires, and elephant ears flapping, he was friends with the habitués. The place might look sinister, the types vicious and criminal, but before long they were buying him drinks, laughing at his burlesques, stories, songs, and sallies, and his quick ear soon caught voice inflections and patois so that shortly he spoke with the accent of his new friends. Later he was quite apt to become amorously affectionate, and then tearful, but his blubbering scenes passed and he was again hilariously comic.

Through the years I had learned to detect at what stage of drunkenness he would tell about his obsession that he was to become a victim of leprosy. By watching him look at himself in the mirror, I knew when he would cringe in fright, sure that a white leprous spot was growing on his hand. It took much argument to convince him that such was not the case, but the mention of Lili—sizable, dark, and luscious—caused him to forget leprosy while he bemoaned her faithlessness and final desertion. He had found her in a brothel, and loving her as an armful of juicy flesh, took her to live with him. She stayed with him for three years, and he believed her faithful. Even when he discovered that she went daily to the brothel, for money and because she was insatiable, he loved her. When one day she disappeared his heart was broken. That she took with her a sum of money, and several of his valuable possessions, was but a minor detail of this tragic love affair. Now, whenever he was drunk he still looked for Lili, or a dark, large girl of equal beauty who could replace her. That Lili had beauty only in his eyes no friend was ever unkind enough to tell him.

When Gaylord's parents were in town, he was fearful as a child of going home alone. Should he believe them to be out for the night, he might invite a friend to go to his studio, for drink, and to listen to him play the piano and sing bawdy barroom ballads, or to look at his paintings. Whenever he discovered that his parents were not out, his approach to the studio was elaborate. Weakening but still hopeful, he would open the door and call "Mother"; if there was a response he wilted, and turned, no longer dashing and irresponsible. Quickly he put out a limp hand and said "Good night" and disappeared. Well past thirty, Gaylord was cowed by either of his parents, or the idea of parents, as few over-punished children of five are.

Few people would believe in Gaylord as a painter of great talent. His clowning and fooleries, and his freak looks, kept them from allowing him to reveal the erudition and responsiveness to color and form that he possessed. Nor was he given to talking theories, whatever went on in his mind. When he seemed to be intellectualizing about theories, he shortly brought forth paintings which proved that he had first accomplished what he thought out, or felt. It is probable that whatever came from him in the way of intellectual impression had come to him more through his senses than through any processes of the reasoning mind. But only in his capacities for mimicry, clowning, burlesque dancing, and the use of argots did he reveal how responsive he was to visual, aural, or any sensuous impression. Except with rare people he was shy of serious moments or profundities.

However, in the past few years he painted most seriously, and his canvasses had a gay warmth, revealing human type and contemporary scenes which took in a good strip of life's panorama. It didn't please him if one commented on his humorous gusto, his irony, or his scope; then, gravely, he would lecture on paint, form, and technique, and the use of all subject matter merely to attain compositional velocity. The swarm and brawl—the gaiety, comedy, banality, or tragedy—of life he was ready to recognize as material for conversation and fooleries, but when utilizing any scene of whatever variety, he insisted that he used it as a painter only, to achieve a formal composition pleasing to the senses. He crammed his canvasses with figures, types, and details, because he loved details, but his cramming was gaily and neatly done, and if he worked over the expression on faces, it was because in so doing he was careful not to have this affect the painting's quality as a balanced production, done for its whole effect.

With me he was at ease, and he never accused me, as other painter friends have, of liking pictures for their literary qualities alone. Whatever his sympathetic tendencies were inherently, he would have it that he was interested in paint as an abstract medium. He fidgeted when someone talked much of Breughel, Hogarth, Goya, Carpaccio, or any painter intent upon caricature, periods and fashions, or representative scenes. As deep as his obsession about leprosy was his fear that his interest in paint was not finally formal and abstract. "M-m-my p-p-painting is d-d-d-dangerous for conservatives," he stammered, "because it looks all right to them, but upon investigation they're afraid they're deceived. It's too g-g-goofy for them. They th-th-think I'm a primitive, an innocent, naive boy, and th-then they get scared I know art history and what I want to do after all."

Generally his paintings were of cafe, sea-town, and fete-day scenes and types. In them one saw the hard-faced bourgeois merchant, the robust leather-skinned wine-shop madame, the inmate of a bordello, drunken sailors en masse, pernod-drinking old soaks, bronchial-voiced veterans of the wine bottle, fanatics of the chess tables, beet-hued bar *patrons*, comfortable from imbibing their own wares, street scenes, mountain villages, or whatever might serve to document and record. He was right, however, in declaring that he used all these for form effects, and brightly, architecturally, with the added use of color and movement. Not to limit himself he essayed the lyrical, did flower compositions which had an ethereal gaiety, mating doves, pompously amorous, and a few surrealist paintings into which anything—clothes, tools, machinery, faces, shop windows, wire, or vegetables—might seem to be tossed to land where they would. He hoped that even in these he kept all things "inside the canvas" as a composition.

Showman's father doubtless made Gaylord keenly aware that he must be able to talk about the why and wherefores of his work. Certainly Showman Senior let his son know frequently that he'd supported him for years, and that soon he should be arriving as a famous artist. Both his father and mother believed implicitly in him, but this did not prevent them from criticizing his efforts. Showman Senior was Jewish. He had made his millions as an agent for second-class theatrical talent, and he had a theater man's insistence upon recognition to prove attainment. Each year he told his son that he would supply him with an allowance for but one more year; then he must shift for himself. Each year Gaylord suffered deep despair, planned exhibitions, painted in a frenzy, and, as soon as his parents were away on a trip, indulged in drink heavily to regain hope. It was useless to assure Gaylord that his father would never desert him. Both his mother and his father depended too deeply on Gaylord to bring interest into their lives to leave him stranded. When Gaylord presented talented friends to his father, the old man relaxed, became a jovial comedian, talked of doing whatever he could to help young talent, and disappeared early enough from any appointment not to be confronted with the possibility of paying their drink bills. He too had belatedly discovered talent in himself, and made money designing patterns for oil cloths, wallpaper, rugs, and soap wrappings. While not wishing to have Gaylord demean himself by doing petty commercial art, he held in reserve the idea that Gaylord too might make money from such designing work.

These days Gaylord talked constantly of varying life. He no longer found Paris fit to live in. The Quarter had become lousy with people who had neither talent nor appreciation, nor even the awareness of their lack. He heard that in Portugal it had been found necessary to pass a law, even in Lisbon, that people wear shoes on city streets. The police there, he understood, were unable to enforce the law. Gaylord longed for a glimpse of simplicity, and the primitive. The mention of insects, poor food, bad accommodation, unhealthy water, with possible bandits in the mountains of Portugal, did not lessen his ardor. He brushed aside such suggestions with the assurance that two such as us could rough it. He knew furthermore that he would soon pick up enough Portuguese to venture safely into the wildest backcountry. If Portugal proved a delusion, we could get on a boat and do a roughing-it trip into strange portions of the world. About that we had talked frequently, as both of us were sure that cities and conservatism offer few advantages to imaginative people.

Gaylord's liver got in bad state again, and he sank into black depression, hopeless of ever getting to Portugal or of becoming a humanly sociable drinking man again. His wail drove my thoughts to Theoule, my tiny fishing village, where one encountered few "bohemians" or "intellectuals," and evaded soul-probing, art-scolding, and truth and religious and spiritual researchings.

A new American bar was opening in the rapidly changing Quarter. The night before I went south I spotted The White Pelican and took a look-see. As I was the first client, the *patron* offered me a drink, hoping to have me bring him clients. The Groper family passed by and, seeing me, came in. The patron invited them to drinks, too. The Gropers were Mr. and Mrs. and Frederica, that is, Poodie, Moodie, and Freddie. With them was Clan, their wire-haired terrier. They were new blood in the Quarter, and good companions with whom to avoid the innumerable sorrows of old-timers. Poodie didn't know what things were about around here, but he was reasonably game to find out; Moodie "wished she had charm," or had awakened earlier to the possibilities in life; while Freddie wondered, didn't know that her parents did right to plant her in Montparnasse at seventeen, but was drily tolerant of her parents' immaturities. She was high-minded, and was not to be taken in by the mangy Montparnassians. Clan followed where he was led. He didn't give a damn so long as there were enough posts to lift a leg against.

A few nights before Poodie had eyed me suspiciously, but allowed Freddie to go dancing with me. When she did not get home till five in the morning, he was worried and taxed her severely. When I assured him that Freddie couldn't have dragged me from Montmartre with a herd of elephants, so that her late incoming was all my fault, he gruffly accepted a drink, and later decided I had no evil designs on his darling child.

While admitting her youth, Freddie had firm convictions. Blond, she was healthy with ripe youth, and if told that she was a Botticelli girl was sure that whatever her appearance she was more sensible than poetic. However, Freddie did not take into account her sentiments about Harlen Winter, the young man who was the guide and solace of Moodie whenever she didn't know what next to see or do in France. Harlen was, Moodie declared, "so sensitive. I don't know whether he isn't too fine to adjust in America."

Moodie intended to be gay this night. She had an absinthe and talked of having another, ready to get spiffy. Eminently amiable and sympathetic, Moodie and Poodie were taking a long-planned year abroad after twenty years of dutiful, hardworking life, in which Poodie made fair money as an advertising illustrator, always hoping for the free days when he could paint what he wanted.

There was much they wanted to see: châteaux regions, cathedrals, frescoes in Italian churches, the galleries in Venice, Rome, Florence, and wherever. Harlen Winter had written Moodie of the Dordogne valley with its châteaux, far more beautiful than the châteaux of the Loire. Betty Winslow had talked of Provence and the Basque countries. Harlen was sensitive to beauty; Betty was a brilliant and travelled woman. Moodie knew what she had to see before she returned to America. Poodie said, "Yes, if the money holds out."

Looking through the door, Moodie was appraisingly abstracted, regarding a real French scene, Le Grande Chaumière terrace, with its evening group of aperitif drinkers. "I was just thinking that is the sort of thing Van Gogh liked to paint. Poodie, how would he do it, do you think?"

"There she goes," Poodie said irreverently. "Now Moodie, drink your absinthe and we'll decide how Van Gogh would paint that when we have more green in our eyes. Do you know, Kit," he turned to me, "Harlen Winter writes that we must not miss the Carcassonne. He writes such a poetical letter. He is sensitive, with such a delicate appreciation of beauty."

"Poodie!" Freddie sulked and then stormed. "Stop teasing Moodie about Harlen. I think you're mean. You know very well he told us of things to see that were what we came over to look at. I hate you when you imply that Harlen is a sissy."

Poodie subsided in chagrin, very vulnerable when his daughter attacked him. He tipped me a wink, however. "Now Kit, you see those bottles over the bar; how do you think Matisse would paint them? They have a Cezanneish waggle. Barman, give us another round of drinks. Jolly old England, boys, hearts of oak. I say, chappie. Drink up, girls. The old man has to go back and earn some more money soon. Let's forget while forgetting's to be had."

Moodie smiled tolerantly, and for a moment wasn't serious, but she did have to ask about Carcassonne. When I told her that the place was ghastly, like the moving picture set of a medieval walled city, she looked at me analytically. "Kit, I like you. You are amusing. I do wonder, though, if you are really sensitive. Both Harlen and Betty Winslow were enthusiastic about Carcassonne."

"Give up, Kit," Poodie said. "You wait. I'm getting a car. We'll see Carcassonne yet. We'll pick you up down South and let you guide us on an auto trip, but you might as well know that Carcassonne is on the itinerary. Harlen says so, Betty says so, Moodie says so, Freddie says so, and Poodie goes. He's the old meanie to talk about Harlen and Betty. Beastly old blighter. Jolly old England, hearts of oak, boys. Moodie hated London worse than I told her she would. So bloody sporting and jolly and conservative and refined. 'But you don't really find running water healthy in your sleeping rooms, my deah. Oah, I understand—in America. But in England we are very set in our ways, and you know, in our way we muddle on through.' Jolly old England."

Poodie's face wrinkled beneath the remnants of his ash-blond hair. Moody and Freddie responded to his hilarity without bothering to discipline him now. The Gropers didn't belie their name, but they groped in sympathy with each other generally. Freddie would have it appear that she was the most seared and cynical of the three. She attended art classes and knew young men who could disdain all art before Cezanne beautifully. They even knew easily that Picasso was merely facile and clever. At the moment these boys, and Freddie, had elected Derain as the profound painter. Freddie could look at a picture and value it as nothing quicker than Joseph Duveen. What she didn't know about painting she didn't know she didn't know, so her calm was unruffled, before Moodie, Poodie, and myself. Harlen Winter, it seemed, could throw her into qualms of confusion which made her not at all positive.

The boys appeared. Ross was very red in the face, and both he and Sudge were unkempt, for them. They had just arrived from Nice, and had been drunk since leaving there. It was natural to think that Sudge at least might take to Freddie, who was near his age. Having grown up in New York among fair-liberals, she was an aware child, and inclined to believe herself incapable of conversing with anybody much under thirty. It was soon clear, however, that she and Sudge did not impress each other. Freddie informed me quietly that she knew both the boys were neurasthenics: Ross had no will or character, and Sudge was just mediocre. She knew too that as soon as they were alone they'd mock anybody they knew. Sudge later snickered about Freddie and pretended to believe her thirty years old, only claiming to be seventeen so that her mother could pass as younger. It had upset him for a moment when assured he thought this only because he knew Freddie had snooted him.

Agreeing to join me down South if I located a villa for them, the Gropers departed. "How did you leave Poggi?" I asked the boys.

"Through the back window and owing him one hundred fifty dollars," Ross snorted, ashamed but being mirthy out of bravado. He was scraping his left hand with bitten fingernails till they had drawn blood. His hands shook pathetically. All of the senile quality of his youth was uppermost. There was none of his rosy beaming merriment. His face was alcohol-flushed, and he was worried.

"What do you mean?"

"We picked up a girl a few weeks back, and she moved into the room next to ours. None of us had money to pay Poggi at last. We went to Monte Carlo and Sudge gambled. The girl, Sanka, had just enough money to get us to Paris, so we came."

"How did you get away from Poggi's?"

"We packed all our things in trunks, and came back at midnight. His rooms are in back, so he didn't hear us getting our luggage. Then we drove to the station, and here we are." Sudge chuckled, but his mirth was mere nervousness.

"That's a cheap stunt to pull on poor old Poggi. He set you up to many a drink, and charged you damn little for your board."

Sudge's baby face grew long. "I know. I hated doing that on Andy Gump, but we owed money at Maxim's and another cabaret. They'd probably have had us in the can before long, and Dad wouldn't send me any more money. I'll send Poggi the money if I can make it here."

"Who's the girl?"

"We found her on the seafront, and she wanted to come and live with us. She's a good sort. I say she's my stepsister."

"You and your little tarbrush stepsister," Ross said bitterly. "We did muck up a good situation in Nice in taking her on. She's a slut. We told her about you, and she'll try and make you now. I found her first, but Sudge had to horn in." He was still scratching his hand, and winced when I pushed his hand aside to make him stop.

"Hell, if you go to Poggi's while you're down South, don't let him know where we are," Sudge said, but he knew I wouldn't squeal. In my superior age I registered disapproval, but I'd slipped out of boardinghouses in earlier days also. I'd have thought myself a rich man to be able to owe a hundred fifty dollars at Sudge's age.

"You might have told Poggi you were broke. He'd have let you come on, hoping you'd send the money later. He'll look funny when he sees his birds have flown."

"We left two overcoats and a trunk," Sudge offered as restitution. "I know it was a crummy stunt, but what were we to do?"

"You didn't slip anything over on people I introduced you to, did you?"

Sudge spoke of Miss Whitman, an elderly Scotswoman I knew. "She guessed we were in trouble, and was worried because she hadn't money to give us. It was she who bought our meals and saw us off on the train. She didn't know we weren't paying our bill."

"Come on, she guessed. That woman's canny. She's too hard up to try and pay your bill, though."

"Poggi's getting used to Russian and other refugees who get away without paying their bills." Ross tried to be amused.

"You've ruined what faith he had in young boys."

The boys snickered unduly, sad in their attempt not to appear helpless. They'd doubtless got themselves into other jams in Nice. "How many bills do you owe there?" I asked.

Sudge was more frightened than remorseful. "I don't know. Sanka owes Madame Excelsior a thousand francs. She pretended a watch she left was valuable. We owe bills at four bars, too. We had to get out of Nice."

"You haven't passed any bad checks? Is there anything the police can track you for?"

"I don't think so. We got drunk so often the last week I don't know what we were up to, and Sanka doesn't give a damn what she does."

"What made you decide you liked drinking so much?"

"Sanka's a slut," Ross said. "One night she'd tell me she loved me, and stay with me, and the next day she'd be all for Sudge. We fought over that hussy."

"You'd better get your *cartes d' identité* up to date. The police don't mind deporting foreigners once they get on their trail. Old Poggi won't likely have you traced. He doesn't want police investigation himself. The cabarets are used to being gypped too. You didn't steal anything?"

"Oh no," Ross said. His eyes grew large with surprise and reproach.

The boys went to their hotel to clean up. Having no money they were in one room with the girl, whom they shared. I loaned Sudge two hundred francs and said they could move into the studio but not take Sanka with them. I wanted no tricks played on the concierge, who was a fine old woman, easy to impose on, and far too useful to have ruined by mistreatment.

It was eleven that night before I saw the boys again. Sanka was with them. She wore a coonskin coat, and looked like a plump little mulatto wench, though her hair was light brown, and her skin white. Sudge was sure, however, that she had no Negro blood. Her voice, too, had a Negro flapper timbre. As soon as she came into the bar she started throwing loose coquetry and sex appeal to whoever wished to respond.

Sanka was a product of release, perhaps in Harlem, Greenwich Village, or just speakeasies. She looked no older than her avowed nineteen, but a more loosely voluptuous face could not have existed among the decadent Romans. It was the face of a person without discrimination, and born to abandon. Vice was merely what she would naturally drift into. At once she revealed phrases used among free souls who talk of self-expression because they have no thoughts to express. Sudge and Ross looked apologetic and left her with me while they wandered into various bars to see if anyone they knew was about.

Sanka ogled me, and giggled confidingly as she squirmed nearer. Her speech was a strange combination of well-bred English and flippant slang. "Sudge tells me you're clever. He thinks you might like me. It'd make me feel good if you did. I got an inferiority feeling and always get scared I won't be liked."

"Sure, Sanka, you'll do," I said, but she was ogling Gaston, the barman, planning to become friendly with him for free drinks. In her coonskin coat she looked more a soft-faced anthropoid maiden than a being far up on the evolutionary scale. Before long, she had her foot on the rung of my stool, and was pressing my leg, while assuring me that she wasn't promiscuous or whorish. "I just like who I like, and I'm not a teaser. What I do isn't so very bad, whatever you hear people say."

"You believe in love, though, don't you, Sanka?"

"What did Ross say about me? He's furious at me. I ought not to horn in on those boys. They're chums and friends. Each of them thinks he's in love with me, and last night I told Ross it was him I loved. He's mad at me because I flirted with Sudge all day. They're too young for me. I'm no older than they are, but I like older men who know what everything's about. I feel sorta lousy horning in on them, because—I didn't see it at first—they're in love with each other. Ross is with Sudge, anyway, and I just mess things up. I gave them all the money I had. It got us here. I won't get more allowance for two weeks, but I don't care. I'll get on. I know people on the Right Bank, and can cable father to send me more. He's fond of me and afraid not to send money if I insist. I'll go home with you tonight; should I?"

"That's to be considered, Sanka. I go south tomorrow and may not bother to turn in at all tonight. I take an early morning train."

"Don't you like me?" Sanka appealed. As a loose and indiscriminate tart she had her attractions, but she still was on that honest woman side of the line, and so had no card giving even mild assurance of her health. It was best to ignore her slight appeal to the lower senses.

Sudge and Ross returned, and Sudge soon went away with Sanka. Ross looked embittered, and kept glancing toward the door with a hunted wolf air. "Where did he go with that little slut?" he asked.

"To the College Inn to dance. Sanka said she wanted to hear jazz, and sing some blues."

There was dry blood on Ross's left hand, which he scratched constantly and unconsciously. Such a mixture of pathetic and fragile boy and soured broken old man was distressing to regard. There was not health or tense reflex action in him. He was born old, ancient physically. As he went to the door restlessly to peer across the street, his body looked like a frail old man's.

"Be calm, Ross," I advised. "They'll be back. Sudge won't ditch you for the tarbrush. You've all drunk so much you can't see things straight, but Sudge knows she's sloppy."

"To hell with them both," Ross said savagely. "I have to make a decision. I can't go on living off Sudge. We fought like hell last week, and he almost struck me. I'll go back and be a cheap clerk in some office." He snarled in bitterness of defeat as he spoke. One wondered how deep his emotion for Sudge was, detached from the fact that Sudge's small allowance did give him economic security, however trifling. It was the first remark he had ever made to me which indicated that he knew himself a drag on

Sudge's freedom. It was also the first time, obviously, that a fear clutched him. Before he had sublimely believed it impossible that Sudge did not need him and want him.

"But Sudge can't make up all your life, or you all his, unless you both want your existences miserably limited."

"It's money." His voice was harsh with soured resentment. "We wouldn't have to be together every hour of every day, talking over only ourselves, if we had enough money. At that our lives aren't as crummily stupid as Sudge's parents'. Poor little Sudge. He doesn't know what he wants. I don't want to break with him. He so damn beautiful to watch." His voice was flooded with soft tenderness again.

"Maybe Sudge feels what he wants more than you grant. He's hampered by feeling responsible for you, and that's hard on him, at his age. He isn't past childhood, and has to pretend maturity and competence, for you both."

"What did he say?" Ross asked, fright growing in his eyes.

"That you criticized whatever he did, and grew resentful if he suggested the finances were low when you were tormented and wanted a drink. He swears he's always careful to say 'our money' rather than 'my money,' so he thinks you're unfair to accuse him of trying to make you feel like a leech."

"To hell with him!" Ross turned violent. "He'd be festering away with that cheap family of his if it wasn't for me. He wouldn't know anybody if it wasn't for me. He'd be married to some little slut like his brother is by now."

"Supposing that is his natural destiny? He seems to scorn his father enough, and his millions. No one could laugh with more ruthless contempt at the recent newspaper article on his old man as a forceful and broad-visioned Canadian patriot. It's no matter for great wonder, though, if he feels fed up about his own affairs now."

Ross might have been declared a true product of the after-war generation, but it's probable he was another repetition of a biologic-psychologic type which exists and recurs. In his mental attitudes he had no patience with the lost-generation, barren-leaves-on-the-wastelands apprehension of life. Somewhere in him was hardness and disdain. His attitude toward Sudge was perhaps not so much sentimental as calculating. He wanted, maybe needed Sudge, but, more important, he intended to avoid coping with economic situations if he could. At times, his belief in himself as an artist was so supreme and his contempt for money as any kind of standard so complete that, however he solved the economics of life, he was justified to himself. But now he was merely a helpless wreck. Restless in his misery, he left me, surely to look for Sudge.

Sitting on the terrace among a group of tourists was a successful stockbroker who had once lived in a mangy rooming house next to me. We recognized each other, but the people with him looked bible-belt-minded to me, and I wasn't sure he wanted them to know he was acquainted with me as I might show the effects of drink. However, he came into the bar, and his apology informed me that he'd feared to speak to me before, afraid I'd think him too low-brow to remember. Evidently he had decided I couldn't have become the sort of fellow who'd cut a man he'd been drunk with. I explained that I was concerned his party would disapprove of me; we had a drink together, and joined his party on the terrace. There the ladies supposed that we in the Quarter thought them Mrs. Babbitts and too unintelligent to bother knowing. One of them admitted that she "wasn't clever herself but adored bright people." Of course she didn't drink much, but in Paris she was slipping a little. There is never any use trying to explain what one may actually feel or think to people who have preconceived notions of what every person about the Quarter thinks. I drank the drinks offered me, and said I'd probably soon be back in the States to live for a while. The remark was only conversation. I had no belief I'd settle down anywhere for many years.

"O'Malley," Bromson said, looking bothered, "somehow I hate to think of your doing that. I'm stuck, but it's good to think I know somebody who sticks by the banners. Every year I say I'll collect a few more coupons, and come over here to live cutting coupons. But I don't suppose I ever will."

"No, Bromson tells me you've been here ten years. Why would you retreat now?" a middle-aged man said. What the banners were they thought I stuck by, and from what I would be retreating, I couldn't know. I did know my remark had been wily enough to keep the party from proving to me how we deracinated exiled expatriates weakly fled from reality to the disintegration of European life. Still, they did discuss what Europe did, and what America did, to people, and talked of this or that sort of thing as typical of here or there. It was a discussion in which one could say little. Where had expatriates come from and why, and why did so many come and go back, and mainly where did this group get the idea that the Quarter originated types? It might be an easier place for lost souls to exhibit their lostness, but that sort of exhibitionism is indulged in anywhere. It was good to see Sudge and Sanka coming across the street, intoxicated, heading toward me, undoubtedly to discuss Ross. They would not indulge in generalizations or tags. Ross was a definite problem and would not be placed readily.

Sudge was drunker than I ever saw him, but he was merry and inclined to be quippish. "We're going to be married," he said chirpily, his head wobbling, and his lips making him look comically a dazed bird. "I want to be married. You be our best man, Kit."

"We'll get a license and be married tomorrow," Sanka tittered. "Won't Sudge make a cute husband?"

The older women exchanged glances to register protective fear for the young boy in the clutches of an impossible girl. They were calmed when assured that quick marriage in France is hardly possible, but they wouldn't have it that boys get into drunkenness and messes quite as much elsewhere as in loose Paris. Sudge looked and acted like a fifteen-year-old, cute in his drunkenness, and elaborately polite toward the older people, with the politeness he used on dull people he disdained as belonging too much to his father's kind of world. Sanka revealed more knowledge of Sudge's family than she had previously. Sanka was hard to appraise. She wasn't talkative when Harlem was mentioned, but she talked freely of Chicago, of theatrical circles in New York, and of various racy young men. I guessed that she was the daughter of a rich white man by a mulatto mother, of whom Sanka said little. "I don't like her, and won't talk about her. Sure, I can get money so Sudge and I can marry. If Dad doesn't send it when I cable, he knows what I can do. He's fond of me, but he's careless. So am I. Sure, he has plenty of money."

The older people left by one o'clock. There appeared no incentive for me to stay up through the night and take the train south sleepy enough to doze through the boring trip. Sudge, however, didn't want to be left alone with Sanka. He knew Ross would be along and make a scene which I might prevent. Ross did show up before I could leave. He was sullen and sulky, but pretended to chuckle when Sudge and Sanka talked of getting married. Sanka would handle Sudge, and Ross fidgeted. Suddenly he exclaimed, "You're a bitch. Yesterday you said you loved me, and now it's Sudge, and you tried to make Kit."

"Sure, I like all I can get," Sanka said gaily.

Ross jumped at Sanka and caught her throat, or possibly he merely pushed her. At any rate, her chair was turned over, and she slipped to the pavement. Sudge rose quickly and struck at Ross. "That's a nice way for a gentleman to act," Sanka said. Her accent and manner now were surprisingly ladylike and reserved. "I knew you were no gentleman. You don't even make a good gigolo, so strike me if you want to. I'm not hysterical, and am sorry for you." Her well-bred boarding-school manner and her reliance on dignity at that moment were amazing, coming from her.

Sudge and Ross stood in front of the cafe gesticulating in each other's face. "I told you not to hit me. You said you'd never hit me," Ross wailed, tears running down his cheeks.

"You shouldn't have hit Sanka. I didn't want to hit you. Are you hurt?" Sudge said, taking his handkerchief to wipe the blood off Ross's face below the eye. "My ring cut you." Sudge began to cry. "Ross, precious, forgive me. You know I didn't want to hit you. You know I don't care for her. It's you I love, but you don't leave me alone, ever. I want to take care of you, but you don't work, and you don't let me know anybody."

"To hell with you," Ross said viciously. "I won't stay in the room with you two tonight." He swaggered toward the Dôme, not so much wistful now as rather skulkingly bad-tempered.

"I have the key and he has no place to stay. I hit him," Sudge sobbed. Sanka and I exchanged glances, and she was sheepish. She patted Sudge's face and shoulders when he sobbed against her. Now she was maternal and protective, and looked ashamed. "Sudge, baby, I'm not horning in on you boys. I just like fooling and having a good time."

"I hit him, I hit him," Sudge wailed. He leaned over and put his head on my shoulder and kissed my cheek, needing to cling to someone he knew for solace.

"You're a good friend, Kit. You know how Ross isn't fair about anything when he's in a temper. I hit him." Sudge kept weeping like a five-year-old. "I loved you like hell once, Kit, but you would think I was only a little boy. You look after Ross, won't you? I know it made you angry when he said all you were good for was to pay our bills, but I didn't think that."

Sudge's last remark was a new one on me. It hadn't occurred to me that Ross had that attitude, and he'd never expressed it in my conscious presence. I patted Sudge, and looked at Sanka in chagrin, indicating that I'd try to find Ross and send him and Sudge to the hotel together, while she and I drank on through the night. Sanka didn't arouse any emotion of admiration or affection in me, but clearly she had no evil intention to ruin the boys' friendship. She was merely silly and loose, and her sympathies were easily stirred. "Buck up, Sudge," I said, "Ross will come around. He can stay at the studio, or you can. Maybe you hadn't better see each other anymore tonight. You'll be hitting each other again, and since it breaks both your hearts, why do that?"

"I want to get married, but who will look after Ross if I do? Sanka wouldn't mind if he stayed with us, but most girls would."

"Rot, you don't want marriage at your age."

"It would look better, and people wouldn't have rotten ideas about Ross and me."

"You and Ross can't stand the kind of people who bother about having rotten ideas, so what do you care? You have no need to explain to anyone if things are right as you feel them."

"And I only want to take care of Ross so he can write. He'd die doing any work he can get," Sudge wept, overcome again. "I don't know how to go on helping him. We have done nothing but fester for six months. He didn't even try to write. You take care of him tonight. Tell him I love him, and we'll forget what has happened and move into your studio tomorrow."

"You're talking, Sudge," Sanka said. "And I'll see friends on the Right Bank and not come over here for a week, and then I'll have a lot of men with me."

"All right, Sudge," I said. "I'll have a beer at the Dôme and look out for Ross. He can come to my hotel and get the key to the studio."

When located Ross was mild and knew that Sudge had only struck at him to keep him from hitting Sanka. We started toward my hotel beyond the Gare Montparnasse. "I have to make a decision. I'll catch the first boat to Canada and get a job," he laughed bitterly. "And be a goddamned clerk or bookkeeper. Sudge can go back to his family and be known as a commercial genius off inherited and graft money."

"You might do better, later," I said mechanically.

"But Sudge shouldn't have hit me." Ross came back to his grievance.

"Really, if he likes Sạnka he couldn't sit and watch you choke her."

"Oh to hell with you," Ross said savagely, and swung away to stalk back toward the Dôme. He refused to turn when I called. It was only three o'clock, but I decided I wanted a few hours sleep. Ross could come to the hotel for the studio key, and if he didn't, he had spent other nights out in the name of entertainment. In any case, his fragile and wistful quality was either not operating or my sense of humor made me see the situation as comic rather than as essentially tragic. Mere pathos ceases to appeal to one's protective impulses.

CHAPTER FIFTEEN

THE SEA OFFERS COMPANIONSHIP, AND ON STORMY days its sonorous mutterings and roars inspire desolate emotions which have a profound appeal to the aesthetic sensibilities. In Theoule one could live easily. During the day fishermen drew in their nets to reveal a variety of fish, octopus, gaping gelatinous brutes, and masses of sluggish seadogs. Nights the fishing boats reconnoitered the bay, their torchlights popping up and disappearing with the wave rhythms in the mist. Beneath my window was a huge rock, in the hollow of which waves pounded and made gurgling roars. At first, awakening me in the strange room, they had dread portent, but soon these noises were company. Below the balcony the fishermen had a wooden table upon which they ate their meals. Beneath the rock they built a fire to cook their food. One old fisherman could flop a full pan of whitebait without losing a fish. He delighted in having someone praise his skill, and looked up to show how nicely crisp the fish were on both sides. "*Pas mal, non?*"

Dockie had gained size and personality since I had seen him four months ago. His mother was a small black bitch who walked jerkily because a stray rock had broken her spinal cord. This did not ruin her vivacity or popularity with other dogs in town, and the Theoule dogs lead more imaginative lives than the bourgeois human inhabitants.

Still a puppy, Dockie was already twice his mother's size, with nonchalance and supreme belief in himself. His father was a sizable hunting hound, and he had taken after that gentleman. His paws were still twice too large for his frame, so that he bobbed up and down, and rolled left and right, in his gait. While good-natured, he didn't care much about being fondled, and he disdained puppy cringings. An older police dog liked him, but one day, when Dockie was too insistently playful, the older dog snapped at him, and continued the attack. Dockie retreated not an inch. At once he bared his teeth and countered the attack savagely, angry indeed that any dog should presume to impose on his seemingly easy-going disposition. I grabbed him to safety, having sympathy for beings who have little discretion. After that Dockie decided that the kitchen employees were beneath him, and came to my room nights to sleep. Dockie was well bred. At seven he waited for me to wash; then we took a stroll to the beach where it was understood I was to sun myself while reading or swimming till lunch-time. Once on the beach Dockie's social duty toward me was accomplished, and he wandered about investigating smells until other dogs arrived for their daily consultation. Dockie was the only dog in town who dared venture into the preserve of Sultan, a vicious, solitary wolfhound. Sultan didn't even attempt to discipline Dockie, and would even exchange smells with him now and then.

For a dog who was hardly likely to develop into a Casanova, Dockie had an amazing appeal to all the other town dogs, though he was quite unawakened to the wonders of sex. His lumpy body got all tangled up with his feet, and he generally liked leisure. He was a lazy dog who would develop into a vagabond lover at best. At moments he pranced a bit, but gradually subdued his activities to a sagging walk down the beach. Once he saw Sultan involved with a lady dog, and it puzzled him only until a flea on his ear needed discipline. Then he walked away, forgetting all that silly business.

Other people came to the beach. There was an aged American woman who was *folle*, the bistro madame said. She had gambled away a fortune at Monte Carlo, wore sandals, a bright wrapper, a hat with a jaded ostrich plume, and came to the beach carrying a basket from which she loosed a hen held in leash by a long cord. Whenever she felt affectionate, she pulled the hen to her, embraced it, and whispered into its ear. The hen appeared not to mind or even care. She had an egg to lay now and then, and sometimes laid it in the old woman's lap. The woman's daughter, Gladys, also came to the beach, but ignored her mother. She hadn't been much of a mother, and Gladys was also *folle*, the kind natives said. She sat one day to tell me a grand tale of having gone boating with the fishermen, who tried to have her. She then plunged bravely overboard and swam, by her account, no less than ten miles to safety. Instead of heading toward Theoule, but three hundred yards away, she had gone to La Napoule, thus making more valuable her hard swim for honor.

Soon a luscious white lady, an actress, came to sun herself on the beach. She carried a white lace parasol to protect her luminous skin from the sun's rays, and she made a fine point about having the hotel men servants place her chair exactly right upon the sand. But they knew too little about the delicate chivalries to which a woman of her capricious charms was accustomed, and she dismissed them, making me very aware that she, the charmer, had arrived, while appearing ignorant of my existence. Things didn't click between us, because shortly after she appeared the bistro madame arrived. She was an edition de-luxe: tall, large, handsomely made, with purple black hair, a handsome gypsy face and bearing. She knew she resembled Renault's Salome. Many artists had wished to paint her. With her dog Sultan she would swim out a mile, aided by the rhythm of his powerful progress. She too was friendly, rather than queenly with caprice toward which any man must pay homage, as was the actress.

The town's pastimes were few but sufficing: walks up the mountainsides, swimming, sunning, drinking pernod with gardeners and fishermen, gambling on the franc slot machine, and wondering about the background of the beachcomber who managed to get money enough on which to stay constantly drunk. Three exquisite boys—one Dutch, one English, one French—lived in a villa on the hill, and the Dutch boy did not realize that makeup failed to conceal the fact that his charms were no longer youthful. They all came into the bistro to buy cigarettes, and were not unready to be charming if nobody was annoyingly humorous. It was only tourists who mocked them. The natives were simple people, lacking that form of sophistication which makes some people flippant.

One night a travelling circus appeared in the town square, but, the headman announced through tears, the performance was to be sad and incomplete. They were one family, and their twelve-year-old boy, the star, had died three days before, but they must carry on, for they hadn't money enough for funeral expenses. The story touched the Theoule citizens, so that they contributed more sous than usual for this kind of show. Afterward, they drank in the bistro, dancing to the mechanical piano. At first the girls were shy with me, but when my drunkenness revealed me as also *fou*, they looked upon me with kind understanding as they looked upon Gladys and her mother with the hen.

By the time the Gropers arrived all but a small middle strip of my body was brown. Even in Theoule, tradition ordained that portion should be covered. Moodie declared herself happy to learn that I did take care of myself. In Paris I had looked pale and nerve-worn. She had almost presumed to advise me not to drink so much. It was strange to hear of the things that happened in Paris. The people there must be a lost set of fumblers. In Theoule we had our madness, but it seldom interfered with the goodwill and balance of the community as a whole.

Freddie now came to the beach soon after Dockie and I had stretched ourselves on the sand. She was inclined to be abstracted, wondering about the value of things, or if she was to have or even wanted an "interesting" life. She feared she was lazy. Soon the clear flesh on her ripe young body was biscuit brown, except where a backless orange bathing suit covered her. We swam out to the raft to sit, dive, or swim in deep water. By and by Poodie and Moodie showed up, with Clan, who always found he had another engagement when Poodie threatened to throw him into the water. The villas on the hills were receiving their summer inhabitants, who were there surely because they too liked an unpretentious seaside place. Various children, young men and women, swam out to sit on the raft. They were reticent, and Freddie looked nonchalant, but by the simple expedient of rocking the raft and slipping to push Freddie into the water, the boys and girls got acquainted with her. Possibly I looked a bit haughty because at first none of the fresh girls would push me off the raft, and I was reserved before their youth. At last a clear-featured, blue-eyed nymph rather admitted she knew I liked her looks by a quick shove. I was bright enough to clutch her around the waist and into the water we fell together. A seaside summer was well underway, with nobody bothering to act any age.

Occasionally Freddie yearned to talk about art and emotion, but there was wonder rather than frustration or neurasthenia in her questionings. And her questionings were held much in reserve with me, while she awaited the arrival of Harlen Winter, with whom she could have really sensitive discussions. In the meantime she had Moodie and Poodie to keep in order, and books to read.

Harlen had told her that *The Turn of the Screw* was a horror story of real obscenity, so Freddie was aloof toward any of Henry James's novels; however, she listened to Poodie chuckling over Gogol's *Dead Souls*, and read it gravely to declare it really profound writing. *Taras Bulba* nevertheless brought forth more authentic enthusiasm. The sensuous, virile, and debonair fatalism of its onrush stirred awakening emotions in her. Moodie sat listening to Freddie and me talk books.

"I wish I had read some Thomas Mann," Moodie said yearningly. "There are so many books I have never read. How have I lived all these years knowing so little about the really fine things in life?"

"Mother," Freddie was fretful, "do stop talking like that. You can simply read something of Thomas Mann. You make me furious when you pretend meekness, as if you didn't feel very sure of yourself."

When Freddie had these attacks of bad temper, it was almost a sure sign that she had not heard recently from Harlen Winter, or his last letter had displeased her. She talked of getting some painting done, and went to Cagnes and Vence, to return with water colors which had the authentic child, or primitive, quality which showed that Freddie hadn't listened too foolishly to pedantic instructions. To me she confided that Poodie was too literal. His water colors done while they motored through the châteaux region of the Loire were charming, but they had the limitation of striving to emulate colored photographs. Freddie was devoted to Poodie, and would never let him know that she thought his years of advertising illustration had enslaved and conventionalized his vision. And though she didn't believe in commenting on other artists' painting, his method was not hers. Poodie, however, was charmed that Freddie's paintings were still naive, without manner or technique or merely fine painting and craftsmanship. Moodie had long since given up painting, but was pleased to know that dresses that she designed for Freddie were admired by ladies who went in for elegance. Moodie was all confused about what she liked, should like, or if she liked. She thought that when she tried to paint, the effects were all muddy and dull and unimaginative. However, having visited the Ingres museum at Montauban on the way down, Moodie had moments of rapturous analysis.

"I know he was so anatomical that his figures were just anatomical machines, but he loved to work, just to work, and he loved to paint legs, arms, and hands; he loved warm flesh tints. He wasn't dried up by discipline and technique, don't you agree?" Moodie would talk, worried and reflective. At these moments she would sometimes confess that she was too intense about analysis. "I wish I had charm and abandon. Some people exude life; it radiates from them, and they draw experience to them. They understand and feel things by being alive."

Freddie always squirmed when Moodie talked so, and sometimes Freddie scolded. Poodie looked away uneasily, or made a facetious remark.

"I wish I had lived in a town like Arles when I was young," Moodie continued. "The people are so beautiful and proud, a pride of life, and a bearing. I do wonder if I didn't spoil the best, the young years, when one lives with joy, by being dutiful, and worrying. I do wonder if I haven't missed . . . the sensitive things."

Kate and Hal Meng arrived to join the colony. Kate was much underweight and had a fallen stomach; Hal was inclined to stomach ulcers, so they both were on a diet, and real affinities as well as man and wife. They rented a villa on the hill, intending to stay months to regain health. Kate could do her fashion designing from there, by taking trips to Cannes, Juan-les-Pins, Antibes, and now and then Paris. She had long since realized that fashion journals' versions of an elegant and modish world were mainly fiction. She wasted little time looking for gowns or women whose smartness would devastate her, or give her ideas. Seated before her drawing board she invented designs, admitting that styles bored her, but she needed money. Evidently her attitude proved that she knew what she was talking about, for she had offers to do more work than she could manage. Fortunately for both her and Hal, Kate had no superior attitude, and Hal didn't feel cowed, because she could earn many times the salary that he could hope to earn for some years, if ever. He was a painting-writing boy, not long out of college, and neither playing the stock market nor being an advertising man with fair success had decided him as yet that a working life is superior to one of leisure.

With them was Woo-Woo, a tiny griffon, who insisted that he was one of the dogs of the town even if he did look as though he were the result of kangaroo bit by a mosquito and scared by a lion. Regardless of prenatal influence, Woo-Woo pranced like a stallion, assumed the fury of a lion, and was ready to have dishonorable intentions toward anything which could be suspected of being a dog. Leap and sniff as he might, he could not get higher than the ankle of any other dog in town, but this did not quell his ambition. At first it never occurred to him to have fear. He felt goodwill toward everybody, even children if they didn't try to catch or handle him. They upset his nervous nature, and he distrusted their competence to treat him as his dignity deserved. Disillusion was in store for him, however.

At the bistro was an orange and black mother cat of Persian and alley cat lineage. Irrespective of protecting her kittens, she hated dogs, and every dog in town but Woo-Woo kept off her preserve. One night Woo-

Woo saw one of her kittens and bounced, joyfully yiping, to play with it. At one swipe from the mother cat's claws Woo-Woo ran down the road screaming murder. After that he remained trembling upon Kate's lap whenever he was in the vicinity of that cat, and never again could he gaze on a kitten without having his entire nervous system in a turmoil.

On encountering Dockie he succumbed to Dockie's charms, and Dockie was bemused at Woo-Woo's minute jackrabbit leaps. He would learn that a swat from his huge forepaw sent Woo-Woo rolling, and yiping with real pain. Woo-Woo always forgave him, however, but became wily in their games. Theoule inhabitants were reluctant to admit that such an animal as Woo-Woo really existed, or they didn't at first approve, but his general playful gregariousness and lack of moral attitudes did at last appeal to their tolerance and sympathy. The French are not keen on righteousness, or noble talk about justice, but they do understand weakness and dislike unjust prejudice and interference.

Harlen Winter arrived, and Moodie appeared more excited about his coming than Freddie, who had in stock a quantity of nonchalance. Harlen had a quantity of postcards, views of various châteaux, cathedrals, and reproductions of Italian primitive paintings by Cimabue, Giotto, Pierra della Francisco, Massaccio, Gozzoli, Carpaccio, and Cosima Tura, as well as of Greek sculptures in the Naples museum. He would withdraw the cards from his pocket and point out beautiful designs, forms, and faces, with caressing tenderness. Moodie grieved for him, wondering if he was not too idealistic to cope with the vulgarities of real life. He was too sensitive, his perceptions so delicate that mere austerity necessary to exist was lacking in his nature. Poodie was generally silent when Moodie talked this way, but once he was humorous.

"How dare you, Poodie!" Freddie turned on him savagely. "Harlen isn't just a pretty boy. I hate you when you talk so, and insinuate that Harlen's . . . I won't say the word. You're like all beastly advertising men and Americans who think that making money and being a success is all that matters. How dare you! I hate you. And your attitude is cowardly. You're ashamed to admit that you're sensitive yourself. It's horrible the way men pretend they aren't sentimental. Harlen isn't a sissy. He just isn't afraid to admit fine emotions."

Poodie escaped by swimming out to the raft, but he came back soon enough to hear Moodie talking. "I do wish we had enough money to let

Freddie marry Harlen, and get her to realize that perhaps Harlen hasn't much force of character. He is sensitive. I love Harlen." Moodie gazed at Freddie and Harlen who were out on the raft talking sensitively and earnestly to each other. "But I don't think the marriage would last. I'm not a prude. Freddie is healthy, and Harlen isn't very virile, but she might as well marry him and find out that he's a dear but not what she wants as a husband or lover. Of course Poodie doesn't feel about things as I do. I do believe men aren't as free-minded as women about things."

Poodie looked uneasy, but Moodie ignored his presence and went on talking. "Poodie would be furious if he thought Freddie didn't wait to be married to find out about love, but I'm not sure that girls shouldn't go ahead before they try marriage, and often make a failure of it."

Poodie squirmed and walked around in circles, then walked hesitatingly toward the water. Indeed, he did not feel about his darling Freddie as Moodie declared she did. I had little doubt that both of them would be decidedly upset if Freddie listened seriously to Moodie's talk about freedom. Poodie was inclined to look with severe suspicion upon young men who showed too great an interest in Freddie. Nevertheless, he had Moodie and Freddie to cope with. Whatever he felt or thought, he didn't argue. Obviously, however, he didn't take very seriously what Moodie had said, since day in and out he was present to witness that Moodie kept an observant eye on Freddie's activities.

The day before Harlen's departure the Gropers were despondent. Moodie and Freddie grieved for him. Moodie knew he was in for a siege. Harlen was twenty-five now and would get no more allowance from his family. No one knew what he could do to earn a living without being miserable. Poodie sympathized with Harlen there all right. What would he do? Would anyone choose to work at a job that doesn't interest him? All the sad men, young and old, of the working or of the leisure class, know or can recall the days when wonder about what to do with life devastates the emotional being.

Harlen made a brave leave-taking. His finances were low enough for a young man returning to America to confront wage-earning. Still, when the Gropers and I drove into Nice to see him off on the train, he insisted upon offering farewell cocktails. He was not permitted to pay, but his offer was meant. The party seemed very gay until Harlen stood on the end car of the train waving goodbye. He looked desolate and forlorn, and prettily romantic and wistful. Poodie had turned away in discomfiture. Moodie was going to bear up well, and talked to Poodie about how Rousseau would have handled the group of people standing at the depot bistro. But both of them were guardedly observing Freddie, who was unaware of everybody but the departing Harlen. As the train dropped out of sight she turned sobbing and made no attempt to conceal her emotions. Poodie fidgeted and looked miserable, and then started out of the depot toward a cafe across the way. Moodie hesitated, as though to chide Freddie, but she too left. Freddie grasped my shoulder when I put my arm around her to direct her toward the door.

"I know I'll never see him again. I know so, and if I do we won't feel the same way about each other," she gasped, in an agony of tears. "I know that rotten commercial attitude in America will spoil him, or break him. I know he hasn't much will or character. He doesn't even want to succeed. I'm terrified. They'll just make a gigolo out of him, and he's better than that."

"You'll feel differently later, Freddie," I said, knowing the remark was trite. "Think, there are so many people to be sorry for and have emotions about. Save a few emotions, Freddie. Come on, buck up. We'll join Poodie and Moodie and have beers. You don't want Moodie to be able to accuse you of being unable to control yourself."

"I know. Moodie was hateful. She acted as though Harlen had come to visit her, and wanted to talk to her all the time. I don't care. She might know I loved him, and he's the first one. She might have left us alone." Freddie didn't bother to look where she was going, but the idea of not showing herself in tears before her parents helped. We went across the street slowly to give her time to control herself. At the cafe she was wan and not talkative. Poodie still looked miserable but was quiet, and even Moodie said nothing, though several times she breathed deeply, wanting to express some bit of her philosophy. Experience had taught her, however, that Freddie would snap back fiercely at such a time.

The next day Freddie wasn't on the beach. Long past her regular appearing time Poodie showed up, and said that she intended to go up the hill path to search some scene to paint. "She wants to think, and get herself together. I suppose she won't paint anything, but we won't ask her tonight to see what she's done."

A few minutes later we saw Freddie climbing the steep mountain path.

She waved a detached greeting and went on with her painting materials. That evening when we had dinner together, she had two water colors to show, and was easy-spirited. She could talk about Harlen and wonder just what he would do in America. The next morning, she was out on the beach again assuring me that she believed I was right. There is no use in believing too much in sentiment. Freddie had decided that I was good for her education, even if I had been ironic and cruel in my comments about Harlen. He had discovered the châteaux and paintings of which he had postcards. Henry Saylor had told him what things to see, and what was fine in art, but she knew very well that he had a feeling about things himself. As I had made no remark about Harlen for several days, I wondered if Freddie was deciding that Harlen got enthusiastic only about the things he thought the right people admired.

"Freddie, you're revealing things about yourself," I chanced to remark. "You aren't so sure of Harlen's idealism and mind as you were."

"I hate you when you say things like that." Freddie turned on me much as she often turned on Poodie. "You know I adore Harlen."

"Sure, sure, Freddie. Do you know what a lech is? You had a grand one on Harlen, but now that he's gone, you find yourself interested most in painting. You've done a great deal of talking about your art the last two days."

"How dare you! I just know now that Moodie is right when she wonders if you are sensitive," she said, but with less firm indignation than she used on Poodie. "Maybe I wasn't deeply in love with him. What of it? Life has more color and interest if we have emotions," she said weakly, and got up and ran into the water to swim out to the raft. It wasn't until that afternoon that Poodie informed us that a rich American had rented the villa which was Theoule's palace.

"Four Yale boys are visiting the family. They're all members of Skull and Bones, and Freddie knows one of them. She saw him this morning and forgot all about Harlen. Moodie's all excited, too."

When Freddie came back from the raft, I let her know I had heard the news. She smiled and blushed, and revealed that when she was fifteen she'd been much taken with Neil Ringer. "He's shy, though, and the château has its own beach. I don't think those boys will come to this beach at all."

"Freddie, give me your mitt. To that beach we go. It's not private, and we'll wander absent-mindedly along, you know, hunting for seashells. Don't suffer frustration."

"Oh, I can't do that. I'm a well-brought-up young lady. I'd feel embarrassed. No, no, Kit. Don't force me."

However, Freddie stumbled right along. Within five minutes of not very subtle tactics we had run into the Yale boys, and Freddie had arranged for her friend to meet our aperitif-gathering at the bistro that evening. She didn't talk about Neil's sensibility. She merely thought he had very nice blue eyes. "He's of a fine old family, and wealthy, but he isn't pretentious at all. He just thinks of me as a little girl, because I was the last time he saw me."

"At cocktail time, Freddie, I'll help you reveal yourself as a poised woman of the world. He may be an old man to you and himself, but he's only another collegiate to your grandfather. I get you, Freddie. You're not so lacking in social ambition that you can't give a young heir the once-over."

"How dare you talk that way!"

"But you didn't let me finish to say: as long as he's good-looking and likeable. That's right. That's adjusting yourself to life."

"Sometimes I think I'm foolish not to go back to America and stay with Aunt Jess, to meet people my own age. Travel and being bohemians is all right for Poodie and Moodie because they have planned this trip abroad for years, but I'll be out of everything if we stay here too long. I do want to be gay and have fun, and not be bored stiff with what young people do when I do get back. Maybe I'll tell Poodie I'll go back and stay with Jess. He and Moodie would be freer to do what they wanted then. There can't be complete harmony when they want to do things I don't want, and they feel responsible for me."

CHAPTER SIXTEEN

WHEN KATE AND HAL MENG CAME BACK FROM one of their trips to Paris, for Kate to take in fall fashion shows, they found us restless. Mediterranean sunshine has its glory, but after seven months of it our souls had become less Mediterranean. And devastating as all of us had felt Paris to be before leaving, like so many who cannot learn by experience, we were planning, even yearning, to return. Past horrors never have a definite reality, unless it is a bawdily comic one, once they have been talked and laughed about by skeptical people knowing the need for unseriousness.

With the Mengs had arrived Ross Campion. Sudge was visiting his parents who were on their annual trip to London. The Mengs turned up at the fishermen's bistro, and Kate told Freddie and me that Ross had stopped off at their villa. "He looked so miserable in Paris. Helpless without Sudge. We hadn't the heart not to ask him down with us, but no sooner had we driven out of Paris than he began to worry."

"He's scared that Sudge will be angry not to find him in Paris when he returns," Hal said drily. "They're both afraid Sudge's dad will cut off the allowance. I didn't like Sudge once, but he's worth two of Ross. Ross won't do a thing about himself. I see myself doing typing for money, and letting Ross spend that and most of my allowance, too. Ross is a weak fish. His wistful charm doesn't get me anymore. He's too damned selfish. Hell, he couldn't even decide for himself what he wanted to eat as we were driving down here."

"But he's a poor wreck," Kate said, her voice flooded with just such comic sympathy as she bestowed upon the minute Woo-Woo.

"He looked a broken old man in Paris, and is so terrified that if Sudge doesn't find him there he might seek new interests."

"As he might," Hal said, as he sipped a pernod.

Freddie listened. Politely, she refused to comment on the Mengs' guest, but I knew that the snooty young Freddie refused to think that the boys were worth all this sympathy. The conversation shifted to Paris. Sensibly I, and even Freddie with her four-months experience of Paris, should have known that Paris was going on as usual, being another of the world's quarters, so far as Montparnasse is concerned, of lost souls. We, certainly I, should have valued the tiny bit of bourgeois or countryman contentment which I had possessed in the past several months. Nevertheless, the faraway had its glamour. I began to think of an Indian-summer Paris, casual contacts, late nights, hilarity—general drifting. Again, for the millionth time, I decided that the problems of other people couldn't possibly depress me. I was a satirist.

The Mengs left us, saying that they would return later with Ross to dine at my *pension*. After a pernod, Freddie and I agreed that as the Mengs had admitted doing a short run this day, they could just take us into Cannes for some dancing. We had lived a very quiet and dutiful six months and needed an outing.

The Mengs didn't come back. We each had another pernod. "It's that Ross Campion," Freddie wailed. "I know he's the sort who fusses and can't get ready."

Soon Poodie appeared. "Where's Hal and Kate?" Freddie demanded, knowing she could bully her father. "Kit and I want to go to Cannes and dance."

"You're out of luck," Poodie said heartlessly. "Hal and Kate drove that Ross boy into Cannes half an hour ago, and your old man's too tired to act as your chauffeur tonight."

"Why didn't they take us?" Freddie complained. "I think they're hateful."

"The Ross boy was afraid of losing his boyfriend and had the heebie-jeebies. He just had to go back to Paris." Poodie was irreverent. Nevertheless, seeing Freddie's face, he decided he didn't want an aperitif and discreetly sneaked away. He could be obstinate, but it made him creepy when Freddie accused him of being a heartless father. He was afraid of giving in if she begged him to drive us to Cannes.

"Poor Poodie," Freddie laughed. "He's funny. He would take us to Cannes, but he's tired. Did you notice the expression on his face when he didn't have his drink because we were in a temper."

"Yes." I was cheerful. "He looked like Clan when he's afraid he's going to be thrown into the water. Damn the Mengs and Ross, though. They knew we'd damn well like a night out."

"Ross makes me furious," Freddie said sternly. "He's nothing but a silly weakling. He's worse than a gigolo. You defend him, but I can't help despising him. Nobody who has as little character as he has is anything but a selfish pig. I won't admit that he's the least bit attractive or intelligent. He simply uses his wistful manner. I won't feel sorry for him." Freddie broke off, and looked nonplussed. I wondered if she hadn't suddenly recalled what she said to me about Harlen Winter's lack of character, and how she admitted her own indecision.

After another drink Freddie and I began to wail our grievances, and evidently, through a course of drinking, they became very inclusive. In the room above the bistro lived an elderly American woman who knew all of us. Freddie and I forgot she was there, which was an error, as she was the town newsmonger. The next day the Mengs and the older Gropers had heard that Freddie and I didn't think too highly of any of them. Our failure to achieve Cannes and the Boeuf sur le Toit for dancing had apparently embittered us. On the Mengs and particularly Ross we had been severe. Moodie and Poodie had come in for rather light criticism on my part, but Freddie had cut loose with all her sad tales of how parents can cramp a girl's style.

Except to take the attitude that anybody who gossips is too low to believe, Freddie and I were discreetly silent. Both of us had too much of a hangover to be energetically ashamed, apologetic, or defiant. Too much drink after months of little drink can have a devastating effect. At the aperitif hour the Mengs so delicately helped Freddie and me through this touchy situation that they were back in our good graces, had we not already felt that remorse which comes from not being able to remember what one has said in one's cups.

"Freddie, we just went in to get a prescription for Kate, and then only because Ross was in a panic to get back to Paris," Hal Meng explained, proving that he had felt dastardly for having deserted us the night before.

"Yes, Freddie," Kate crooned, letting me know that I, the older, was the real culprit, "it was tragic. The poor boy was terrified that Sudge wouldn't join him down here. He knew Sudge would be despondent after visiting his parents, and might get drunk and into trouble. Once we got Ross on the train we stopped to have one—only one—drink at the Boeuf."

"We didn't hear your car coming down the road," I countered.

Hal Meng laughed most disagreeably, I thought, and Freddie affirmed with a glance. "We sat inside and listened to you two give the town populace the razzle-dazz. What you called all of us was nobody's business, but we decided you were too many drinks up on us to be solaced."

"I don't care," Freddie said, quickly covering our night before. She was very red in the face, but did her best. "I think Ross is a disgusting weakling." The Mengs laughed with gentle restraint, which made it necessary for me at once to offer Freddie a drink, and for her to accept.

"Don't you care," Hal said paternally to Freddie, "we'll drive you to Juan-les-Pins tonight. By the way, Kit . . ." So as not to further embarrass Freddie, Hal talked about Gaylord Showman, who might actually arrive in Theoule within a day or so.

Autumn was deeply into the atmosphere on the day Gaylord appeared, and the mistral was blowing. Whether it is primitive emotion, or neurasthenia, the blowing of the mistral has a disintegrating effect, and I was wanting to be away. Gaylord's arrival, however, calmed the unrest for a moment. With a roadster, he was now vehemently intent upon the trip to Portugal. There we could get back to the Middle Ages, drink with the peasants in mountain fastnesses, and if disappointed, we could venture eastward, into Turkestan, Tibet, or the Gobi desert. Gaylord was drunk and his mind was ready to go anywhere, regardless of what his energy and resistance might let his body submit to.

He and Poodie were disposed, before meeting, to think antagonistically of each other. Gaylord was a "modern" and Poodie was "academic" and both "painted." Hal and I were all right with either of them; we only wrote, and of course we drank. Poodie thought Gaylord would be pretentious and patronizing, while Gaylord thought Poodie traditional and full of conservative disdain. Gaylord, however, was too drunk to join in the night of his arrival. He went directly to bed, boisterous but pliable. In the morning he made his first appearance on the beach.

Gaylord had a talent for, and delighted in, garbing himself in strange costumes. At one costume ball he came as a riverboat gambler of the 1880s, with a velvet-collared coat, a ruffled white shirt with lace cuffs, and a brace of pistols. That early in the evening a weeping drunk-on had belied his bad man get-up is of little moment. Where he had found the bathing costume he wore this morning no one discovered. It was horrifyingly modest and demure. White, with circular red stripes, it buttoned down the front, had half-length sleeves and legs which went below his knees. His stomach protruded gently, and the suit's bag gave his already loose legs a knock-kneed look. As he was still intoxicated, he did not stutter or assume a pompous manner to cover his uneasiness among strangers. Instead, he did fluttery and girlish dance steps on the sand. Poodie watched and found his preconceived resentment toward Gaylord completely gone. When introduced to him Gaylord was out of breath, looking like a winded bullfrog after a pursuit by a snake. "H-h-how do you do. Kit has t-t-told me about you f-f-folks down here. L-l-let's have a drink. It's h-h-h-hot. H-h-heat gets me." Poodie could not know that Gaylord's speech was not stuttering, for Gaylord. When he really stuttered a listener needed a windshield or a veil. Sober, he was careful not to blow bubbles, but drunk he forgot such niceties.

Over pernod Poodie and Gaylord waxed eloquent about paint mediums; these they could discuss. Gaylord became enthusiastic about starting research at once and writing a book on the history of paint mediums: their varieties, preservation, durable color, uncrackable and resistance-to-the-elements qualities. Poodie, as an advertising illustrator, had done some reflecting himself, and agreed that it was terrifying to think one might paint a masterpiece that wouldn't stand the ravages of time. Strangely, for Hal and me, who sat drinking with them, Poodie didn't indulge in leg-pulling or comedy. He and Gaylord had struck it off as twin souls. Not to leave Hal and me out of the conversation, Gaylord, after bestowing a juicy kiss on each of our cheeks and declaring his devotion, said we must all get together and edit an ABC magazine. A for articles on art, anthropology, astronomy, archery, aviation, and animals I have seen in delirium tremens. B for boxing, biography, bitches, boating, and badgering. C for clippers, Calvacanti, circuses, cooking, crime, and so forth.

The idea immediately took with the four present, and we devoted three pernods each to thinking of articles which might be written for this novel, contemporary, and alert journal. The eating, drinking, sleeping, and love-making habits of all countries and peoples were good for a series. Comedians, clowns, pantomime, documents, hunters, and studies of high-class pathologics would fill much space, properly investigated and reported. Hal Meng was keen on showing up the fallacy of case reports in psychoanalysis, as he had a grievance against neurasthenics who go in for confessing or being father confessors in the name of psychoanalytic research. I added that we might as well investigate the bunk in metaphysical books, and such works as *The Golden Bough,* in addition to examining the lives of prophets and mystics, such as Blake, Dostoyevsky, Nietzsche, and Whitman. Too many of them had hovered near enough to insanity to indicate that frustration, lack of extrospection or vital energy, or some defect, had invalidated their right to prophecy. This point caused Gaylord to insist that we must study the effect of dope and drink on the artist and on imaginative people in general.

"You k-know Kindler and his whale s-s-story?" Gaylord said. "He'd been hitting the hop, and he said to me, 'Look, let's get into that boat out in the sea.' I went with him to the chamber pot, and we climbed in and rowed across his studio to the whale. Entering, we found a staircase, and this we descended."

No longer frightened of Poodie, Gaylord had ceased stuttering completely.

"At the foot of the stairs we found a man sitting. 'Ah, Jonah, I presume,' Kindler said, most meticulously. 'Yes, and gentlemen,' Jonah told Kindler in a perfect Oxford accent, 'I wish you to understand that I am not staying here for an indefinite period of time.' Yes, I can tell you enough stories about the hopheads to make an article myself," Gaylord triumphed. "*Garçon, encore quartre pernods.*"

"And there are freak inventors and bugs to write about," Hal chuckled merrily. "And famous old practical jokes, types of whorehouses all over the world."

"And the aesthetic side of means of transportation," Gaylord added, taking out his pocket case full of cards where he kept all ideas and information catalogued.

Unfortunately, Gaylord, who had been gay and comic, encountered something in his card index that depressed him. He suddenly became quiet and stared dolefully into space, his lower lip drooping. I suggested another drink, but he touched me in the ribs with his elbow, and slid one of the index cards for me to look at under the cover of the table cloth. It was under "A": "Artists, psychoanalysis necessary to bring back to norm. Self, suffering from abnormal fear of having to earn money for self-support."

And a second "Artists" card: "Tragic lives and insanity of genius. Van Gogh, Stendhal, Dostoyevsky, Nietzsche, Winslow Homer, Poe, Odilon Redon, etc."

There was little use saying much to Gaylord, and silent sympathy would not cure him of his moment of phobia. He might have another drink and become gay and clownish, or he might weep, or depart in Hamlet-morbid silence. I had one of those idiotic, rational, and practical instances of skepticism anyway, and inquired who would do the research, write the articles, and finance a magazine of such agnostic and science-insistent type as we were advocating. My three companions were rightly disgusted, and my question drove Gaylord to another drink. The last Hal and I saw of him that night he was staggering down the road arm in arm with Poodie. For the moment they were again intent on comedy and trivialities, but Hal and I knew that before long Gaylord would be telling Poodie of the psychologist-doctor who would analyze him and set him right with life. They would surely also talk paint and paint mediums.

The next morning, Gaylord had little interest in a trip to Portugal. Having the night before managed to have become a town character among the natives, he liked Theoule, saw scenes and types he wished to paint, and was most serious about laying off the drink to allow his kidneys to repair themselves. Yet he still talked to me of Bali and Cambodia; recalled a cinema he had seen in which a herd of ten thousand reindeer moved across the snowy tundra of Lapland; considered Prescott and wondered about Peru, Mexico, the Mayan, Toltec, and Aztec civilizations; swore that someday we must take a freighter and visit a few of the world's brawling, colorful seaports. Customs, costumes, taboos, and religions had never been properly studied, and he wanted to do research into mediums and ethnography as well as to paint. The glamour was not in his enthusiasm this day, however, because I knew he was talking for me, not to let me down.

Migration season had finally come. When the mistral starts blowing dismally about the cliffs of Theoule, desolation and unrest settle into the hearts of such as us. Paris and its wild life was a known quantity and quality. New places have their romantic appeal so long as one remains unaware of the fact that their habits and qualities are prosaic enough to their natives. Though Gaylord intended to stay on in Theoule, I hopped a train to Paris, sure that the others would feel the migratory urge before many days had passed. Freddie was restless; Moodie, Poodie, and the Mengs were swearing at Theoule, Paris, and France in general; and each of them was ready to start a mass stampede toward New York. I felt obstinate, having from news accounts and from letters gathered the idea that no New York day was complete that didn't have its quota of brokers, editors, or nerve-shattered people leaping out of skyscraper windows, to fall in front of pedestrians already jittery enough because of the pressure of economic and traffic conditions.

CHAPTER SEVENTEEN

SUDGE RETURNED FROM LONDON AND THE BOYS led a quiet life, but in some way they had become Sudge and Ross, rather than a dual entity, the boys. During a sojourn in Luxembourg they had collected a dachshund bitch, Sadie, and whichever one Sadie might be with at any time, she seemed to supply his need for companionship. Their manner of coming and going was still reticent, but it had less of a secretive, tiptoeing quality than before; and no longer did they twitter and snort in joyous world-mocking confidence to each other. The words "sound" and "stout" had gone out of their vocabulary, and Montreal, with their old-time friends, no longer supplied them with diabolic amusement when familiar incidents were recalled. Ross scarcely ever indulged in his rosy-beaming smile; he was instead wistfully sour and waspishly critical. Meanwhile Sudge was developing impatience, and actually looked skeptical or irritated at some of Ross's statements. His visit to London had given him a scare, and purpose.

"Father and I fought, and I struck him," Sudge confided shortly after I encountered him for the first time in months. "He kept making cracks at the way I lived, and one night, over the whiskey, I told him what I thought of him. He hadn't any helpful advice, didn't advise my returning to college, and had no ideas what I should do but come back to Montreal. I told him that I'd typed several novels in the last few months, and that was a more intelligent job than being an office clerk, as Pinky is. Father kept drinking whiskey and picking at me. I know he is bored with mother, and she with him, and he thinks I'll be company for her. Finally I struck him."

"Were you pretty drunk?"

"No. When he asked me what I was going to do with my life, I asked what he had done with his and hoped I'd avoid being such a dull fart as he is," Sudge said bitterly. "He got damned righteous and British as though his kind were the backbone of the Empire. Temper was gathering in me."

"Did he hit back?"

Sudge looked bitter, and then giggled weakly, but there was little spontaneity in his mirth. "He said how much money he had made in the last year, investing money Pinky, my sister, and I inherited in trust from mother's family. I broke loose and told him that every cent he had he'd inherited, married, or had thrown at him, and that he was such a rotten lover, mother had to take on sea captains to escape him. That jolted him. He didn't realize I knew, or that I knew he'd kept his ugly secretary as a mistress. He made a pass at me, calling me a young cub, and I struck him. He was going to hit back, but I think he realized I'm stronger than he is. The next day, he said he was sorry and acted fairly decent. I was leaving for Paris, and he said he'd continue my allowance until he'd considered further."

Hilaria was passing and joined us at our table on La Coupole terrace. She was now living with a German lover who had conservative-snob ideas, and he wanted her to be a great actress. Hilaria looked elegant and was inclined to be aloofly detached with a grand-lady manner. She deigned to be ironically amused by an old barroom friend such as myself, but she would still have it known that she was now a serious woman. "Kit, I work now in a cabaret, very fashionable. Later I will act in a play which is being written for me."

"Do you think you'll stand the racket of being serious that long, Hilaria?"

"I am no longer fool young girl," Hilaria said with an air of fatigue that so serious a woman as herself should be teased.

"You'd better let down for today, Hilaria. I'm just back. You're doing the poised and haughty lady well, for the moment, but I'm beered-up. Relax a bit."

Hilaria sat erect and gazed about her, registering gentle disdain and tolerance. She knew me as *fou.* "You'd better have the drink you intended to have before I doubted your seriousness," I suggested. She shrugged her shoulders to imply anger; then she permitted herself to smile. She looked about and suddenly gave in.

"*Oui,* Kit, I haf a drink weeth you. *Merde. Garçon, un Bacardi cocktail.* What is art in the life when one is young and beautiful girl like me? I am no woman to act gracious to dull people who come to cabarets because they no can amuse themselves. I am woman of the heart. Yesterday I thought to marry my young man, but *merde*, marriage is not all in the life. I think today he begins to bore me with his wish that I be one tamn fool respectable girl. I am woman with the spirit; also I am young."

"That's the idea. You know you could be a great woman if you wished, Hilaria, but what for?"

"*Oui*, Kit." Hilaria was tenderly coquettish. "A dramatist has writ a play he wish I should play in. I told him yes, but now I have me a new idea. The play has symbols, a woman being all things to all men—mother, lover, baby, and saint. When he talked, because he had the pretty, innocent eyes, I have thought me his idea veree grand and beautiful. He has such nice small-boy smile. But today I think, 'The play with the symbolism. It is old-fashioned, banal.' Why for Hilaria becomes stupid and think such ideas great because their author pleases me? I sleep with him, and to hell with his play. I am no woman for the foolish acting of one repertoire of human emotions. That is not art. Only the stupid woman thinks herself a great actress to do such things."

"And Indian summer is on in Paris, too, Hilaria. I feel that things will be rather sociably nice for a week or so. You couldn't miss real life for anything so stereotyped as a naive young dramatist's idea of symbolic womanhood, could you?"

"*Non*, Kit," Hilaria said, looking around. "And now I go. Tonight later maybe I see you. Here comes one tamn fool writer and he's looking for you. Him I can't stand and I have been rude to him, but maybe he is friend to you, so right now I go not to make scenes."

"It's Flannagan," Sudge said as Hilaria left in a flurry. "Paris has him floundering and he knows friends of yours and hopes you'll give him some tips."

Flannagan approached from a distance, and he was headed for our table. As he walked his heavy shoulders sloped and his head dangled forward, weighed with ponderance. His hands were clasped behind his back, as though he used them in some way to help propel his plump stomach before him. I thought of an Irishman wheeling cement up an incline, or Rodin's *The Thinker*, and of the way Dockie, my Theoule puppy companion, used to stage-set himself against the sea and skyline. On windy days Dockie wobbled to the beach to sit, a figure of dramatic contemplation, in an attitude suggesting that he knew all experience and had in sage sorrow resigned himself. When he got up to wobble down the beach, he too, as Flannagan now appeared, looked world-weary with the futility of pondering.

Flannagan spoke reticently to Sudge, but apparently was going on. Sudge had probably indicated no liking for him. Now, however, Sudge was gracious and called to him. "This is Kit O'Malley, Flannagan. Come and have a drink." Quickly to me Sudge said under his breath, "Ross and I showed him around Paris, and located an apartment for him. Gaylord took him to a prizefight, bought him drinks, but Flannagan hasn't bought any of us as much as one coffee."

Flannagan's smile was winning and a trifle shy, or he was on his guard before Sudge and a new acquaintance. He didn't in any case appear to have quick reflexes. The word had come to me that he "had a goiter on his hand" and could never get it into his pocket to pay for his own drinks. Particularly Gaylord had been sour about Flannagan, who had allowed him to pay for an entire evening's entertainment at a prizefight, with not an offer to buy even a beer. I wondered if Flannagan, a small-town product, wasn't merely bewildered by the Paris pace and his inability to speak French. He hadn't been with us two minutes before he was recounting a tale of his boxing match with Pemberton. The match was already history and a source for comedy about Paris. That Flannagan should, as Pemberton declared, imitate his writing style and also be a boxing literary man was too much. Taller and heavier than Flannagan, Pemberton had nevertheless been defeated in the boxing contest.

Flannagan was obviously puzzled that he was able to outbox Pemberton, who received much newspaper notice as a writer with professional boxing skill. Pemberton, the day before, had been confused and declared that only because he had been drinking too much had Flannagan bested him. Dutch Kelly, who had held the watch, had not stopped the fight at the proper time. He had been too astounded to see Pemberton, whom he was disposed to heroize, getting the worst of it. In all, the three literary men did not know what to think. Did Flannagan's superior boxing ability make him also a better writer than Pemberton, or just a roughneck? Or did Dutch's inability to box at all make him the best writer of the three? Pemberton was suspicious of Dutch, too. Why hadn't he stopped their boxing at the time to call the round? Was his old friend a double-crosser, and did he want to see Flannagan win?

Sudge left us after finishing his drink, and before long Maggie Flannagan arrived. She decided she was hungry and must have a pastry. Flannagan chided her that she had already eaten two within the hour, and that if she had another she'd have to do without dinner. They couldn't afford too many pastries. Maggie had the pastry nevertheless, and to my amazement later meekly went to watch Flannagan eat dinner, which she had forfeited because of that pastry. Through the course of several days the Flannagans revealed little passion for any drink but beer, but a great passion for pastries, and Flannagan had an equally great passion for meeting great men, as long as they were successful—in the ten thousand to fifty thousand dollar class—as he intended to be. Today, however, he had to talk about his boxing match with Pemberton. It had puzzled him in a variety of ways. Until his own medium success with a book, he had tended to make a hero of Pemberton, but now he thought himself the less clever but the deeper writer. When I admitted that I knew little about the science of boxing and was but mildly amused by prizefights, he looked disapproving, and offered to teach me how to box. My response was lukewarm. He wouldn't understand that it didn't interest me; and Maggie showed a flicker of Irish understanding when she spoke.

"But if he doesn't want to bother about boxing, he doesn't, Shawin." Her voice indicated that she may have heard too much about the subject.

Flannagan thought over her remark thickly, but soon was talking again of the thrill, science, and physical kick of boxing. "Were you inclined to be sickly or undersized as a child?" I asked.

Maggie shot me a quick, illumined glance, and turned away so that Shawin couldn't see her flash of a grin. Flannagan looked puzzled, trying to think. "I didn't grow fast. I'm under average height now, and too fat for my age. Why do you ask?"

"Mild curiosity. So much is made of athletics in the schools in America that I find they rather bore me. That happens when one knows or has known several All-American football players, Olympic champions, and athletic stars in general."

"But with all the fights that start in bars and speakeasies, a fellow should know how to defend himself," Flannagan said.

"Quick thinking is as apt to win a barroom fight as boxing ability. Such fights don't have any rules to direct them."

Maggie was fidgeting, but Flannagan was intent upon his obsession.

"Pemberton was funny the day we boxed," he recounted. "He didn't seem to try to hit me or to win. He looks all right when he's shadow-boxing, but he has no science of defense or attack. I thought he was aggressive."

"Oh no, Pemberton's real nature is probably gentle or tender. He's afraid that might be discovered, so he acts as he writes: hard-boiled realism. The sentimental public feels the softness in his work, though. He's giving them the frozen corrugated gelatine that looks steely they desire."

James Fernley John appeared and, seeing us, came to the table. It wasn't possible to understand clearly what he mumbled through his walrus mustache, but we did understand that he invited us to try a British drink, a black velvet, a mixture of stout and champagne. He had recently returned from the States, where, he assured us, his lectures on tour had been formidably successful. As neither in conversation nor in platform lecturing John's speech is more than one-tenth understandable, any audience could think he said whatever it wished.

"You'll be going back soon then," I surmised.

"But O'Malley, they want me," John said, modestly plaintive about the demands made on him by a public voracious for his books and addresses. "When I was speaking for the radio, I was given fifteen minutes to talk, but at the end of that time the announcer said, 'Mista John, they like you so well. Continue speaking as long as you wish.'"

As I pictured the breathless millions in America sitting in their quiet homes intent upon the words of James Fernley John, so intent that their interest psychically transferred itself to the radio announcer, Maggie Flannagan shot me a glance, or either blew her nose or suppressed a titter. Shawin looked puzzled as if all the story had not been told.

James Fernley John cleared his throat and shifted his corpulent frame to be better able to sip his black velvet in comfort. He breathed heavily, and looked very snorting-old-Britisher, and he mumbled again. Only because I had heard this one from him before could I inform the puzzled Flannagan what Mista John had said. "He has, you understand, more readers for any one of his books than H. G. Wells," I explained, as gravely as possible in spite of the fact that Mrs. Flannagan had a female's inability to comprehend a genius such as Mista John. "But people are ready to wait and get his books from the library, even if they must wait ten years. Any book of Wells they must read at once, or it is out of date. He is translating his own books into French too, which Wells could not do."

Flannagan looked at me with an air of panic, at his wife with wonder, and then at James Fernley John. Plainly Flannagan was becoming incredulous. Slowly an illumined look began to creep over his countenance. Neither Maggie nor I was taking Mista John's tales too seriously, and that I, a writer, had such an attitude toward the great prose stylist of the day was something to ponder. Later Flannagan surmised that it had been a good thing John hadn't taken to him in New York. "My publisher thought he might do a foreword or say something complimentary about my work. I guess that would have been a good thing only if he'd done it a few years back. People seem to doubt him now."

Maggie snickered a completely shanty Irish giggle because her husband made this comment with such pained seriousness. She didn't say anything, however. She always let Shawin be her lord and master and do her thinking for her. Although she seemed fond of him, one guessed that she didn't take him very seriously, either. Evidently her interest in art and literature was nonexistent.

"But you don't realize, as John will tell you, that he is a genius, brought up in the tradition of genius. His parents, uncles, aunts, and cousins were geniuses. And kind produces kind. No big public could go appreciating hereditary genius through too many books. It was only a short time back that people with so much insight as the reviewers discovered him as a prose master. For years he had been doing Georgian novels, or free verse, or modern writing, as he was fostering young talent while an editor."

"Do you mean what he says is just . . . imagination." Flannagan was happy with his own brightness. "I wouldn't think a man with his reputation would lie."

"Think of Benvenuto Céllini. Fertile minds need some outlet."

John, who had left us rather quickly, passed by the terrace again. This time I noticed that he was aging, looked lonely and dismal. He was minding then that his third wife had finally rebelled and quit him. She could, she declared, allow him all the romances with fat and aging women he desired; but she would not tolerate any longer having him come back to boast about his conquests. As I was looking at him I sensed that Flannagan was also observing him.

"Why the poor old boy got it that we chuckled at him, and he's wanting somebody to sit with," Flannagan said. "Will you ask him over again? I didn't like him but I'm sorry for him now."

Since I was inclined to be amused by and possibly to like Flannagan as a small-town type I'd known in schooldays, this touch of humanity in him appealed to me. "No, the old boy was needlessly rocky about me without reason, and his adenoidal breathing bores me. Pathos is too usual in the Quarter. I can't stand too much of him; he breaks my heart," I answered callously. "Let's have our literature without too much of the politics and megalomanias of professional writing people."

Maggie shot me a quick look, and Flannagan's expression was worried with reflection. But his expression changed when he saw Reyner, editor and bookseller, approaching, his face bright with his usual benign expression of cordial geniality. He was, he informed us, bringing out the next number of his modern English quarterly with translations from a variety of Polish authors. His chief find and contributor was also giving him a section from his huge book on American literature. I recalled Sudge's prophecy that this contributor, Isaac Steingold, was brilliantly analyzing and destroying all American writers of the past, with however enough acumen to have prepared a background for the time in the history of American letters when he had appeared on the scene. From Mista Reyner and Mista Steingold, one gathered that literature in general is in the hands of the Jews, mainly Polish or Russian, and that no book has depth unless its main characters are Jew-race-conscious mystics.

I finished my drink and left, hearing Mista Reyner comment to Flannagan that these young writers of today pose problems but offer no solutions. He was very jovial, beamingly suggesting that we were all young rascals. Then I saw Ellery Saunderson bouncing down the street like a surreptitious balloon. With him was the Rumanian best-seller of the season. Mista Reyner, Flannagan, Ellery, the Rumanian, and what other arrived authors who were apt to collect on the terrace this mild autumn night, would be too much on their guard toward each other to make easy drinking companions. I decided to search for Hilaria, or a *poule*, or some mere barroom hound. The conversation of a group of successful writers too often is cagey and discomforting rather than intellectual.

CHAPTER EIGHTEEN

SUDGE HOVE INTO SIGHT, WALKING IN HIS ABSENT-minded, daydreaming way of youth. Suddenly he made gesticulations of delighted recognition, and soon was coming toward me with a large woman who was, however, well made and smartly dressed. It wasn't until they were on top of me that I recognized Margot Lindstrom, from Nice. Sudge looked at me in sly joy, indicating that Margot still "excited" him, and the fact that she was in the Quarter meant that she was a more understandable quality to him than she had been as a rather loose but conventional woman in prosaic Nice.

Margot revealed that she was in Paris to extend her fields of adventure. She was penniless, and mildly regretted having lost her Chilean boyfriend, Anatolio. Still, that romance had paled on her, and she was hopeful of gaining employment in some cabaret as a *diseuse.* When Sudge introduced her to a passing acquaintance, he called her "Countess Margot."

"Don't be a countess in this Quarter, Margot," I told her. "That's bad news. There's one Italian countess given to smashing glasses in people's faces, and she's been bad news on the continent for years. There's an English Lady, who's a wreck of pathos gone stale, and a Belgian countess, originally South African, and any of the three would take the last franc of a blind grandmother when the thirst for a drink is on them, which is always."

"If I have to be an adventuress the title will help," Margot chortled. "Possibly I have work at a smart cabaret, but my voice and my style may be too refined, or the smoky atmosphere may kill what voice I have left."

Sudge was restless, and spoke to James Fernley John, who invited him to his next Thursday evening intellectual gathering. Margot laughed lightly and said softly to me, "The little boy is coming to tea at my apartment, and I have the curiosity. *Moquer,* he has lively ideas. I have bored myself with too much quiet life. *A bientôt.*"

Margot might say she was, and look, devilishly uncaring, but I wondered if she could make a foursome with the three other titled dames of the Quarter. The Italian countess had cadged, played with blackmail, and staged cabaret and barroom brawls, in Germany, Italy, England, and France, for years, since before the war. Lady Mart, the desperate, driven, and lost heroine of Pemberton's novel, had twelve years experience as a city beachcomber. Now and when she had been with her English lover, she had been ready to borrow from, strand bills on, or talk suicide to any tart, barman, proprietor, or susceptible young or old person she encountered; and all in the great old British-aristocrat tradition: "We don't let each other down." "You're one of us, and we don't do this or that."

Neither of these Ladies was apt to appeal to Margot as types to copy, and the Countess Diana, South African ex-music hall star, and versed in the nightlife of Argentina, Mexico, Cuba, and Panama, was a bit rough-spoken for Margot, who still had conservative-lady ideas of how to present herself. Diana drank heartily, doped frequently, and used a vocabulary that drove "nayce" and "refeened" people out of whatever rendezvous she was in. Gypping taxi drivers, spoofing barmen, and appealing to the ribald sympathies of gendarmes or cynically sentimental old soaks was Diana's program for navigating her rolling seas. She knew the value of a wisecrack that drew a belly laugh. Pale and in a fervor, she rushed one night into a bar to announce that she'd made a great decision; she was going to take up literature and write her memoirs. Again, when some wit wondered how many balls of twine it would take to place a net around Montparnasse, Diana responded, "Balls, balls, and balls, and that's the answer to all your questions." She knew her Cockney, her music hall, and her American showgirl types of rough comedy, and she did not, unlike Lady Mart, wail and weep. Instead, she was scornful of such damn fools as listened to her sad tales of need. Such people deserved to have money taken from them, unless they were drunks who understood thirst as she did, and then Diana was a pal. No, it was doubtful that Margot would find Montparnasse her grazing lands. She might talk, but she wasn't hard enough or trained enough to stand the racket.

For several days Sudge and Margot were in little evidence, but Ross was about, in a state of abject nerves. Sitting in a cafe he watched the door constantly, and with each person entering who was not Sudge, he sank again into his misery. Sudge had left him to his own resources for the longest period of time since their arrival in Paris. The once I chatted with him for a few minutes, he talked bitterly of getting the first possible boat back to Canada. "Sudge doesn't need me anymore," he complained. "He thinks he's in love with that slut from Nice, and she's old enough to be his mother. She's only playing him." He was scratching his hand again, and vehement in his disgust that Sudge's father didn't grant Sudge a larger allowance. And too, Ross informed me, Sudge had placed a novel in America, and was to get a hundred dollar advance. Ross took the attitude that the novel must be cheap to have placed, for his own book wasn't even written to be submitted to a publisher as yet.

As we talked Sudge came into the place with Margot. He took Ross aside and talked quiet confidences. Ross had spent what money he had on him getting drunk the night before so that he hadn't eaten today. "But Ross, dear," Sudge said fretfully and regretfully, "how could I know you'd do that? You know we had to live on that two hundred francs for a week."

"You didn't show up for two days. I had to get drunk," Ross said, in a temper. Margot looked at Sudge meaningfully, but Sudge didn't respond to her glance. In a minute he and Ross went out the door together.

"Will he come back?" Margot laughed mockingly.

"I doubt it."

"I was wrong about him," Margot chortled, "in several ways. He doesn't mock the world so much as he defends himself with his wit, and then he does not know, always, how mocking he sounds. He speaks like a boy who is allowed no freedom."

"He isn't allowed much by Ross, it would seem."

"Yesterday he came to my apartment," Margot confided. "He was not at ease with me, but when he wished to get back to Ross, I felt a devil in me. I asked why he must always return to the other boy. He was going to kiss my hand in saying goodbye, but I drew him to me. It was cruel, but touching for my heart, too. Whatever, he is no lover of the other boy. He is male, and a woman can play with him, easily. He is affectionate and tender, but he is male, and not a frightened boy like the other."

"Yes, and a predatory male at that. His attitude toward Ross is that of an adolescent male who pities suffering. Torment and neurasthenia and helplessness distress him."

"He is tender, too," Margot said with wonderment. Suddenly she exclaimed, "Oh, I am not falling in love with him. It was only I was sure the boys were everything to each other, and I felt vicious. Perhaps now I am cruel. Before I have chosen always never to interfere with other people's relationships, unless I want one or the other, but perhaps Sudge needs to be free of the other boy. It is strange. Now the little boy says he would leave Ross, for me, as he would not before have left him for anybody else." She laughed, puzzled. "But he would want me to stay with him, and I am too old, and not old enough a woman to take on a boy. I have seen Lady Mart with her young American boy, and that was too much for me to think upon. She is older, she drinks more desperately, she is not healthy as I am, but never will I let life drive me to become what she is. But perhaps I would get to want and need Sudge; oh, no, no. I saw Lady Mart make a scene in terrified jealously because her young man was merely talking to a young and pretty girl. She was in agony that she would lose him, and her last chance. I believe I must move to the other side of the river, or return South. I wanted to be reckless and gay, but not involved in complications."

After dinner, some hours later, Sudge peered into the Falstaff to find Margot and me very cheerful over whiskey. He too looked secretively merry, and said he'd as soon get drunk this night. Good news had broken, for him and for Ross. His check for a hundred dollars on his novel had arrived. Ross had a letter from his mother telling that his sister was being married to a young millionaire, and that Ross might spend the next summer with the young couple on their lake estate in the north of Canada. And more tickling to Sudge than everything else, he had received a letter from a university offering him a position instructing freshmen and sophomores in Elizabethan and Restoration literature.

"Ross is home writing letters to his mother, sister, and brother-in-law. We both knew him as a merry drunk and nightlife lecher. He'll loan Ross money to get back, to keep him from talking too much." Sudge rocked on his stool and snorted with infantile delight. "Ross is going back to Canada on the first boat available, and I'll go back in the fall, in time to take the university job."

That Margot, I, and others at the bar joked and laughed at the thought of the childish-looking Sudge lecturing to college students didn't dampen his joyous mirth in the least. It was only when somebody asked if he might not have to quell his modern impulses and tastes somewhat did Sudge become scornful. He regretted his past indiscretions, when, coming over on a freighter, he had talked of *Ulysses* to the captain and officers. Quickly brushing aside all experimental and "modern" movements, he lectured like an eighty-year-old dean of literature at a sectarian university. He spoke of sanity and balance and getting back to sound English prose. He scorned modern poetry, and praised Milton, Wordsworth, Byron, Shelley, and Browning (but slightingly). After a third brandy and soda he turned, for old time's sake, to me and talked soothingly to reform me. Had I read Thomas Love Peacock? There was a man who could say more in a sentence, or in a page, than any modern says in chapters and whole books. Peacock had been his model in the novel that had been accepted. His message was that he had been a boy with curiosity, but that now his tastes and attitudes had matured, and ripely he lectured on. Sudge had no intention of waiting until he stood before a classroom of college students to lecture on English letters and morals and the lasting qualities in art. His young sagacity had everyone at the bar defenseless, and the barman, and all bar clients, could only ply him with drink to let him prattle on. Too often had he and Ross appeared as wistful little boys for it not to please old-timers to see Sudge so merry. Plainly too, to me, he was merry about the idea that all was set for a romance between him and the ripe Margot, as soon as Ross had sailed for Canada. He had pined for a romance with a woman of mature experience for years.

"I am moving tomorrow to Passy," Margot told him, smiling strangely. Sudge, a little drunk, followed her gaze and his face fell. She was looking at an evidently wealthy Swedish man of middle age. "He was a friend of my husband's years back," Margot informed Sudge, seeing his expression grow dour. "I talked to him at the Vikings bar and he will give me an apartment. Montparnasse is not for me. I need money. I have been thinking that it is better to regard what position I have left. You, Sudge dear, I am ahead of. You will be a respectable professor of English, but tomorrow I will be already no longer a bohemian."

Sudge looked disappointed, but his merriment did not fall completely from him. When Margot departed with her Swedish friend, he confided that he understood: Margot was full of wile and caprice and intrigue. She wanted to be a courtesan de-luxe. The Swede was no friend of her husband's, but somebody had told her he was rich.

"She wouldn't have wanted to wait for Ross to get on the boat, either," Sudge snorted. "She tried to make me say I'd see little of him if she lived with me. Dear Ross. He will be terribly lonely on the boat and in Canada until I get back. Kit, I'll bring you Peacock's book tomorrow. You must see what prose he writes." Sudge was earnestly serious now. A shadow, however, had come over his mirth as he began to wonder whether Ross could stand Montreal, and whether he himself could actually stand being a college instructor.

CHAPTER NINETEEN

TEN DAYS LATER, ROSS HAD ACTUALLY TAKEN A boat back to Canada, slipping way quietly. It was surprising that he went without Sudge, but he was supremely confident that Sudge would soon follow. Sadie, the dachshund, was left to keep Sudge company.

As the season deepened into winter, the usual Paris pall weighed upon people's spirits, with chill driving them into the interiors of cafes. Consuela Lutyens decided to have her long postponed marriage; Felix Lutyens and Dale Burke retired to a cottage in the country as Dale was to have a child. The summer lot of Quarterites returned to England and America, went to Italy, the South of France, or Spain, or retired to little villages outside of Paris. The small "American bars" took on their winter qualities, too.

Daniel, a French journalist who had been drinking absinthe and pernod for twenty-five years, hiccuped and belched over his drink, talking to himself and his fingers and figments of his imagination. Brussier, who hated and cursed Americans, started nightly brawls, which never became quite as deadly as the combatants promised. Myron Tomson drank his pernods and went to sleep standing up, his huge black-haired head drooping, and his protruding dark eyes making martyred accusations at the world should he be awakened.

Mike Murphy, with a terror of policemen, and a great admiration for gangsters, talked constantly of racketeers, while reading every book and newspaper account of crime he could get his hands on. He read aloud to the bar at large. He punched the air, and banged a fist into a palm, shouting, "Zowie, bam, another knockout. Nice friendly boy, what? Pow, and down she went. Nice people, what?" He talked too much one night and fought with a newspaperman until the fight became a free-for-all. In the uproar an old French soak screamed, "*Vive la France. Merde à l'Angleterre et l'Amerique.*" A young American patriot leaped into the fray to defend his country's honor. Several of the combatants were arrested and spent the night in the gendarmerie, but they were released in the morning to have more pleasant evenings.

The Gropers were back from Theoule, as were Gaylord Showman and the Mengs. Gaylord was at once disgusted with Paris, and again gave up drink to save his liver. The Mengs, still on a diet, came seldom to the old haunts; and when the Gropers appeared, Freddie was disgusted with the Quarter's mangy futility, while Poodie talked of wanting to work and get back to America, and Moodie looked as though she hoped someone would encourage her to have a second pernod so that she could feel release and have magnetism and charm. Freddie, attending art classes given by Léger, had discovered that a fifth person who could influence her life had arrived. Beyond Léger, Harlen Winter, and myself, she didn't reveal who the other influences were. She did, however, read newspaper accounts and letters telling of dances and parties which she might have attended had she been in New York. These made her sad, feeling that she was letting youth pass by without the proper gaiety.

Colette Godescard had come back from Tahiti with her young Frenchman, and she had gone in for speaking baby talk and being most clinging vineish. They had been stranded and had taken up beachcombing in Tahiti, Colette swore. Phillipe earned their passage back by working as kitchen boy on the boat, and for this Colette would marry him and remain mildly faithful. Upon encountering Hilaria, she naturally had to have a night of drinking to celebrate her return. Then Colette and Hilaria seldom appeared on the scene.

Iron Smithy, a girl who consumed quantities of alcohol amazing to the most hardened drinkers, passed out nightly at some bar, but not before telling various people what she thought of them in very rich and racy language. A featherweight champion began appearing at the Falstaff with his manager and trainer. They were dudishly clean, washed behind the ears, and smoked big black gussies. They spat on the floor out of the corner of their mouths, drank copiously, but soon stopped coming. The wrong legends had reached them, or it was out of season, for they evidently found no romance or adventure here. Soon other Quarter habitués spoke of trips they wished to take, and two actually did leave to investigate the Russian situation firsthand.

The Flannagans were about, though they had talked of going to Monte Carlo, or Italy, for months. Flannagan was confused, and seemed unable to get across the river to buy tickets for anywhere. Having discovered that his school French did not function, he was scared of other foreign countries, and, little as he liked the Quarter, people there spoke English. Apologizing to himself for having done no work since arriving in Paris, he talked of doing a story on the boys. They puzzled and bothered him. The Brinkers, who had a siege of head-hunting, had taken up with both the Flannagans and the boys, before Ross's departure. Mrs. Brinker had quickly determined that she didn't like Flannagan and had let him know. However, the boys pleased her. She didn't care for reading, and their glib irony and erudition helped her out of situations in which the conversation had become too informed. Because the boys had politeness, she liked having them at her teas and cocktail parties whenever she had collected a rare species of known success or genius.

Flannagan and I sat by a charcoal burner on the terrace of a corner bistro on a dampish afternoon. Sudge appeared with Sadie. She, as usual, had her nose pointed toward the Falstaff. There were three men in white coats, and white coats meant a kitchen and food to Sadie. She had long ago discovered that by mounting a bar stool, placing her forefeet on the bar, and sniffing with tender wistfulness, she obtained food and caresses. The caresses didn't mean much to her, but for food she had always a weakness.

Sudge looked dejected. It was six weeks since Ross departed, and still Sudge had no definite plans for his return to Canada. He had apparently forgotten the idea of being an instructor; a reluctance to leave Paris or to return to the bosom of his family governed him. He was lonely, but he had Sadie, and he seemed not to miss Ross as much as he had expected.

Sudge and Flannagan didn't care for each other, but Sudge joined us at my invitation. It was too dismal a day for much but grayly staring into space until the night lights came on, and drink may have warmed or solaced our commiserating hearts. "I'm festered," Sudge confided to me. "You know that Jew lecher, Abramson, who I wrote about in my memoirs? He's in town, doesn't know anybody, and his version of French doesn't operate. He wants to be with me all the time. I know he's lonesome, but he festers me." A childish plaint of helplessness was back in Sudge's voice.

"What did you ever do with those memoirs, Sudge?"

"Tore them up. They were disgustingly idiotic," Sudge said, having one of his moments of remorse about past indiscretions. "I wish nobody had ever seen a copy of them."

"You used to think Abramson funny."

Sudge, with tea before him, Sadie cuddled warmly in his lap, and somebody to talk to, began to look less dejected. He snorted his mirth. "Yes, he wasn't around us much in Montreal, and he furnished some good laughs with his hopefulness with broads he picked up. Now he's about with a copy of Ovid's *Art of Love* in one pocket, and a book of brothel addresses in another. That's what Ross put him up to, pulling his leg. Ross told him once to read Petronius, and now he's discovered *The Golden Ass*, the Marquis de Sade, and several French books he can't read but that some other Jew had told him were erotic. Having just read a bit of Huysmans he must have a spell of luxurious perversity and eroticism. He'll be turning Catholic mystic next. Now he says that Paris disgusts him. They know nothing of the subtleties and nuances of love here. The *poules* don't want him at any price. He's too mangy, a dumpy little mucker with rat yellow teeth and dandruff on his coat collar. I can't tell him how his breath smells. What can I do about him?"

Sudge was helpless again, but bravely managed to snicker as he observed Flannagan regarding him with perplexity. Flannagan couldn't decide. Was Sudge a mere little twirp, and if so why did such a variety of people seem fond of him? Also Flannagan had surely seen that Sudge was generous and quick with his sympathies as well as with his money.

"Can't you make Abramson understand that you're working and want to be alone in your studio?" I offered as indifferent comfort.

"No." Sudge was burned up with disgust. "He came home with me last night, and stuck around all day. I started to read *The Anatomy of Melancholy*, thinking that would bore him. It did." A comic idea struck Sudge and he gurgled. "Burton must have been a merry soul. Think of being so bored as to compile every thought on melancholy ever written."

Flannagan confessed his disillusionment with Paris, and said he must leave soon. He was bothered by the way we flaunted sophistication as though cynicism is profound. He wanted to get back among the real people.

"The ones you write about?" Sudge said, a flash of temper in his birdlike face. "You've been around Paris quite a time yourself now."

"Yes, but where do all these people come from? They're only pretending to be released."

Sudge's eyes blazed, not because he wanted to defend Paris people, but because he detested Flannagan's mind and writing. "Don't you suppose some of your characters are in Paris now looking for life, dumbly following fate? If they aren't, I don't know where all the morons about come from. Anyway, some of the types about have reflexes enough to go away if they don't like it here."

Flannagan didn't bat an eye, but Sudge had struck below the belt, if Flannagan understood his implication. He looked sluggishly puzzled, but perhaps that was his mask, and plainly no he-man author writing about prizefighters, thugs, gangsters, and toughs in general, as he did, could protect his characters from a priggish young boy as Flannagan believed Sudge to be. After a silence he said he wished he could make the train to London tonight, but his bags weren't fully packed. They had been in this condition for a week, but whenever the time for final packing and departure came, neither Flannagan nor Maggie was capable of decision. London, too, would be a new problem to cope with. As we sat there in bad humor, Reyner, the editor-bookseller, came by. He had more or less taken Flannagan under his wing, since Flannagan appeared ready to listen to his editorial opinions and advice. Reyner wanted his genial gestures appreciated by such young authors as he would discover suitable for appearance along with his gentle-spirited editorials.

"Well, well, what's this?" Reyner asked, twitching his ferretlike eyes and beaming a crinkled smile. "I thought you and your good wife intended to be off to London tonight."

Flannagan's slow mind groped for an explanation, then gave up to apologize. "We waited until three for our laundry, and it crowds the suitcase. Maggie doesn't know how to pack. I guess we won't get away until tomorrow."

"You're babies, complete babies." Reyner was paternally jovial and decisive. "I promised to see you off this week. Come along now. Get your bags and I'll take you to the station. I'll even buy the tickets for you and take their cost out of what I owe you for the story you promised to send me for the magazine." Flannagan was slow, perhaps reluctant, to move and go to another new and bewildering great city. Still, the decision was being made for him. He went with Reyner. Sudge chuckled and wondered if even Reyner could galvanize Flannagan and Maggie into action. They were the breed of Irish that dislikes activity.

Suddenly Sudge moaned, "There comes Mrs. Moodlow. I promised to give Sadie to her, thinking I'd go back to Canada in a few days. Poor Sadie. She'll be heartbroken to leave me. She was only a poor starved stray when Ross and I picked her up in Luxembourg and nobody had ever fussed over her."

Mrs. Moodlow came to the table, and Sudge, quickly brave, handed her the leash with Sadie on its end. "Please don't feed her too much. She's healthier if you don't. I do hope she learns to like you soon," he pleaded.

"Oh, Sadie and I will get on," Mrs. Moodlow said. "I'm sure such a charming old matron as she is loves food more than any sentimental attachment. I have to go. I have an article I must write to catch a midnight boat, and how I hate it."

Sudge disapproved of the idea that Sadie would not miss and long for him, but as Mrs. Moodlow started off, Sadie turned back with a vaguely questioning look, wagged her tail and body, the lengths of which ran into each other, and then pattered merrily after Mrs. Moodlow. Sudge looked sadly disgruntled. Somewhere from the depths of him a thought spoke itself. "Ross has been gone six weeks, and I have had only one short letter from him. He's staying with his sister and her rich husband. I was sorry he had to go back. We thought he would be so lonely, but he doesn't even bother to write me news."

"Sudge, don't recline on the idea that old friends and places are best; both change, and you have to find the qualities you liked in the old in the new."

"But Ross was with me for five years." Sudge was reluctant to accept my attitude, but now did not, as he once would have, accuse me of cynicism.

"And in those five years you did too much for him, letting him be chiefly dependent on you. Away from you, do you think Ross will forgive you that?"

"I'm going to have a phobia if I can't get drunk tonight," Sudge said, very infantile and attempting to be brave. "I haven't any money either."

"Drink, I'll set you up. Hell, you're in your normal state if you're in the midst of a phobe. All's well with the world, and you can't be as superficial and sophisticated as Flannagan implies."

"I ought to go back to Montreal, I suppose, but I don't want to. I really don't want to be a literary man anymore, but I'd rather write than do any other work I can do until I inherit my money." Sudge's melancholy was becoming philosophic and a bit analytic as he sipped another brandy and soda.

"And if you had your money now, Sudge, you might be so bored by the time you're twenty-five that you could never realize your ambition to be a rakish old man. As it is, you'll have years, after twenty-five, to be a naughty old roué, and not begin now that slow form of tortuous suicide which monotony and ennui are. Having to calculate a little is some mental exercise."

Sudge wasn't responsive to my facetiousness. "I think sometimes now I'd have ambition, if I knew what to have ambition about." He was grave, but chuckled after a sip of brandy. "I'll stop. I know, Kit, it irritates you to hear somebody soul-torment themselves and ask for solutions. People who do that sort of thing are fearful asses and generally mangy."

Within an hour Reyner came back looking hot, somewhat fretful, but triumphant. He had to prove that he had managed to get the Flannagans on the train. "I got them off," he said breathlessly, doing his overworked genial smile beneath which grinned irritation and wonder at the indecisiveness of such people. "I tell you, it was a job. They're babies. Never have I seen such helpless people in my life. Mrs. Flannagan hadn't packed the laundry, and the bags were full, and we had no time. I took the bundle and hurried them and the baggage into a taxi. We hadn't space to get the laundry packed, so at the station I told them to get it in some case while I got the tickets. They hadn't when I returned, but three cases were open and the train was pulling out. I bundled them into a carriage, and pushed the laundry and open bags to them through the window. At once the train started rolling. What will become of those babies in London? They also want to visit Ireland, but they are likely to be on a boat to Australia and not know it. It was a job, I tell you."

Reyner felt efficient and triumphant. Lacking much sense of comedy, he decided he must be amusing as Sudge was chortling in his nostrils. To quiet himself, he had a whiskey and offered us drinks. Soon he hurried away, Sudge swore, to give the impression of being an overworked editor who had little time to waste at cafe tables. "He feels more important if he's sitting with Steingold or Ellery Saunderson. He does intend to be literary and a serious patron of letters, but I wager he likes pornographic books mainly. Otherwise, why does he have so many German photographic studies?" Sudge tried to control his snorts, and bubbled, "What is his private life? I feel like going around and talking to his concierge. I nearly exploded one night when he and Saunderson competed with each other in telling dirty stories just after old Ellery had been complaining that the intellectual people of Paris don't get together often enough."

It was dinner time. Sudge and I moved down to the Coupole bar to eat, and to see who was about. Dale Burke was there with Felix Lutyens, Consuela and her French husband, and three young French surrealists. Dale was feeling joyous, as her novel was out in England and America and getting fine reviews as "lovely, and true feminine prose at its most sensitized." Sudge rather drily inquired if she wasn't a bit too deliberately poetical, with her moons swooning on the lawn while the nightingales cadenced harmonics to the warm, brightly tragic night.

Dale didn't mind. She insisted on buying the bar drinks out of the check she had just received. She was accustomed to telling Sudge that "he wasn't important," as he was inclined to suggest that she dripped beauty all over the place pretentiously. She wasn't Sappho to him, and however much soul she had, Sudge claimed himself soulless when Dale became too vaporized with fluttering sensitivity.

Consuela soon introduced Katherine Montoon to Sudge and me. I knew about her from Gaylord Showman, with whom she had lived for a time. She was thirty-odd, a painter who talked well enough the contemporary patter, and who swore she was the best woman painter of the day. From Consuela I gathered that Katherine was on the loose at the moment, though generally she stuck much to her studio and worked. Apparently Sudge's humor and birdlike twitterings and suppressed snorts amused her, for soon she was deep in conversation with him. He was confiding to her that he wanted to fall in love, to know what it meant.

"You do want trouble in life, don't you?" Katherine said, smiling at Consuela and me to indicate how amusing she found this child. "Do you watch some of the love matches about?"

Sudge insisted that he must be in love. Things were too empty unless something happened inside him. Katherine grew engrossed in him as he talked. Consuela wanted to do some wandering, so she and I left to go dancing. At midnight I returned to La Coupole for a snack, but looking through the glass door I saw that the bar was empty except for Sudge and Katherine who were sitting in the corner. They were glued together in a long kiss, so not to interrupt them, I went on to the Dôme for food.

CHAPTER TWENTY

BUSINESS TOOK ME TO AMERICA, AND THERE I decided to try a little of the normal, balanced, and sane life which various elders are prone to advocate. It wasn't in New York, Chicago, Boston, or the Southwest to be found, and those who talked about it, deploring the lives of expatriates, seemed neither happy, contented, interesting, nor interested. In an isolated town in Mexico, there was an interval of tranquil days, with the more or less primitive natives *mañana*-resigned and often gaily indifferent to time, problems, or mortality. However, after some months, I felt isolated from kinds I knew, and hearing the call of French terrace cafes, good beer, wines, and spirits, as well as the summons of the Mediterranean, I returned to France.

On the boat I encountered an English novelist and thought myself pleased until he started a popular discussion about which the world will have—Catholicism or Russia. He was only into his third whiskey before he was muttering darkly about the forces of evil that were collecting in the world; and on imbibing a fourth whiskey he confided that he had ruined his life by too many love affairs in his youth, unromantic sexual experiences which had deadened what sensibility he had. I was sure I detected him as a hophead, too, for his mutterings were soon soddenly dire in a way one does not connect with mere alcohol. He nodded and muttered and hallucinated so that I could not know whether or not he agreed with my remark that to revive a corpse such as Catholicism would be an error. Corpses walking in the sunlight always stink; and the Russian business could be allowed its experiment for fifty years and could not easily fail more dismally than had religion.

"Yes, you're right," he mumbled. "Religion is dangerous. Individuals and groups interpret to their own ends. What is to become of us all? The dark forces are gathering."

Whatever dark forces were gathering in his mind, I fled to the salon, where dancing was going on, feeling that what Hamlet, saints, philosophers, and scientists can't solve is not my problem. Those who want to may retreat into the moldering caves of religion, but one has the right to be unserious or indifferent, when there are a quantity of mediums and pastimes in which energy can be better utilized.

The English novelist liked somebody to drink and chat with, and there was a dull assortment of humans on the boat. Because I understood his feeling, instead of avoiding him, I practiced the listening look while paying little attention to his serious searchings. He was with me on the train to Paris, and checked into the same hotel, as it was reasonable, but I knew Paris would let me avoid him if I felt inclined. It was four in the afternoon when we arrived at the hotel, and he had to have one whiskey, and then a few more, to buck him up. Understanding his state all too well, I stayed with him until restlessness and curiosity made me insist on going to Montparnasse. He came along, a bit wobbly, and rather morose from drink.

Fortunately I ran into Sudge seated in front of a small bistro on the Rue de Vaugirard, far from his former haunts. He was having tea and toast, frowning over a volume of Proust. He stirred, vaguely remembering me, and irritated perhaps to be recalled from his ponderings, much as his dachshund bitch had vaguely remembered him after she had been with a new owner for a few days. Quickly, however, his natural courtesy asserted itself. "You, Kit, I thought you'd never be back, that you were settled in Mexico."

"No, I won't be settled anywhere for many years, if ever until the old boy pops off. What's the news?"

"Really, I don't know," Sudge said rather plaintively. "Katherine and I never go near the Quarter. She ought to be along any time now. She'll be fearfully glad to see you."

"And Gaylord, is he in town?"

"No, he's down South," Sudge laughed, and his laugh had become less of a snort, more subdued. "And Lili is with him again. He forgave her various infidelities, doesn't drink much anymore, and talks constantly of the new painting technique he has developed."

A strange emotion, or more properly, sensation, went through me. "And Ross, is he still in Canada?"

Sudge was vague, remembering with some difficulty, it seemed. "Oh, he's an instructor at the university, the position I was to have, I guess. He seldom writes to me."

Distress, the slight premonition of depression, fluttered into my heart. I ordered a calvados. They were all "settling down." The calvados bucked me up to ask Sudge, "What have you been doing?"

"Reading, studying maybe you call it. Katherine has a good many books and I've read them all."

"Any good ones? I'm going to try Paris quietly this time."

"Not many new ones. Trollope, Smollett, Sterne, some Elizabethans, and a good many of the Loeb Library Greeks and Latins. Athanasius is fearfully jolly. I've been reading Berkeley and Descartes and Kant and Aristotle too; they're frightfully much better than one would ever know from college courses."

A fleeting impression ran through my mind that Sudge was becoming terribly British, and perhaps reversing the order of reactions in usual youth. Just a year ago he had been a staid, balanced, old man, advocating Peacock and Restoration prose with its neat orderliness; before he had fancied himself as a naughty boy; and now, did he reveal a phase of going through a metaphysical or religious crisis? He seemed painfully earnest.

I picked up the volume of Proust. "Are you liking this?"

Sudge looked sour, and for the first time at this meeting regained some of his boyish scorn. "He's too fake-analytic with his delicate soul fainting under the perfumed anesthesia of what he feels about art and physical beauty. As the *London Times* would say, 'This is prose at its finest, synchronized to the mood of the author's emotional intuition at the height of realized sensation which is sensibility quickly quivering.' No, I'm trying to read through him, but I can't stick him, or Joyce, or Virginia Woolf. They work too hard digging moldy delicacies out of their subconscious. I've been reading Trollope. He's a rollicking old port-wine hound, hypocrite, and commercial writer, isn't he? I'd die trying to live among characters such as he writes about, but he's snortingly comic. There's none of that 'The shadows were but pursued phantoms of what he tried to believe he remembered from his all-too-precocious childhood.' I can't stand fine writing." Sudge looked pained. "I hope you didn't read that idiotic book they published in the States last year. I should have waited."

"I liked it, Sudge. Don't be uppish. Even if it's bad or mediocre, you aren't the only writer who has done rotten work."

"I know. But I don't want to write now; I want to live." Sudge's tone became childishly plaintive. "I'm so bored with authors trying to imply significance where there is none; and being intellectual or poetic when they aren't poets and have no intellect. It's been all right till the last two weeks, because I had great fun reading, but now father's writing to me again to return home. I'm tired of fighting with him to think or feel what I do. He says I don't know what I want, and he doesn't know what I want because he never had what he wanted himself."

"You get on with Katherine all right, I take it. You've been with her for almost a year now, haven't you?"

"Yes, but she's restless, and neither of us has enough money. We talk of taking a freight boat and going—anywhere—to be on the sea for two or more months. Tonight we're going to the border of Spain, and maybe to Morocco, if we don't find a freight boat that's doing a tramp trip we can take for what money we have."

"Good idea. Perhaps you've both done too long a siege of Paris without variation."

Katherine came to join us. Before she had been seated many minutes, I guessed that her manner might upset Sudge. She was older-patronizing and amused, somewhat, in her treatment of him, but she was fond and affectionate. Sudge left the table for a few minutes. I wasn't quite at ease, and wanted to look up other people I knew before going south, as I planned, in a few days. Long ago I had become used to the idea that one has to become reacquainted with old friends on encountering them after a time and a different variety of experiences than they have been having.

"Sudge appears to be suffering growing-pains," I commented.

Katherine smiled. "He needed to, from what he has told me. He was two years in France with Ross, without either of them having gotten far away from Montreal and the school memories."

"What's his next phase to be? He's skeptical about most writers, and literature in general; and a bit scornful of philosophy. Has he had a prophetic streak yet, or does he remain usually disdainful and mirthy?"

"He still wants to be in love," Katherine laughed.

"And he isn't, with you?"

"We're fond of each other." She was noncommittal. "He bothers because of the others I've lived with. I once didn't think so but he has jealous and possessive emotions, the real old-fashioned male kind. He's distressed about his own past, and mine too. No, he's still a boy-romantic. His obsession about being in love puzzles me."

"Does it really?" I asked shortly, thinking of Ross. Katherine's gaze caught mine and she grimaced, and then smiled ironically and answered: "Certainly not; don't be silly."

Sudge came back to the table from downstairs, and said, "We'll have to go if we're to catch the eight o'clock train. We haven't all our packing quite done. But, Katherine, let me buy Kit just one drink. I'm so sorry. We'd have waited till tomorrow night if we'd known you were coming back to town."

"But darlin'," Katherine said in her manner of dropping final g's, "have we enough money or time?"

"But yes, for Kit," Sudge said, wavering. "Don't you think so, dear?"

"Yes, if you think so, darlin'."

"No, don't bother. We have to go on to meet somebody. Don't wait if you're rushed. I'll catch the bill," I said, wanting to be away, and aware that the English novelist was going to sleep in his chair, while Sudge eyed him with distaste.

"If it's truly all right, Kit," Sudge said, plaintively apologetic.

"Of course."

Katherine picked up her bag and arose, waiting for Sudge to finish his brandy quickly. He hesitated. I took his hand and Katherine's to bid a casual goodbye. "Drop me a line if you feel like it. Let me know what you think of wherever it is you settle in."

Sudge still hesitated, feeling that he ought to offer me a final greeting and farewell drink, and sensing, too, I thought, that I was pondering whether to leave the novelist asleep in his chair, or wake him up and assume the responsibility of presenting a new old soak to the Quarter barmen. However, Katherine spoke up: "Are you comin', darlin'?" It was certain that the mature Katherine looked on the young Sudge as an easy solution to her love life. He had youth and physique, courtesy and wit, and let her do the managing as some older men in the past had not permitted.

"Yes, dear, we can get a taxi at the corner," Sudge answered. As he went away he had again that rather hurried, tiptoeish walk which was secretive or reticent. Possibly he wanted to object to being managed, but if he wished to be "in love" he had better resign himself.

I shook the Englishman, and he came torpidly awake. "Let's go on to the Quarter. There's an Irishman, several Russians, and a Pole there, all of whom delight in talking religion, mathematics, higher thought, and the power of evil. I'll locate one of them for you surely, and then I must be on my way, doing the rounds."

ANNOTATIONS

PAGE

CHAPTER ONE

1 "Duse or Bernhardt": Eleanora Duse (1858–1924) of Italy and Sarah Bernhardt (1844–1923) of France were the greatest actresses of their era.

2 "Comte de Lautréamont": Isidore Ducase (1846–70), whose novel *Maldoror* influenced such French surrealists as Radiguet.

2 "Blaise Cendrars": Blaise Cendrars (1887–1961) was born in Switzerland but left home at sixteen to seek adventure. Poet, novelist, and autobiographer, he was associated with the early cubists in Paris. After losing an arm in the trenches during World War I, he returned to Paris, where he became part of the avant-garde poetry, music, and art scene. Having lived in New York, he was on good terms with the American expatriate writers.

3 "Gaston": barman and part owner of La Coupole; admired by the Americans for his understanding and kindness to artists and writers.

4 "*corps comme*": body like

7 "*cochon, ordure, putain*": pig, filth, whore

7 "Madame Select": the *patronne* (proprietress) of the Select, who looked after the cash register. The Select catered to mostly the same crowd as the Dôme. It was the first café to stay open all night, and Madame Select was considered too quick to call the gendarmes at the first sign of trouble.

CHAPTER TWO

10 "Laforgue": Jules Laforgue (1860–1887) was born in Montevideo, where his father taught French. A major French symbolist poet and inaugurator of *vers libre*, Laforgue wrote in colloquial language and even used slang. His ironic tone undercut conventional values and romantic notions. His poetry strongly influenced the modernists, especially T. S. Eliot. He died in poverty of tuberculosis.

14 "favorite actor": John Barrymore (1882–1942), great stage and silent screen actor of the period whose aquiline nose in profile was much photographed

and celebrated. McAlmon resembled Barrymore not only in profile but also in being a heavy drinker.

14 "American novelist": Sinclair Lewis (1885–1951). McAlmon develops the incident here, which is noted only in passing in *Being Geniuses Together*, where the unnamed Caridad is referred to as a "tough flapper."

CHAPTER THREE

23 "Elagabalus": Varius Avitas Bassianus was made Imperator of Rome in A.D. 218 at age 14. As hereditary priest of sun god Elagabal, he took the name Elagabalus. His appeal to Sudge and Ross was undoubtedly that he was a dissolute youth who appointed inept friends to high office. The Praetorian Guard killed him and his mother in A.D. 222.

CHAPTER FOUR

26 "Muzzie-Cat": Hemingway's nicknames for his wife Hadley ("Olive") were variously "Feather Cat," "Feather Kitty," and "Wicky Poo," while son John Hadley Nicanor (b. 1923) was called "Bumby." Hemingway signed his letters to Hadley "Waxen Pup" in the early years of their marriage. They did have a dog named Waxen Puppy, but he had to be euthanized in 1923. In the typescript of "Nightinghouls," "Feather Kitty" is crossed out, and "Muzzie-Cat" is written in above.

27 "Lord Mike": Pat Guthrie, model for Mike Campbell in *The Sun Also Rises.*

27 "Jewish bookdealer": Harold Loeb (1891–1974), novelist and founding editor of *Broom*, was the model for Robert Cohn in *The Sun Also Rises.* Sisley Huddleston quotes Loeb (without naming him) as saying: "I am the Jew in Hemingway's book. . . . I don't mind who knows it. At least I am made to knock out the other man. He was a poor fish. As for the girl, she was better than Hemingway described her. Still, he makes me of real flesh and blood, and I don't mind" (*Paris Salons*, 123). Loeb offers his side of the story in *The Way It Was* (1959).

28 "Dutch": F. Scott Fitzgerald (1896–1940). Did McAlmon pick the name Dutch Kelly for Fitzgerald from *The Sun Also Rises*, given that Spider Kelly was Robert Cohn's boxing coach at Princeton and that Fitzgerald was a Princetonian?

31 "Howard": Harold Stearns (1891–1943). Hemingway calls Stearns "Harvey Stone" in *The Sun Also Rises.* Journalist and racetrack tout, Stearns was notorious for cadging drinks. He tells his hard-luck story in *The Street I Know* (1935).

32 "Philip Danbury": Richard Aldington (1892–1962), English poet, novelist, critic, and biographer; his antiwar novel *Death of a Hero* was published abridged in England in 1929 and unexpurgated in France in 1930.

32 "sound romanticism": McAlmon writes of Sisley Huddleston in *Being Geniuses Together* that he was "always ready to talk about the literary clock turning back to Romanticism and away from Sordid Naturalism" (Boyle, *Geniuses*, 250).

34 "The goodwill editor": In *Being Geniuses Together*, McAlmon is also caustic toward Titus: "The pompous and trite editorials Titus wrote in his endeavor to be a parental editor, indicating the way the young should write, killed interest in the venture [*This Quarter*]" (Boyle, *Geniuses*, 283). Titus challenged Morley Callaghan and McAlmon to write a story about homosexuals for the magazine. Callaghan produced "Now That April's Here" about Glassco's and Taylor's fight over Sibley Dreis (Stanley Dahl in *Memoirs* and Sanka in "Nightinghouls"), but McAlmon demurred.

34 "Reyner promised": Graeme Taylor (Ross) published two extracts from a novel (uncompleted) based on his experiences in and around Montreal in *This Quarter* 4, 1929.

CHAPTER FIVE

35 "studio down the hall": In *Being Geniuses Together*, McAlmon mentions that down the hall from his studio apartment lived Yvette Ledoux (Colette Godescard) and Gwen Le Gallienne (Laura Bradley).

36 "Raymond Duncan": Duncan (1874–1966), brother of dancer Isadora Duncan, founded a neo-Greek colony on the outskirts of Paris into which he recruited young women, dressed them in togas and sandals, and made them sell gewgaws to support the colony. Kay Boyle entered the colony, and McAlmon helped her and her daughter Sharon to escape.

37 "Princess of Faraway": Englishwoman Gladys Palmer Brooke, the Dayang Muda of Sarawak, cousin of Archie Craig (see Eustace Cross below). Boyle and Glassco both had a hand in writing her memoirs, *Relations and Complications, Being the Recollections of H. H. the Dayang Muda of Sarawak* (1929).

38 "André Boissard": Richard Brault, Kay Boyle's first husband.

38 "invalid editor": Ernest Walsh (1895–1926). Badly injured in a plane crash as an Army Air Corps pilot in World War I, he was a poet and co-editor, with Ethel Moorhead, of *This Quarter*, and a great admirer of McAlmon's writing as well as Hemingway's.

38 "Eustace Cross": Archibald Craig, pen name of English poet Cedric Harris, cousin of Gladys Palmer Brooke, who was, in addition to McAlmon's description, homosexual.

CHAPTER SIX

42 "Quarts Arts": a licentious costume ball held annually in the Latin Quarter.

46 "young surrealist": Robert Desnos (1900–1945), French surrealist poet and novelist. Active in the Resistance during World War II, he died in a concentration camp in 1945. Most of his poetry was collected in *Domaine Public* (1953).

48 "colored writer": Claude McKay (1890–1948), Jamaican-born poet and novelist of African-American life, "in whose honour," according to Huddleston, "one of the most memorable parties of the Quarter was given." Among the notables attending was McAlmon (*Back to Montparnasse*, 107).

49 "Jimmie": Jimmie Charters (1897–1975), originally from Liverpool, was the American expatriates' favorite Montparnasse barman. With Morrill Cody he wrote *This Must Be the Place: Memoirs of Jimmie the Barman* (1934). He and McAlmon were good friends and looked after each other in brawls. In *Djuna: The Life and Work of Djuna Barnes* (1995), Phillip Herring quotes Charters's account of a drunken "internationally known American newspaperman" becoming enraged when Barnes rebuffs his advances and slugs her. At a nearby table with a friend, McAlmon is decked too, but gets up and knocks the man down and sits on him. When McAlmon lets him up, the guy starts swinging again. Now Jimmie, having a drink on his night off, jumps into the fracas and floors the guy three times (*Djuna*, 139–40).

51 "Brick comforted me": In *Being Geniuses Together*, McAlmon recalls drinking with Bricktop one early morning at a cheap bar where black expatriates gathered after hours, and she treats him to "an uproarious description of how I looked the day she got Jimmie the barman and me out of jail" (Boyle, *Geniuses*, 317).

CHAPTER SEVEN

54 "Oxford-Irishman"; "famed English sculptor"; "famed English painter and lover": J. W. N. Sullivan (1886–1937); Jacob Epstein (1880–1959); Augustus John (1878–1961).

56 "Armenian": Michael Arlen (1895–1956), born Dikran Kuyumjian, author of the vastly popular novel *The Green Hat* (1924), whose heroine, Iris March, was modeled on Nancy Cunard, with whom McAlmon was intimate and who provided his model for Hilda Gay in "The Lodging House." He profiles her in the "Neurotic Correspondence" segment of the long poem "The Revolving Mirror," collected in *Portrait of a Generation* (1926).

56 "master of prose style": McAlmon says much the same about Ford Madox Ford in *Being Geniuses Together:* Ford told "the world that he was the

master of prose style in the English language," that he was a "genius" from a "family of geniuses," and that he had more readers than H. G. Wells. Despite scoffing at Ford's "mythomania," McAlmon grants that "he had many likable and admirable traits . . . and gave some very amusing parties" (Boyle, *Geniuses*, 127–28).

57 "His face was a landscape": In *Being Geniuses Together*, McAlmon remarks that he had known Hilaire Hiler since 1920 (1921?), and in spite of his odd appearance, he was "beautiful in his way." McAlmon also praises Hiler's linguistic and musical skills, as well as his painting, designing, and scholarship.

58 "Boeuf sur le Toit [Cow on the Roof]": The Boeuf sur le Toit, established by Jean Cocteau in his surrealist phase, became a gay and lesbian hangout in 1928.

CHAPTER EIGHT

65 "Irish tenor voice": James Joyce (1882–1941), with his long-suffering wife Nora.

69 "present girl . . . with her sister": Pauline Pfeiffer Hemingway (1895–1951) and Virginia "Jinny" Pfeiffer (1902–1973). In the spring of 1929, with Pauline, Jinny, and Uncle Gus Pfeiffer, Hemingway came to Paris for an extended European stay that included a tour of Spain.

69 "the Jew and the blond villainess": Kathleen "Kitty" Cannell (1891–1974) (Elsie Mime) was the model for Frances Clyne in *The Sun Also Rises*. A good friend of McAlmon's, she was mistress to Harold Loeb ("the Jew") in 1925.

71 "Olive": Hadley Hemingway. During the spring of 1925, when Hemingway was infatuated with Duff Twysden, he would sometimes take Hadley home from late dances and parties to relieve Bumby's babysitter and then return to be with Twysden. According to Michael Reynolds, "Time and again he [Hemingway] would make his wife miserable with foolish and insulting public behavior . . ." (*Hemingway*, 289, 291).

CHAPTER NINE

77 "hack-reviewer husband": Courtenay Lemon, whom Barnes would refer to as her husband although there is no record of a legal marriage. For an accounting of Barnes's romances, with men and women, see Herring.

CHAPTER TEN

83 "Margot Lindstrom": Brian Busby conjectures that "Margot Lindstrom is either Margaret Whitney or Marguerite Lippe-Rosskam, who are thought

to have inspired Mrs. Quayle" in *Memoirs* (Busby to Smoller, November 17, 2004). Given the similarity between their names, Lippe-Rosskam is the more likely model. In *Character Parts*, Busby observes that "Glassco once described his relationship with Lippe-Rosskam as his 'first experience with real love'" (210).

CHAPTER ELEVEN

92 "given birth to a child": Here McAlmon is probably referring to Sharon, Boyle's daughter by Ernest Walsh.

95 "Felix Lutyen's Rolls Royce": McAlmon is mistaken about the make of Laurence Vail's car. It was a Hispano-Suiza, a gift from Peggy's mother Florette. Vail drove it as if it were a racing car (Gill, *Art Lover*, 121–22).

96 "Her sister died": Peggy Guggenheim's sister Benita died in childbirth on July 21, 1927. Peggy grieved deeply, causing a rift in her marriage. Here McAlmon skews the time line, for Benita died almost two years, not "a few months," before the events Consuela describes. Perhaps McAlmon was recalling an earlier conversation with Clotilde. A photograph of McAlmon, Peggy Guggenheim, Clotilde Vail, Kiki (Man Ray's favorite model and mistress), and surrealist writer Louis Aragon, taken at Le Canadel, is among McAlmon's memorabilia at the Beinecke Library.

98 "trying to flirt with": According to Anton Gill, Vail had an "obsession with his sister," and would become jealous and (especially when drinking) violent when men flirted with her. An exhibitionist (evidenced by his attire), he liked to make "scenes" with Clotilde as an audience (89). McAlmon's account of Vail's manic outburst therefore accords with the facts. Vail received a lenient six-month suspended sentence—doubtless, as Kit says, because of Peggy's wealth.

CHAPTER TWELVE

103 "granted him a degree": Gnarowski notes that McGill University does not list Graeme Taylor among its graduates (232).

105 "Married to a man": John Reed (1887–1920), Louise Bryant's first husband. Reed reported on labor strife for *The Masses* and other radical journals. His reporting on the Bolshevik Revolution was the basis of his seminal book on the Revolution, *Ten Days That Shook the World* (1919). He helped to organize the first Communist Party of the United States, and when he died in the Soviet Union in 1920, he was honored by burial in the Kremlin.

CHAPTER THIRTEEN

110 "young Frenchman": Gnarowski identifies him as the painter Georges Malkine, who was also the lover of Caridad (222).

111 "sailors don't care": an allusion to the title of Edwin M. Lanham's first book, which McAlmon published in 1929.

113 "Elihu Law": Ezra Pound (1885–1972). Perhaps McAlmon is punning ("Law") on the fact that Pound's father was a judge in Idaho.

117 "Mr. Bradley": Richard Le Gallienne (1866–1947), stepfather of Gwen and father of the actress Eva Le Gallienne. Born in Liverpool with roots in the Channel Islands, Le Gallienne was a member of the Rhymer's Club that included W. B. Yeats, Lionel Johnson, and Ernest Dowson. He later wrote a romantic novel and a memoir. From 1901 to 1927 he lived in the United States, spending his last years in southern France.

CHAPTER FOURTEEN

123 "The Gropers": the Meyer family. Fredericka "Freddie" is Felicia Meyer. A photograph of her, McAlmon, and Edwin and Joan Lanham in bathing suits in Theoule is among McAlmon's memorabilia at the Beinecke Library.

125 "Joseph Duveen": Sir Joseph Joel Duveen (1869–1939) was the foremost art dealer of his time. He helped to build art collections for J. P. Morgan and Henry Frick.

126 "Sanka": Sibley Dreis is called Stanley Dahl in Glassco's *Memoirs*. Her father immigrated to Winnipeg from the United States in 1919, and she became a naturalized Canadian citizen in 1922 (Busby to Smoller, February 16, 2005).

128 "coonskin coat": Gnarowski, in his edition of *Memoirs*, includes a photograph of Taylor, Glassco, and Dreis in Nice, in which Dreis, with dark skin and close-cropped hair, is wearing a fur coat.

CHAPTER SEVENTEEN

158 "This is Kit O'Malley": Morley Callaghan's account of first meeting McAlmon, Glassco, and Taylor differs from McAlmon's version. Callaghan and McAlmon had corresponded before Callaghan came to Paris in April 1929. He was grateful to McAlmon, whom he called "this generous man," for encouraging his writing. At the time, McAlmon was living in the Paris-New York Hotel (leaving Glassco and Taylor occupying his studio). When Callaghan comes to see him, McAlmon is "laconic" at first, "studiously unimpressed," but loosens up and tells him he is going south in an hour.

He also informs him about his countrymen Glassco and Taylor, "two bright boys from Montreal." Callaghan confesses to a "strange sneaking liking and respect for him no matter how badly he behaved" (*That Summer*, 81–85). After McAlmon leaves for the Riviera, the Callaghans move to his hotel, and then, as Sudge tells Kit, Glassco and Taylor help them find an apartment on the Rue de Santé. Callaghan's impression of the two young men is similar to McAlmon's: "bright little devils . . . inseparable companions, very understanding of each other, soft spoken with a mocking opinion about everybody" (91).

158 "outbox Pemberton": Although McAlmon's tone is ironical and detached, he was probably delighted that Hemingway, who to him had "a boy's need to be a tough guy, a swell, boxer, a strong man," took his lumps from the shorter, rather pudgy Callaghan (Boyle, *Geniuses*, 180).

159 "several All-American football players": McAlmon's older brother Will was a football star at the University of Minnesota, and Gene Vidal, his boyhood pal in South Dakota, was an all-American quarterback at West Point. Hemingway tells Callaghan that McAlmon's "trouble" (envious and insecure?) was that his brother "had been an idolized football player, and McAlmon had been no good at games" (*That Summer*, 233). In *Death in the Afternoon* (1932), Hemingway sneers at McAlmon's ("X.Y.") reactions at their first bullfight in 1923, then adds, "Does not care for sport of any sort. Does not care for games of chance." To Hemingway, devoted to both, McAlmon was clearly unmanly.

162 "Isaac Steingold": He may be Ludwig Lewisohn (1882–1955), German-born novelist and critic who in 1932 published *Expression in America*, analyzing American literature from a Freudian perspective.

CHAPTER EIGHTEEN

163 "a *diseuse*": a talker, mistress of ceremonies

163 "*Moquer*": a scoffer, a jester

165 "placed a novel": According to Gnarowski, Glassco claimed to have published books, of which there is no evidence. One such is *Contes en Crinoline*, supposedly published in French in Paris in 1930 (214).

CHAPTER NINETEEN

169 "actually taken a boat": There is a discrepancy between *Memoirs* and "Nightinghouls" as to why Taylor returned to Canada. In the former, it was to tend to his sick father; in the latter, it was to take a university teaching position originally offered to Sudge. In Busby's view "Glassco's is more probable,"

as Taylor seems not ever to have taught (Busby to Smoller, February 16, 2005).

169 "*Vive la France. Merde à l'Angleterre et l'Amérique*": Long live France. Shit on England and America.

170 "Colette would marry him": Gnarowski notes that Yvette Ledoux married Georges Malkine in 1931 (227).

175 "I got them off": Callaghan retained only a vague memory of this mad scramble to catch the train: "Our leave-taking of the Quarter and our departure to London seemed to have been rather hurried and crowded." He quotes a letter from Titus, who says, "[F]rankly, I have never before seen such an experience as we had getting you off." However, Callaghan cannot remember the "cause of the confusion" (*That Summer*, 239).

176 "nightingales cadenced": Sudge's (that is, McAlmon's) parodic "while the nightingales cadenced harmonics" and so forth may be a gentle pun on the title of Kay Boyle's first novel, *Plagued by the Nightingale*. If so, McAlmon telescopes time because the book was not published until 1931. He might also have punned on her title in selecting his own. Because Glassco appeared to him "birdlike," and he and Taylor seemed furtive and spectral, McAlmon may have envisioned them as "nightinghouls." There is evidence, however, that McAlmon came up with this felicitous descriptor years before he met them, for the fourth chapter of *Being Geniuses Together* is entitled "The Nightinghoul's Crying." (Boyle deleted all of McAlmon's chapter titles in her edition.) And this chapter centers not on Paris but on McAlmon's experiences among writers in London's bohemia in 1921. So perhaps he simply recycled it for Glassco, Taylor, and the other denizens of Montparnasse in the late 1920s.

ROBERT MCALMON was a prominent American writer in Paris during the 1920s. In addition to his two novels, three story collections, and three volumes of poetry, McAlmon published stories and poems in the leading expatriate literary magazines. In 1923 he founded the Contact Publishing Company, which brought out major avant-garde works by (among others) William Carlos Williams, Ernest Hemingway, Gertrude Stein, H. D., and Djuna Barnes. He was one of the most flamboyant and recognizable figures in Montparnasse. In 1938, *Being Geniuses Together*, his salty memoir of his experiences in bohemian London, Berlin, and Paris, was published in London. His friend Kay Boyle revised it, adding her own autobiographical chapters, in 1968.

SANFORD J. SMOLLER is the author of *Adrift among Geniuses: Robert McAlmon, Writer and Publisher of the Twenties.* He has contributed essays, articles, and reviews on American, British, and Continental literature to scholarly and literary journals. Until leaving teaching in 2002, he taught literature and writing at Florida International University. He previously taught at Dickinson College, University of Wisconsin campuses, George Mason University, and the University of Miami.

The University of Illinois Press
is a founding member of the
Association of American University Presses.

Composed in 10.3/14 Janson Text
with Meta display
by Celia Shapland
for the University of Illinois Press
Designed by Dennis Roberts
Manufactured by Thomson-Shore, Inc.

University of Illinois Press
1325 South Oak Street
Champaign, IL 61820-6903
www.press.uillinois.edu